The Expert's Guide
to Veterans Benefits

Robin Alford

Library of Congress Control Number:		2010911618
ISBN:	Hardcover	978-1-4535-6500-1
	Softcover	978-1-4535-6499-8
	Ebook	978-1-4535-6501-8

This book was printed in the United States of America.

To order additional copies of this book, contact:
Xlibris Corporation
1-888-795-4274
www.Xlibris.com
Orders@Xlibris.com
78048

Contents

Acknowledgement 7

Prologue 9

About the Author 11

Resources and References 13

Introduction 15

Section 1
How the VA System Works

Chapter 1   Eligibility 19

Chapter 2   Filing Your Claims..42

Chapter 3   The Appeals Process 59

Section 2
Taking Care of Our Own

Chapter 4   Transitioning from the Military............................81

Chapter 5   Disability Compensation and Pensions....................89

Chapter 6   Military Retirement..126

Chapter 7   Examining VA Health Care 146

Chapter 8   Health Insurance 178

Section 3
Educational Benefits

Chapter 9   The GI Bills 207

Chapter 10 Additional Education Benefits..............................235

Section 4
Life after the Military

Chapter 11 Employment 255

Chapter 12 VA Home Loans..270

Section 5
Discounts on Shopping and Travel

Chapter 13 Bargain Shopping and Veteran Discounts....................287
Chapter 14 Travel Benefits..299

Section 6
The Golden Years and Beyond

Chapter 15 Planning for your Retirement.......................................325
Chapter 16 Military Funerals...333

Appendix A..357
Appendix B...366
Index..369
Limit of Liability/Disclaimer of Warranty 375

Dedication

To my loving husband, whom without his love and support this book may have never been written. I would also like to offer a special acknowledgment to the sacrifices of Kenneth Peck, Edward Campbell, Allen Megginson, and the loving memory of SCPO Thomas Spence. Each of these outstanding veterans has had a major impact on my life and, over the years, has helped to forge my perspective on the burdens that each veteran shares. Finally, I would like to offer my sincerest gratitude to everyone that has ever worn the uniform, and acknowledge the sacrifices that each veteran and their families have had to endure in the name of freedom.

Acknowledgement

I would like to give a special thanks to Michelle Brown, for the cover artwork. She is an amazing artist, who specializes in computer graphic, graphic design, and animation/illustration. Her ability to take an idea and concept out of my head and turn it into a beautiful work of art is truly an amazing talent and one that is greatly appreciated. I am grateful for all of the sacrifices she has made and the countless hours she has spent making the cover of this book. Thank you Michell Brown. Additionally, I would like to thank Ronald L. Russo who greatly assisted me with the interior graphics. You are both amazing!

Robin Alford

Prologue

If you have picked up this book and are reading this page, then chances are you're in the same position that my family was once in about fifteen years ago. Either you have been trying really hard to get your veteran's benefits and have been continually denied, or you are getting ready to start the long process of applying for them and have heard numerous nightmare stories about others who have tried hard and failed. In either case, you're going to need some help, which is why I am here for you.

I'm not going to waste your time with hundreds of great historical quotes or a long diatribe or history lesson of how the VA or the DOD came into existence and became the way that it is today. After all, that is what high school and college is for. What I will do is teach you how to get your rightly deserved veteran's benefits in the most efficient way possible. By teaching you how to work within the current system that is in place, at this time, and teach you how to put yourself in the best possible scenarios and situations for success when it comes to getting your benefits. The real trick when it comes to being successful at getting your veteran's benefits is being able to see what is coming at you ahead of time and being able to clearly identify the land mines before you step on them.

About the Author

Being the wife of a severely disabled veteran over the years has given me plenty of insight as to what the average disabled veteran goes through on a daily basis. Between the struggles of just getting out of bed in the morning to receiving numerous crushing rejection letters from the VA. That is how I became involved in the plight of disabled veterans.

Being a bail bondsman in my professional career, I have become quite accustomed to thinking outside the box, coming up with different strategies to achieve different objectives and a strong background in researching the different laws and statutes. These skills coupled with a strong love for my husband have made me truly committed to helping other veterans not have to go through what he did.

After watching my husband struggle with the VA system over the years, and realizing how imperative it was for him to receive his benefits, I found myself getting involved with his case. Shortly after that, he started to become very successful with his claims! As exampled by his 100 percent and 70 percent disability ratings decisions!

I then took my knowledge and understanding of the VA system and began to realize that my husband was anything but alone when it came to having difficulties with getting his benefits. Many of my bonding clients and their family members had experienced the same or similar situations when dealing with the VA as well. While I am not a lawyer and am not claiming to be one. I merely began to share the information that had made my husband successful, much to my surprise, by sharing with them the exact same techniques that my husband had used. They began to have success with their claims as well. Over the course of the last ten-plus years, I have finely tuned my system, building entirely off what I have seen that has worked well with others in the past, then adapting that information with the applicable laws to meet each different veteran's circumstances.

Over the years, many of these veterans began to express to me that writing a book would be a great way to help many other distressed veterans with teaching what is available to them and how to achieve success with their claims as well.

I really hope that this book assists you in your quest for receiving your veterans benefits. Additionally, I run a page on Facebook called "veterans benefits support" to assist veterans and their families with information about the VA and I use it as a forum to speak directly with veterans that are having issues with understanding how the VA system works. If you have any additional benefits related questions please feel free to join us at "veterans benefits support" on Facebook.

Resources and References

While much of the content of this book will be coming directly from the VAs, DODs, SBA, TRICARE, Delta Dental, AFRH, OPM, each of the military exchanges web sites as well the DECA web site, the AMC web page, AFRC, military.com, militarynewsnetwork.com, usajobs.gov, and the social security Web sites, as well as from researching the laws and statutes concerning each benefit. A large portion of the information throughout this book is original, though, and is based solely on my ideas, tools, and techniques that can help you to understand the processes that the VA uses.

While other resources such as Web sites and many of the other books about veteran's benefits strictly rely on the information that is provided by the VA. This book will not only provide each veteran a basic understanding of the applicable rules for each benefit, but will also provide an understanding of many things that the VA will not share with you. This knowledge and understanding can truly help each veteran to overcome the barriers and conquer the system.

Although no publisher in their right mind would allow me to give any type of expressed warranty, the information contained throughout this book will almost assuredly be of assistance to those that need help with understanding how the system works.

Introduction

Over the years, I have spent my share of long hours in the VA hospital waiting rooms, as well as on the phone, for my husband with the VA. I have also spoken with thousands of veterans and their spouses over the years, and realized that what stops the majority of veterans from getting their benefits is that most of the time, they don't know what benefits they qualify for. Many veterans simply do not know how to get them. Most people feel it takes too long and it is too much of a pain in the neck. The majority of us were denied for a benefit or several at one point or another. The one thing that we all have in common is that we have all heard the horror stories!

Three Rules for Receiving Benefits

I came to realize a few things over the years when it comes to getting your VA benefits. They are as follows:

1. Make sure you are entitled to what you are asking for. This often requires extensive research, which I am doing for you. I will do my best to explain who qualifies for what and when, in plain, easy-to-read English.

2. Documentation. I will help you to keep track of what you will need to qualify for each benefit, how to apply for and, in some cases, how to track the benefits you've applied for. I will also tell you which forms you will need to apply for each benefit, how to get them, and where to submit them.

3. Know what is out there for you. You will be amazed by the number of benefits you may be entitled to because of your service to our country. As I researched for this book, even I was amazed with several of the things that I found that are out there for veterans and their families.

I will also from time to time be putting in my thoughts on certain subjects (often using examples). Giving you the reader the benefit of my numerous past experiences, often hard learned past mistakes, and thousands upon thousands of hours of research. In order for you to understand how the system works. This will give you the best opportunity to be successful in filing your claims.

The benefits that are out there for you can often be found online, but you often need a law book and a Dick Tracy decoder ring to figure out if you qualify for them. Then there are the not-quite-as-frequently-used benefits and the ones that are within the private sector for veterans. Such as discounts at businesses and nonprofit companies that offer great deals and sometimes even free things for veterans. For those of us that live on a fixed income, or just like to keep more money in our pockets, these savings can be huge if you learn how to use them efficiently. They will cover the cost of this book hundreds, if not thousands of times over!

I have a very simple philosophy: If you were ever willing to raise your hand and take the oath to protect and defend our country, go through the trials and tribulations that every soldier, sailor, or airman goes through, missing holidays, birthdays, anniversaries, and everything else for a part of your life. Then you deserve *everything* that you qualify for. You served your country, now let's allow your country to serve you

Section 1

How the VA System Works

If you ever wanted to learn how to play baseball, the first thing you would need to do is learn the difference between a ball and a strike. Why, because learning the basic rules is a very important part of how the game works. The same thing can be said when it comes to veteran's benefits. By knowing the rules, it can assuredly make all the difference in the world when it comes to if you get your benefits or not and the amount of benefits that you are entitled to receive as well.

The chapters within this first section are all about the rules and procedures the VA goes by and how to start making them work to your advantage. Oftentimes by knowing little things like which supporting evidence they are looking for and how to overcome and avoid problems with their appeals. Veterans can greatly reduce the number of problematic situations that can occur throughout their cases. By reading these chapters carefully, you will come to understand how the entire process works: which can save you plenty of time and aggravation as problems arise.

Chapter 1

Eligibility

Did you know that there are over 23 million veterans currently alive today? Yet there are close to 70 million people that are potentially eligible for VA benefits and services because they are either veterans, spouses of veterans, widows of veterans, children of veterans, and even in some cases parents of veterans. That 70 million people make up nearly 25 percent of our country's population. That's almost one out of every four people in the United States that are eligible to receive at least some VA benefits.

So who is eligible for these benefits, you may ask? Well, in this chapter, we will answer these types of questions. In chapter 1, you will learn:

- Who is eligible for veteran's benefits.
- How to check your eligibility.
- How to make yourself more eligible.
- Who is eligible for which benefits.

Where It All Comes From

So where does all of that money come from? Well, each year the President and Congress will approve an annual budget for the VA. You are probably wondering how much that is, right? Well, in 2010, the VA had an annual budget of $112,800,000,000.00. Yes that's $112.8 billion. In 2011, the VA is going to continue to grow and modernize as the VA's budget will reflect. In 2011, the VA's budget is $125 billion.

Now that's a lot of money, but also a lot of veterans! Then there is the Department of Defense more commonly known as the (DOD), which has its own budget and resources. They handle the retirement pay for veterans who have completed twenty or more years of military service, as well as several other various benefits for veterans.

So who qualifies for all of these benefits? Well, chances are if you separated from the military with a discharge that is not dishonorable, then you probably are entitled to at least some benefits!

Destroying the Myths

There are so many myths about the VA. I can't remember how many times I have heard "I don't qualify for any benefits because I only served for four years, not twenty" or "I tried, but my VA rep said that I probably couldn't get it, so I gave up!" Then there is my favorite "My buddy got a certain benefit, but they denied my claim, so I just quit pursuing it."

*Listen carefully: There are over 23 million veterans, with 23 million different sets of circumstances, and 23 million different start and finish dates from when they joined the military. Each person having a unique and different set of circumstances. Some may have a bad back or leg, while others may have lost a limb or hearing. My husband came out of the military with Guillain-Barré syndrome, idiopathic hypersomnolence, a polyneuropathy, and rheumatoid arthritis. Therefore, as you can see, each veteran has a different set of circumstances. Don't go by what has or has not happened with someone else when determining your own case.

Who Is Eligible for Benefits

It all comes down to eligibility. So who is eligible? Well, just being a veteran makes you eligible for at least some of these benefits. A veteran is defined under Title 38 of the federal code of regulations as "a person who served in the active military, naval, or air service, who was discharged or released under conditions other than dishonorable."

Now that we have defined what the federal government considers a veteran to be, which is anyone who served in the Army, Navy, Air Force, Marines, Coast Guard, or Army and Air National Guard's. That wasn't released under conditions that were considered dishonorable.

How do you check to see if you qualify? By dusting off that good old DD Form 214. Even if you think that you may have a dishonorable discharge, chances are you do not. You would be surprised by how many people have said to me over the years, "I had a few bad evaluations or they got into some trouble, so they think they received a dishonorable discharge." Trust me: you would know if you did. Unless you were found guilty at a general court-martial, then spent time in a military prison such as Leavenworth, chances are you don't have a dishonorable discharge. Believe it or not, there are several different types of discharges: (1) honorable, (2) general or general under honorable conditions, (3) other than honorable known as OTH, and (4) entry level separations known as ELS. These are all forms of administrative discharges. These types of discharges make it much easier to qualify when it comes to receiving your benefits because outside of the OTH discharge, they are not typically considered dishonorable service.

Honorable Discharge

To receive an honorable discharge, a service member must have received a military rating of either excellent or good on his/her evaluations. Service members that meet or exceed the required standards of duty performance, and personal conduct, and who have completed their enlistments will normally receive an honorable discharge.

Other reasons for an honorable discharge include people who are deemed physically or psychologically incapable of performing their duties. They often will be given a PEB or Physical Evaluation Board, and then be placed either on the TDRL or the PDRL. This is the Temporary Disability Retirement List or the Permanent Disability Retirement List; these will be covered in chapter 5. With either of these, separation is usually honorable. Other reasons for an honorable discharge include convenience of the government / downsizing and reaching the maximum age. Honorable discharges are the most common type of military discharge and typically allow you easy access to all of your VA benefits without any issues.

General Discharges or General under Honorable Conditions

This discharge is typically given to those who have either gotten into a little bit of trouble or failed to meet the individual service branches performance or conduct standards. Failure to maintain the military's standards for fitness, weight, dress, hair, and appearance are all reasons for this discharge characterization. Also, those with less than average evaluations or several minor infractions would qualify for this type of discharge. With this discharge, you can access most but not all VA benefits.

Other than Honorable or OTH

This would be the worst type of administrative discharge. This type of discharge is for service-members that have a serious departure from the conduct and performance expected of all military members. It can be given for fraternization, abuses of authority, and serious misconduct. This discharge is typically also given to those convicted by a civilian court. After you are found guilty, if the military feels the conduct leading to your conviction brought discredit upon the service, they will often be given an OTH.

It can also be given as the result of certain civil hearings, like a divorce due to adultery. Often this particular discharge is accepted in lieu of a court-martial at the service-member's request (kind of like a plea bargain). Those who receive an OTH are barred from ever reenlisting into any of the armed forces branches unless they can get an exception-to-policy waiver. Also VA benefits are not usually going to be granted unless you can get a VA determination, which is explained later in this chapter.

Entry Level Separation or ELS

This is an uncharacterized discharge. It can only be given to those who have served for less than 180 days. It's like the military version of a grace period. It's neither good nor bad. It is used if your commander does not wish to retain you because you just were not working out. It doesn't carry an honorable, general, or OTH. Do not just assume though that if you served for less than six months, this is what you have because your commander has to ask for it specifically. If you fall into this category, you may qualify for some VA benefits, but you will need the VA to make a determination, which is explained later in this chapter.

Punitive Discharges

These are the discharges that can really limit you throughout your post-military life. These types of discharges are typically handed down as part of your punishment and can really hurt you when it comes to getting your benefits. These include:

Bad Conduct Discharge or BCD

Also known as the big chicken dinner. This is a punitive discharge that can only be handed down by a court-martial (either special or general) as part of the sentence. Bad conduct discharges are usually given out after release from a military prison. It is given after you are released and the appellate review process is complete. It can only be given out to enlisted service members.

This is usually handed down for such things as disorderly conduct, AWOL, DUIs, or drunk while on duty; things like that. Basically, all VA benefits are forfeited under this discharge (if it came from a general court-martial). Unless you can get your discharge upgraded, which will be explained later in this chapter.

Dishonorable Discharge or DD

This would be the worst discharge you can get. It is also a punitive discharge and can only be handed down as part of the sentence if convicted at a general court-martial. If the Manual for Courts Martial authorizes a dishonorable discharge for the charges you are convicted of, such as murder, sexual assault, rape, or desertion. Chances are, you will be going away to a military prison first. Then, if you are released, you will lose your ability to own a firearm, and in most cases, you will forfeit your right to vote as well. As for VA benefits, there is really nothing that is available to you.

Dismissal

This is the officer's version of a BCD. It can be given either at a special or general court-martial. For veteran's purposes, you really won't qualify for any benefits unless you can get your discharge upgraded.

DD Form 214 / DD Form 215

So now that we have examined the different types of discharges, maybe you're a bit more confident about your discharge status. So go ahead and locate your DD Form 214. If you're the spouse of the veteran and have never seen a DD Form 214, look at the bottom left hand corner; it will say either DD Form 214 or DD Form 215. At the top of the page, it will say "CERTIFICATE OF RELEASE OR DISCHARGE FROM ACTIVE DUTY." This is one of the most important pieces of paper you will ever have. At least that's what the PN or personnel man told my husband the day he got out of the Navy. It is definitely true though, so please make sure that you have safeguarded and made several copies of it because this is a major part of the veteran's benefits process.

The day that you process out of the military, along with the million other things that you have going on that day, is the time you will be given this paper. You will receive two copies of the DD Form 214. These are the deleted and undeleted versions. Be sure to check it, and make sure that all of the information is correct, and then make sure that you take steps to protect it.

DD Form 214

The undeleted version has thirty lines on it. This version has your discharge characterization on it. Whether honorable, general, OTH, etc. This is located on line 24 of the paper.

*Remember this is the version that you must use to file your VA claims with. So take a good close look at it. Read the entire form to make sure there are no mistakes that need correcting, and then make several copies and keep them handy. You will be needing it throughout the process of getting your benefits. This form tells you the entire story of your military service and oftentimes what you may or may not be eligible for in the way of veteran's benefits. It tells when you entered, separated, medals you have achieved, your type of separation, your character of service, and a narrative reason for separation as well. Each of these things will become very important and can help you when filing your claims.

The deleted version—the difference between this version and the undeleted version is that this copy only goes to line 22, then it stops. In case you don't want a potential employer to see the type of discharge you have received. Therefore this version cannot be used to file your VA claims.

DD Form 215

The DD Form 215 is used to make corrections and add on additional information. If there are problems after the original DD Form 214 has been delivered.

NGB 22 and NGB 22A

For Army and Air National Guardsman, this would be the same as the DD Form 214 because the National Guard belongs to each individual state and not the federal government. You will need to go through the individual state's National Guard adjutant general's office for the state in which you served in, to get a copy if you lose your NGB 22. If you have a difficult time contacting them, just go to: http://www.ngb.army.mil/resources/states.aspx

Getting a Copy of Your DD Form 214 / DD Form 215

As for Army, Navy, Air Force, Marines, Coast Guard, and reserve component members. If you have lost or misplaced your DD Form 214/215. There is still hope. There are a few ways to get a copy of it.

You can order it online. This usually is going to be the fastest way to do it, but it will cost you money. I don't really like this way, but I have to tell you that it exists, nonetheless. If you just do a quick search online, you will see plenty of companies that will do this from anywhere from $10.00 all the way up to $100.00. Be aware though; the $10-$20 companies typically will only send you the SF 180 which is a Standard Form 180, have you fill it out, and then they will fax it over for you. Wow! That's not a lot of work for $20.00.

Some of the more expensive companies have what are called DD Form 214 researchers. They charge considerably more money often upward of $100, but with your consent, they will physically go to the record center and act as your personal agent. With a signed written authorization, they will go and retrieve your records in person. This is very quick, but rather expensive.

Do it yourself. For those of us that like to keep our hard-earned money in our pockets, that are not in a super big hurry, or that don't need it for a job interview tomorrow morning, I have an alternative. The NPRC, which is the National Personnel Records Center. This is the same place that the other two alternatives were going to contact. So let's do it ourselves. Just go to:
http://www.archives.gov/veterans/evetrecs/index.html

Now fill out the form online, then print it out. You will need to sign it because federal law requires a signature on all records requests, then print your name underneath, then just fax the paper off to fax number (314) 801-9049, or you can mail the paper to:

> NPRC
> 9700 Page Avenue
> St. Louis, MO. 63132-5100

*Remember, the NPRC must receive this paperwork within thirty days of your request, or your request is voided, and you will have to start all over again. The other way to request a free copy of your DD Form 214 is to go online to:
http://www.archives.gov/research/order/standard-form-180.pdf

This will allow you to download standard form 180. Fill out the form, then print it out, and sign the form. Make sure that you meet the criteria at the bottom. (Because some veteran's files are stuck in different places. Due to which branch they may have served in, also when you separated may be a factor. So just read the bottom of the form carefully.) Most people will need to mail this form to:

> National Personnel Records Center
> Military Personnel Records
> 9700 Page Avenue
> St. Louis, MO. 63132-5100

After you have sent the proper forms off, this is usually a pretty quick process. I recently had my husband request a copy of his DD Form 214. It only took eight days to get it. Over the past several years, they have gotten much faster. If the nature of your request for information from your military file is more in depth, it may take you a bit longer. They process an average of four thousand to five thousand claims per day, so just please try to exercise a little patience.

Guard Your DD Form 214/215 with Your Life

So now that you have your DD Form 214/215, or NGB 22/22A, I do suggest that you take certain steps to safeguard it. After losing my home during Hurricane Charley, I quickly realized exactly how important that document really was. We lost everything that night, but my husband had already taken steps that had safeguarded that document. These include the following:

1. Make several copies.
2. Keep them in a safe, lockbox or safe-deposit box.
3. Register the document with the county recording office. It is a cheap insurance policy for you. By doing this, you can avoid ever having to send off for another one. This can usually be done either at the county courthouse, city hall, or county recording office. In most counties, you can register a DD Form 214 just like you would register a land deed or marriage certificate. Then, if you ever need it, you can access it for a few dollars.

*Remember that one question you will need to ask the county recorder is, if anyone can access your DD Form 214. If anyone can access it, you may not wish to register yours because of identity theft.

After Hurricane Charley, we had to buy a new home. We used a VA home loan, and the first question they asked was, where is your husband's DD Form 214. Luckily he had safeguarded it, for such an occasion!

The Importance of Your DD Form 214

The reason this paper is so important is that it's your way of quickly being identified as a veteran. With the fact that our country has had a military longer than we have had a country itself. We have also had veteran's benefits, with so many men and women serving at so many dates. This is how our government has elected to track those who have served. There is no massive computer system that tracks who you are as a veteran, and what you may or may not be eligible for as a veteran, so it is really up to you to be informed as to which benefits you qualify for and which benefits that you need to achieve your goals in life.

How to Upgrade Your Discharge

If by chance you find that either your discharge characterization on line 24 or your reason for separation lines 18, 23, and 28 on your DD Form 214 are either wrong or unfair, here is what you can do to change them. Keep in mind this is far from foolproof, but you can attempt to upgrade your discharge. This is a tool that can be extremely useful in receiving additional benefits.

Fixing Errors in Your Discharge

For example: If you completed your enlistment having given honorable service, never gotten into trouble, had either good or excellent evaluations, and been meeting the requirements for an honorable discharge. Only to find out when you're applying for your GI Bill benefits (which is covered in chapter 9) that your discharge was a general discharge, which would disqualify you from that benefit.

This error may have happened during your separation. After all, mistakes can happen. The day you separate from the military can be extremely stressful, to say the least, so if for any reason your discharge characterization has a mistake that was done in error, you can file to upgrade your discharge and fix any errors that may have been in your military records. There are a couple of different routes you can take to accomplish this, depending on your circumstances. Keep in mind that you need to seriously consider how important this is to you, before you do this.

Don't just wake up one morning and say, "Hey, I want to put myself through as much hell as possible today!" This can be a very long, time-consuming, and in some cases, expensive process, with no guarantees on the outcome. The thing to remember here is that it is a viable option though, and if your complaint does have merit, chances are it can be corrected.

Reasons to Upgrade Your Service Records

A wrongful discharge characterization or improper information in your service record can cause many problems in your life after the military. So here are three different ways to make changes to your service records that can have a positive impact on your ability to get your VA benefits and help advance your post-military objectives as well, in some cases.

1. Fixing the errors in your service records.
2. Changing your discharge characterization.
3. Applying for any medals that you may have qualified for but have not received.

Fixing the Errors in Your Service Records

If after reviewing your service records, you find that there were either mistakes made or there were parts of your record that are unjust. Then you may want to correct them. There are only two reasons that the military will change something in your service records. Either an error or an injustice has occurred.

How to Prove an Error Has Occurred

An error is pretty easy to understand and see.

For example: If you served for forty-eight months on active duty, but your DD Form 214 has an error and says that you only served for twenty-eight months, this may not seem like the end of the world, or worth fighting to get fixed, but things like the active-duty GI Bill requires thirty-six months of active-duty service to qualify for benefits.

In order to receive your benefits, you will have to prove an error has occurred. So how would they determine that an error has occurred in a case like this? Well, after you fill out DD Form 149 (which is explained later in this section). Submit a copy of your active-duty orders that proves that you were on active duty for the time in question, and there is your proof.

Proving an Injustice Has Occurred

The only other reason that the military will amend your military records is if an injustice has occurred. This is often quite a bit more complicated.

For example: At some point or another in each service member's career, you may have had a boss who was either excessively hard on you, moody, or just had it in for you. These types of superiors often love to fill out mountains of paperwork at the drop of a hat in hopes of making an example out of a select few to keep the others in line.

I do agree that the punishment should fit the crime. Although, in some cases, some superiors tend to go overboard, not realizing that all those counseling forms, reprimands, and negative performance evaluations can have an adverse effect on your discharge characterization.

Hence: keeping you from receiving your benefits.
Believe it or not, social networking Web sites such as Classmates, Facebook, and Togetherweserved.com are often great ways to reconnect with the people that you have served with in the past.

They can also be a great way to speak with witnesses, which can submit sworn statements and affidavits that may have seen how your boss has shown favoritism toward some. In certain cases, time may have even healed those old wounds, and if you find your old supervisor and explain how his past actions are harming you even now, they may be willing to submit a letter on your behalf. Stating that their past actions were in the heat of the moment, believe it or not, I have personally seen several veterans take this approach, and it really can help. They each used social networking sites to track down witnesses and get sworn statements to prove that an injustice had occurred, oftentimes several years after the fact. Additionally, over the years I have seen many veterans use these sites to band together which helped them to prove their injuries. Especially when it comes to things like Agent Orange exposure for Korean and Vietnam War veterans. By using these sites to find one another and share information and evidence in their cases these veterans were able to give the VA the overwhelming proof that is needed to overturn the VA's original decisions and win their appeals.

DD Form 149 to Fix Errors or Injustices in Service Records
The first step in this process is to download DD Form 149, or you can pick one up at your local or regional VA office, or you can download this form at:
http://www.dtic.mil/whs/directives/infomgt/forms/eforms/dd0149.pdf

After you have received this form, read it carefully! Both pages, it is relatively simple, but make sure to be clear as to what you are trying to achieve, or you will not be successful. You must fill out DD Form 149 clearly, typed preferably, then attach copies, never originals of any supporting evidence that will help strengthen your claim.

*Remember, the burden to prove your case here is yours. If all you do is send them names, dates, and times that the incident in question happened. You might as well have not even attempted this. The board will not research your claim or track down any of the parties involved. It is your responsibility to provide the proper information.

*Remember that errors are not as difficult to fix. They tend to be pretty cut and dry. If, on the other hand, you need help with filing to have your record amended for an injustice that is in your military record, I do recommend seeking either counsel or representation. I explain this in detail in chapter 3. Even a consultation with a lawyer that specializes in veteran's legal issues can help you figure out if your claim has merit.

Then there are the VSOs. Such as the Veterans of Foreign Wars, Disabled American Veterans, American Legion, and local veterans' offices, they will not be as much help as a private lawyer, but they can certainly point you in the right direction. The people at the VSOs tend to be very overworked, but they live to help veterans and are very dedicated. They will usually look over your paperwork and advise you if anything needs to be changed or added to your paperwork. Lawyers and VSOs are explained in detail in chapter 3.

Make sure that the representative that you speak to has the accreditation from the VA general counsel's office. This is a special certification by the VA that means they have been trained in these types of matters.

Filing Your DD Form 149

After you have gathered your evidence and completed your forms, there are a few things to remember before sending it off. Make sure that your information is correct and you are not planning on changing your contact information throughout the process. This will have been a huge waste of time if a week after you send off this paperwork, you decide to move, change your number, and stop checking your e-mail all at once because you need consistency. They will not track you down. If you do move, you need to notify the Board for Correction of Military Records.

Also, if you are going to retain a lawyer for this matter, I recommend that you do it before you submit the paperwork. If you plan to appear before the board, when your case is reviewed, you will also need to check yes in line 10. Although you will be responsible for all costs incurred by doing this, it may be absolutely necessary in some cases.

*Remember, you only have three years to file the paperwork from the time of the discovery of the error or injustice. The board can excuse your failure to file within the three years after discovery, if it finds it to be in the interest of justice.

Now that everything is completed. Let's send the paperwork off to the Board for Correction of Military Records. Since each branch has its own review board. Each branch's address will be on page 2 of the DD Form 149. Be sure that you send the paperwork to the correct board.

Making Sense of Advisory Opinions

Once you have sent off your request application and evidence, you can expect to receive one, if not multiple advisory opinions from your branch of service.

For example, if you are requesting an error to be amended by the Navy due to the fact that you served for forty-eight months, not twenty-eight months. The Navy's personnel center will send the board an advisory opinion stating that "yes this person served for forty-eight months."

If on the other hand, the request for a change was an injustice, such as disciplinary issues, those would come from the JAG offices. They will send an advisory opinion to the board.

If by chance the advisory opinion is to deny your request, the board will send you a copy of the advisory opinion for comment. This is where you can state your case by responding to the military's stance on the situation. Make sure that if you plan to argue your stance, you have a valid point; make sure you are concise, direct, and clear.

Staying on the Board's Good Side

Don't waste time. You will only have thirty days to respond, unless you notify the board in writing. Then they can grant additional time if needed so that you can collect additional evidence to strengthen your claim or come up with a stronger plan of attack.

Although the advisory opinion is only an opinion, it weighs heavily upon the board. The board is going to be made up of three civilian employees. They will be high-ranking civilian employees that are appointed to the board by the secretary of the corresponding service. If you requested to be at the board when they hear your case, the board will notify you of the time and place of your appearance before the board. This is your opportunity for you and your attorney to speak if necessary. You will be responsible for any and all costs associated with going in front of the board, also your attorney's fees, if you hired counsel, even if you win.

Final Decision to Fix Your Service Record

The final decision rests with the board. If the decision is favorable, your record will be amended. If your request is denied, you pretty much have wasted your time. You cannot appeal their decision, unless there is new, freshly discovered evidence that was unknown at the time that the original application was filed. Then they may or may not agree to reconsider your case. The only other way to change their decision is to file a lawsuit against the Department of Defense, in federal court, but it had better be pretty important if you plan to do that!

Upgrading Your Discharge

Upgrading your discharge characterization is very similar to fixing the errors in your service record. In some cases, if you are able to fix the errors in your service records, you will automatically qualify for a discharge upgrade. Before you attempt to do this, I strongly suggest that you order a copy of your military records prior to submitting your request to upgrade your discharge.

*Remember that you may need it for your case, and if you order it afterward, it will cause a substantial delay in the processing of your application.

DD Form 293 Upgrade Your Discharge

To upgrade your discharge characterization, you will first need to download and print out DD Form 293. There are four pages. Two of which are instructions. Read them carefully. Although this is similar to fixing the errors, there are a few differences though. You have to prove that your discharge was either inequitable or improper. To download this form just go to:

http://www.dtic.mil/whs/directives/infomgt/forms/eforms/dd0293.pdf

Inequitable Discharges

An example of an inequitable discharge would be that my discharge was inequitable or unfair because it was based on one isolated incident in thirty-six months of service with no other adverse action.

Improper Discharges

An example of an improper discharge would be that my discharge was improper because of a pre-service civilian conviction that the veteran openly admitted in their enlistment paperwork. That was later used in the military discharge proceedings against them, which would be improper. These were both just examples as to why someone might receive each of these discharges.

If you are submitting these forms to upgrade your discharge based upon the grounds of inequitable, make sure that you take full advantage of lines 6 and 8. The military isn't going to just give you a pass after a few years, but if your incident was an isolated action, that wasn't that bad; you got out of the military, went on, and made something of yourself. Maybe graduated college and went into management, kept out of trouble, and did something in the several years that have passed since you departed from the military. I would say that you have a pretty good shot at an upgrade. This happens more often than you may think; and many good, honest, hardworking people have used this tool to remove youthful errors in judgment from their otherwise permanent records.

Although the final decision rests entirely with the board, they are usually pretty reasonable. Remember, if the incident was isolated and you have been a model citizen since your separation from the military, time can often tell what type of person you really are.

Discharge Review Board or DRB

Another difference with this type of board is that the Discharge Review Board or DRB has a traveling panel, which is known as the traveling panel of the board, which travels to different locations throughout the United States, this can be a great way to have your voice heard and for them to see that you are a model citizen while cutting down on some of the expenses. You are still responsible for any costs incurred to visit the board on your part. Another thing to keep in mind is that the Navy and Marine Corps don't have a traveling board.

Keep in mind that the Discharge Review Board cannot review or consider any type of discharge resulting from a sentence given by a general court-martial. Also, if the discharge that you want reviewed happened over fifteen years ago, you must apply to the Board for Correction of Military Records using DD Form 149.

Final Decision to Upgrade Your Discharge

Once the board has deliberated, and the determination is handed down, the decision is final. You cannot appeal their decision unless there is new and pertinent information that wasn't available at the time you submitted your original claim. Trying to reargue your same claim twice will not get you anywhere. The only other option that you would have is to file a lawsuit against the Department of Defense. As I stated before, good luck with that!

Applying for Any Medals that You May Have Qualified For

Have you ever watched the news only to see a feel-good story of a WWII or Vietnam veteran who is finally receiving the Purple Heart forty or fifty years later? This doesn't happen by accident or for no reason.

These are veterans that have realized the importance of receiving these medals. Nothing can prove that it happened, like a service medal or badge. If you research the laws under USC, Title 10, section 1130, you will see that you are allowed to:

- Request that a decoration that you received be upgraded to a higher award.
- Request award of a decoration you were submitted for, but did not receive.

- Request award of a decoration you believe you deserve, but for which you were not recommended.

By utilizing this option, veterans that meet the qualifications for certain medals such as the Purple Heart or Combat Action Badge can cut through the red tape when it comes to certain VA benefits such as compensation and pension benefits that are explained in chapter 5. The reason being is that by having these awards it helps to prove a service-connection to your injuries, because a Purple Heart is only given to a service member that is injured at the hand of an enemy combatant and a Combat Action Badge is only given to those that have been in combat. Which can go a long way in helping to prove a service-connection exists with your claims.

Certain awards and medals being the Bronze Star, the Silver Star, Distinguished Flying Cross, Distinguished Service Cross, Legion of Merit, the Meritorious Service Medal, the Medal of Honor, Soldier's Medal, Air Medal, the Army Achievement Medal, and the Army Commendation Medal require you to apply through your congressman's office using a DA Form 638. Anyone that witnessed the action for which the medal is being applied for should also complete a DA Form 638. This can be downloaded at:
http://www.americanwarlibrary.com/forms/da638.pdf

All other awards such as the Purple Heart and other awards, badges, and medals require that you complete a DD Form 149. This was explained in the Fixing Errors in Service Records section earlier in this chapter. Once completed, you will need to send your DD Form 149 and any evidence to justify the award to the Board of Military Corrections.

Now, that we have examined how to get and keep track of your DD Form 214. Fix the errors, clean it up, and in some cases, upgrade your DD Form 214 and other paperwork as well as awards within your military file, in order to put you in the best position to receive your benefits. What types of benefits will all of this hard work get you?

A Quick Look at Benefits
Let's take a brief look at some of the major benefits that you may qualify for. This is just a quick glance at many of the benefits you may be entitled to. In the coming chapters, I will explain each benefit in detail and how they work.

Table 1-1

Benefit	Discharge characterization or requirements	Forms	Chapter of Book
Disability Compensation	Honorable, General, or VA Determination	VA Form 21-526	Chapter 5
100% P&T (Permanent & Total)	VA Determination	VA Form 21-526	Chapter 5
VA Pension	Honorable, General, or VA Determination	VA Form 21-526	Chapter 5
Death Pensions	Honorable, General, or VA Determination	VA Form 21-534	Chapter 5
DIC	Honorable, General, or VA Determination	VA Form 21-534	Chapter 5
SBP	20 year retired	File during out-processing	Chapter 5
Military 20 Year Retirement Pay	Honorable	No Forms to File	Chapter 6
Concurrent Retirement Disability Pay	Honorable	No Forms to File	Chapter 6
Combat Related Special Compensation	Honorable	DD Form 2860	Chapter 6
VA Healthcare	Honorable, General, or VA Determination	Enroll using VA Form 10-10 EZ	Chapter 7
VA Dental Benefits	100% P&T or Within 180 of Separation or by VA Determinatopm	No Forms to File	Chapter 7
VA Extended Care Services	Based on VA Disability Rating Percentages	VA Form 10-10 EC	Chapter 7
Tricare Military Health Insurance	Honorable with 20 years of Service TDRL PDRL	DEERS & Tricare	Chapter 8
T.A.M.P.	Honorable	DEERS & Tricare	Chapter 8
C.H.C.B.P	Honorable	DEERS & Tricare	Chapter 8
Champ VA	Rules Vary Greatly	VA Form 10-10 D	Chapter 8
Delta Dental Insurance	Same as Tricare	Must Call to Enroll	Chapter 8
Active Duty G.I. Bill	Honorable	VA Form 22-1990	Chapter 9

Table 1-1 continued

Benefit	Discharge characterization or requirements	Forms	Chapter of Book
Reserve and National Guard G.I. Bill	Current Service Members	DD Form 2384-1	Chapter 9
G.I. Bill of the 21st Century	Honorable Service after September 11, 2001	VA Form 22-1990	Chapter 9
VA's Vocational Rehabilitation Program	VA Determination of 20% or Higher Service Connected Disability or VA determination	VA Form 28-1900	Chapter 10
VA's Dependants Educational Assistance Program	For Dependants of Veterans with 100% P&T or Have Died	VA Form 22-5490	Chapter 10
Veterans Job Preference	Honorable, General, or VA Determination	DD 214 & SF 15	Chapter 11
Veterans Small Business Loans	Honorable, General, or VA Determination	Apply Directly Through the Lender	Chapter 11
VA Home Loan Program	Honorable, General, or VA Determination	VA Form 26-1880	Chapter 12
VA Home Loan Program for Reserve and National Guard Personnel	Minimum of 6 years of Honorable Service	VA Form 26-1880	Chapter 12
Home Adaptation Grants	100% P&T Disabled and VA Determination	VA Form 26-4555	Chapter 12
Military Shopping and MWR Privileges	20 Year Retired 100% Disability Rating, and Current Service Members	Military ID Card	Chapter 13
Additional Shopping Discounts	All Veterans	Military ID or VA card Required	Chapter 13
Space-A Travel	20 Year Retirees or Current Service Members	Military ID Card	Chapter 14
On Base Lodging and Vacation Rentals	20 Year Retirees 100% Disabled and Current Service Members	Military ID Card	Chapter 14
Armed Forces Retirement Homes	20 Year Retirees and Disabled Veterans that are Unemployed and VA Determination	Apply Directly Through the Retirement Home	Chapter 15
Basic Burial and Memorial Benefits	Honorable, General, or VA Determination	Varies by Which Arrangements are Chosen	Chapter 16
BGLI	Honorable, General, or VA Determination	SGLV Form 8714	Chapter 16
S-DVI	VA Determination	VA Form 29-4125	Chapter 16

VA Determination

As for the words *VA determination*, that means the VA will have to determine if you are eligible for that benefit or not. They go by laws that were enacted by Congress under Title 38, section 3.12.

The rules can often be very difficult to understand to say the least. With millions of different situations, here is a quick way that I have always used to explain it for those of you that don't either have an honorable or general discharge.

*If you have a bad conduct discharge, dishonorable discharge, or for officers that receive a dismissal from a *general court-martial*. Then you are not entitled to veteran's benefits.

If on the other hand, you received an other than honorable, a bad conduct discharge, or a dismissal from a *special court-martial*, then you may have a fighting chance depending on the circumstances.

The VA will have to make a determination as to if you can receive the benefit or not. You will also be limited as to which benefits you may receive.

For example: Say that you were in the Army. You went over to Iraq and got injured (fighting for your country). You came back to the United States and got a DUI on base one night. Well, you are given a special court-martial and receive a BCD as part of the punishment. So the question is, would they be able to receive VA benefits?

The VA would have to determine if you meet the requirements to receive benefits for your injuries. In this case, it was a special, not a general court-martial. So in this case, the VA would more than likely go ahead and grant eligibility for certain benefits, and you would more than likely be limited as to which benefits you may receive, such as health care, seeing as the injury was service-connected.

For those of you that received a dishonorable discharge, sorry, there is not much that you can do, unless, you can get your discharge upgraded. As explained earlier in this chapter.

Three Important Questions to Ask before You Apply

*Remember, for each benefit you are considering applying for, there are three basic questions you need to ask yourself:

1. Do I need this benefit? If yes, continue on. That may sound crazy, but there are quite a few people out there that just like to clog up the system with really nonsensical requests.

    For example, people that apply for Chapter 31 vocational rehabilitation, just because they can. Chapter 31 is a fantastic program, that I will cover in chapter 10. They use it for an educational goal that goes nowhere. All I am saying is make the most of it or save it for someone who will. A person who fights to get 100 percent permanent and total disability rating just so that they can get a free hunting and fishing license, but they don't like to hunt or fish! In other words, the benefits that you apply for should always be consistent with your true needs.

2. Do I qualify for this benefit? Make sure that you qualify for the benefit before you apply for it. Nothing slows the VA system down more than people who apply for a benefit when they do not qualify for it. You see, the VA can't just take your claim and look at it and say yes or no in most cases. If it is a no, they have to make sure that you don't qualify based on the information that you have provided. This is explained in chapter 3.

    Then the VA has to either send out a letter rejecting your claim or ask for more information to help substantiate why your claim is valid. This takes up a lot of the VA's time and resources, creating a huge backlog of other cases. Since each benefit has its own requirements that you must meet. It depends on:

    a. When you served.
    b. Where you served.
    c. Your length of service.
    d. Your discharge characterization.

    Do not worry though. I will be explaining each benefit's minimum requirements as we go.

3. Can I prove my eligibility? A lot of this goes back to just simply having things like your DD Form 214/DD Form 215 handy, which was explained earlier in this chapter. Knowing how the government works though, it oftentimes isn't quite that simple. Although for things like a VA home loan, a DD Form 214 is really all you will need in most cases. VA disability compensation, on the other hand, you will need quite a bit of documentation, to say the least. This will be explained extensively in chapters 2 and 3.

Chapter 2

Filing Your Claims

In this chapter, we will be discussing everything having to do with filing your claims. Everything from determining which agency handles each benefit, where and when to enroll, to picking out the right VA representative or how to do it yourself. What the VA's responsibility is in helping you, how to track down the proper paperwork, to submitting all of your evidence and keeping track of your records.

This can be a very time-consuming process, to say the least, but let me see if I can get you squared away.

Who Runs the Show

For the purposes of veteran's benefits, there are essentially two main government agencies that handle almost all of the benefits for veterans.

These would be the Department of Veterans Affairs, more commonly known as the VA. The other would be The Department of Defense, more commonly known as the DOD.

These two main groups pretty much run the show when it comes to your benefits. If you plan to file for a benefit, you will first need to make sure that you are dealing with the correct agency, so let's take a quick look at each one and get an idea of what they have to offer.

VA Benefits

The VA manages and handles claims for a wide variety of veteran's issues and needs. These are the most commonly used benefits by the VA:

1. VA disability compensation
2. VA pensions
3. VA health care
4. CHAMPVA
5. all of the GI Bill and educational programs
6. the vocational rehabilitation programs including chapters 31 and 35
7. the VA home loan program
8. VetBiz
9. Dependency and Indemnity Compensation or DIC
10. Veterans' Group Life Insurance (VGLI)
11. Service-disabled Veterans Insurance (S-DVI)
12. funeral and burial expenses (in most cases)

DOD Benefits

The Department of Defense has its own benefits that they manage and are responsible for. Here is a list of commonly used DOD benefits:

1. military retirement pay
2. combat-related special compensation (CRSC)
3. military ID cards for qualifying veterans
4. TRICARE, which is the military's health insurance program

5. TAMP
6. CHCBP
7. On-base shopping privileges at the PX, NEX, Commissaries, MWR, etc.
8. Space-A travel
9. armed forces hotels, resorts, on-base lodging, and vacation rentals
10. the armed forces retirement homes
11. survivors benefit program (SBP)

A quick tip that I use to keep track of which benefit goes to the correct organization, it's really simple. If you need a military ID card to access the benefit. It's typically a DOD benefit. If it requires a VA card to use that benefit, it's a VA benefit. Makes sense, right!

Being Successful at Filing VA Claims

When it comes to filing claims with the VA, there is quite a bit that you will need to know if you plan on being successful. It truly breaks my heart when I see someone who has been suffering because they never knew that they could receive benefits or has been demoralized by the system, only to give up because they didn't feel that there was any other alternative. I have seen this happen firsthand on numerous occasions, even within my own family.

Listen up, the system that is in place is the system that is in place. I get that it needs a serious overhaul in a lot of areas, but as someone who has been dealing with the VA off and on for the majority of my life. I can tell you this much: I have seen improvements in quite a few areas. I cannot fix the things that need fixing with the VA, but I can and will teach you how to get things accomplished within the system that we have in place at this time.

Enrollment

The first step in getting your VA benefits is enrollment. Nobody is going to hunt you down and give you your benefits, so since they are not going to come to you, you will need to go to them, ASAP, because the sooner that you apply for your benefits, the sooner you will receive your benefits. If you are seeking compensation for a disability, this can be very important because disabled veterans often tell me that it takes too long, although at times this is true, but you do get back paid from the day that you filed your claims, so think of all that backpay! In my husband's case, when he won his appeal, he received close to $50,000 in backpay.

Locating Your Nearest VA Medical Center

The first step on your journey to getting your benefits is to locate the nearest VA medical center. These are typically hospitals that are capable of handling thousands of patients each day. To locate your nearest VA medical center, just go to:

http://www2.va.gov/directory/guide/allstate.asp?dnum=1&isFlash=0

Once there, you will need to locate the enrollment office inside the center and just walk in during business hours. Bring your military paperwork, any disability award letters you may have received and your driver's license. They will issue you a Department of Veterans Affairs official identification card. It will have your picture on it, with a magnetic strip just like a credit card on the back. This is how the VA will be able to identify you for medical care purposes so that you can start receiving treatment for your service-connected disabilities.

Finding Your VA Local Office

The next step will be to locate your nearest veterans' office. They are not that hard to find, seeing that they are located throughout most cities. If you are having trouble locating your VA local office, you can contact the VA regional office. I have put this in appendix A. Or you can inquire at the VA medical center. Also, you can check your local phone book or online. These offices sometimes move because they are smaller, as did several of the local offices in our area recently, so I am hesitant to publish this information because it often changes.

Now, before you start the process, make sure that you have all of your proper information. Such as your DD Form 214, service records, and medical files, driver's license, marriage certificate, birth certificates (of children), and a blank check to deposit funds. Be sure to make several copies of them. Also never hand over your originals unless they specify as well.

Picking a Veteran's Benefits Counselor

One other item that I feel is very important is to seek out the right veteran's benefits counselor or Veteran's Service Organization more commonly known as a VSO to help with your claims because not all counselors are the same. I encourage you to either ask around with other veterans as to their experiences with their veteran's counselor or drop by or call your local VFW post. They always tend to know the good benefits counselors. It is kind of like finding the right private doctor. You want someone that you are comfortable with, that you can speak openly with. A good veteran's counselor is worth their weight in gold.

My husband is horrible with names. Yet he can always seem to remember the names of any veteran's counselor that he has ever spoken with! Having a good relationship with the right veteran's benefits counselor can make all the difference in the world. There is no law that states that you have to use any particular counselor, so do the work, it can really make the difference and save you several months by getting it right the first time you submit your claims by doing it properly.

Once you find the right one for you, make sure that you keep them in the loop about anything that you feel may affect your claims. The insight that they can provide can be invaluable. I do not recommend switching counselors once you have filed your claims because being inconsistent will do nothing but cause problems with your claims in the end. That is unless you feel the counselor clearly doesn't have your best interest at heart.

*Remember that they do this for a living. They have appointments dealing with all types of often confusing veterans' issues all day long. Our counselor is probably one of the most committed people that I have ever seen at making sure that my husband is armed with the correct information about his claims and rights as a disabled veteran.

Often it may take a few weeks to get an appointment with a specific counselor, but the right counselor is worth the wait because if mistakes are made, it will take a lot longer to fix them.

Transition Assistance Office or TAO

For those soldiers that are intending to separate within the next 60-180 days. I strongly urge you to visit the TAO (Transition Assistance Office).

This is a great new program that has been put into place in order for servicemen and women to be able to start preparing for life after service. This office is similar to your local VA center in that they can help you with filing your paperwork for your benefits prior to separation.

By doing this at the 180-day point prior to your separation date, your chapter 33 (Post-9/11 GI Bill) claim will more often than not, be settled prior to your out date. This way, you can start your schooling immediately! As for your disability compensation claims, this can greatly reduce the wait time involved in receiving your disability rating. Seeing as the average wait time for a new claim for disability compensation and pension is just over six months in most cases, so be sure to take advantage of this help.

Online Applications (VONAPP)

For those of you that are the do-it-yourself types. You can use VONAPP or veterans' online application. This is a way to download and file your claims yourself, but be careful. Any mistakes can cause substantial delays in your case.

Quick Start

For those service members within one to fifty-nine days of exiting the military, you can use Quick Start. This allows a service member with fifty-nine days or less remaining on active duty to file their VA disability claim before separation, retirement, or deactivation from the National Guard or reserves. This can accelerate the receipt of your VA disability compensation benefits claims.

The most important thing to consider before deciding on which method to use to apply for your benefits is that the military employs all types of people, from nuclear engineers to pilots, and even doctors and lawyers. Yet the system in place can be equally confusing to all veterans. So be extremely careful if you plan to apply for these benefits on your own!

VA Form 21-526 Online Application

If you plan to file a claim for veteran's disability compensation on your own, you will need to download and complete VA Form 21-526. Just go to: http://www.vba.va.gov/pubs/forms/VBA-21-526-ARE.pdf

If you are applying online, you will need a valid forwarding address, phone number, and e-mail address. Make sure that the VA can always find you easily because consistency is important. As for submitting your additional supporting evidence, you will need to contact the VA at 1-800-827-1000 to find out where to send your additional supporting evidence. This will typically be the VA regional office in the state that you plan to live in after discharge.

For Guardsman Coming Back from Title 10 Call-up

For certain National Guardsman that have been deployed, if after you have been deployed under Title 10 call-up, which is federal duty to an area such as Iraq or Afghanistan. After your deployment, I strongly suggest that you consult your local veteran's benefits counselor. Provide them with a copy of your NGB Form 22 or DD Form 214. In some cases, you can receive VA benefits such as medical treatment and disability compensation for any injuries sustained while on your deployment, while still maintaining your current status in the guard. This can be an invaluable tool.

Be aware, though, that if your service-connected disability impedes your ability to meet your branch's standards, you may be medically separated; but it can be a great way to plan for the future because by getting a disability rating, even if it is 0 percent for the injury or disability, this is still an acknowledgment that an issue exists and you can receive treatment for it. You can also submit supplemental information at a later date to increase your disability rating, which can provide you with more disability compensation as well. This will be covered in chapter 5.

Different VA Forms

Throughout this book, as I explain each benefit, I will include the information about which forms you will need, how you can get each form, the minimum supporting documentation and evidence you will need, then where you will need to submit your completed claims.

Each benefit requires a different form and often goes to a different place. They often require different supporting documentation as well to ensure that you meet the requirements of that benefit. The important thing to remember here is "making sure that the *i* is dotted and the *T* is crossed" because making sure that everything is correct the first time will help you to complete the process without having extra delays. The VA is often more concerned that the claims process is being completed to their standards than if you have included all of your evidence properly to support your claims. Since the claim is yours, it becomes your responsibility to include what it is that you want them to see as proof on the day they make a final decision regarding your claim.

Factoring in the Ever-changing Congress

Part of the reason that the system is so complicated and you always hear people complaining about it is that many people don't understand that different Congresses make different rules at different times, so depending on your dates of service, this can also affect your ability to qualify for a certain benefit and which benefits you may qualify for as well.

For example: Let's take the VA home loan program. Depending on when you served, some veterans only require ninety days of active-duty service. Others require 181 days *continuous* active-duty service. Then other veterans that served at yet another time period require twenty-four months continuous active-duty service. National Guard and reservists require six years of service to be eligible for this benefit. I know this can be confusing.

This is why people often get so confused when it comes to veteran's benefits such as disability compensation. The rules are complex, to say the least.

Meeting the VA's Guidelines

The VA decides each individual case based on its individual merits. There is no master list that they use to decide how disabled each person is or isn't. Don't misinterpret that statement though. Although there is no master list, the guidelines are very stringent as to what the VA can and cannot offer you for your injuries.

The Ever-evolving VA

Even for those of you who have filed a claim in the past and were either denied or just have given up on trying to work with the VA. I would like to encourage you to try it again. You see, as someone who has been dealing with the VA since childhood with my father and aunt back in the 1970s and 1980s. Now with my husband since the 1990s. I have seen the VA steadily evolve.

I remember back when the waiting rooms were always so overcrowded and everyone was always complaining and often screaming. It could take three to four hours just to simply get your blood drawn. Then they would draw twenty to twenty-five vials at a time. Boy, how times have changed!

Now everything is modernized and computerized. A simple blood draw that used to take three to four hours usually takes maybe thirty minutes to an hour now, with two to four vials of blood. The VA now has patient-driven scheduling, which has greatly reduced the wait times. Nobody likes to go to the doctor, but now at least it won't take all day!

The VA's Duty to Assist

Then there is one of my favorite new laws that have changed the way that the VA works more than any other. Prior to the year 2000, the VA had this great idea to confuse veterans into submission; but in 2000, Congress passed a new law requiring that the VA assist you in every reasonable way possible with your VA claims. This is referred to as the VA's duty-to-assist law.

Although it is still your burden to prove that you are eligible for each benefit. Under this new law, it is the VA's responsibility to assist you in every way reasonably possible, in obtaining the proper information and evidence relating to your claims. Furthermore, you won't need your Dick Tracy decoder ring to decipher the tea leaves that the VA provides you with.

So what does all of this mean? It means that the VA is obligated to inform you in plain simple English terms. Exactly what evidence is required to support your claims? No more needle in a hay stack. This way, you are not having to randomly guess which evidence you should or shouldn't submit. Now the VA must tell you.

They also have to explain in plain English why they have denied your claim, or if and which additional information that they may need to complete the processing of your claim. For those of you who are new to the VA, this used to be a *big* problem.

The other important part of this law is that the VA now has to make a "reasonable effort" to obtain the evidence in your case for you. There are two different types of records.

1. Federal records—these would be things from your service record or from military doctors. The VA can only stop pursuing these records after they are reasonably sure that they either do not exist or that further pursuit of the records in question would be futile. In other words, either it no longer exists or it is classified! The VA will inform you of any possible alternatives such as asking if you have any copies of said paperwork.

2. Nonfederal records—these would be medical records from private doctors and sworn statements and such. Although the VA will request that your private doctors turn over any and all medical records and medical opinions on your behalf, after you sign a release form. This oftentimes doesn't work out so well since private doctors and hospitals often charge either one or two dollars per page and the VA isn't allowed to pay for copies, so the doctors' offices and hospitals often disregard these requests. Although the VA is obligated to resubmit a records request a second time after a few months. I recommend that you be proactive and purchase a copy of any medical records needed to help substantiate your claims. This is a small price to pay to ensure that your documentation is readily available, and once you have your complete medical file, you can make additional copies at home for the cost of paper and ink.

What Is Supporting Evidence

Supporting evidence is probably the most important thing that you need to understand when it comes to being successful at filing your claims. This is a very important section, so please read it very carefully!

Although the VA has a duty to assist you in filing your claims, I can't stress to you enough that the person who is responsible for proving that you are eligible for your claim is *you*!

Many benefits such as the GI Bill do not require very much supporting evidence. Usually, a copy of your DD Form 214 is evidence enough to prove that you are eligible for that benefit. Seeing as it states how long you served and your discharge characterization, which needs to be an honorable to qualify, see it's not so hard. That was easy, right?

Then there are other benefits such as burial and memorial benefits that are still not that difficult to prove eligibility for. To qualify, you need a discharge characterization that the VA doesn't consider as dishonorable. Then if you served as an enlisted person on or before September 7, 1980, you can have served for as little as one day to be eligible. After September 8, 1980, you need twenty-four months of continuous active-duty service. Both of these things can still be proven by a simple look at your DD Form 214.

We still have to prove that the veteran has passed away, so the additional supporting evidence you would need is a death certificate. Then, there are the things that in the legal world are referred to as the loopholes. These are the things that fall outside of the norm.

For example, let's say that the person who died was an active-duty soldier that dies while serving his or her country, over in Iraq. After all, this is the military. The soldier has only been in for less than twenty-four months, so will the government cover the soldier's burial expenses? Of course, they will be covered.

Even though they have been in for less than the required twenty-four months, the government often puts in a slew of other qualifying alternatives, which makes it so that those who fall outside the minimum qualifications can qualify. Additionally, if this scenario were real, then the service member's family would qualify for numerous additional benefits on top of the normal burial and memorial benefits.

*Remember, to qualify for the benefit, you would have to either qualify by meeting the minimum requirements or meet the qualifications of the loophole.

So in a case like this, your supporting evidence would be the casualty report that proves that the service member died while on active duty, on active-duty orders, in a combat zone, with the coroner's report. This would be sufficient in order to meet the requirements.

Then there are much more complex cases, which often tends to happen in disability compensation cases. These can get really confusing in a hurry since there is no official list as to what can or cannot be used as supporting evidence in each case. People often get confused, so I would like to try to take a common sense approach to this.

The Importance of Supporting Evidence

Don't, and I mean don't, think that you can pull a fast one by trying to send a letter from a co-worker, your best friend, or anyone else that really has nothing to do with your case! One hundred letters, one from every person that you know, although they may be notarized. They are not going to carry the weight that one medical opinion from your licensed doctor will carry, so don't waste your time. You can on the other hand, write a "stressor letter" that states in your own words how your condition came about, the severity of your condition, and how it impacts your day to day life. A good stressor letter should be about five to seven pages long and should explain in full detail how your medical condition occurred, how it impacts your daily living and reduces your ability to function normally within society. The stressor letter should be direct and powerful. It should explain in detail what caused your injuries and how it impacts you. Look at it as your opportunity to write a letter to the judge in your case. Think about what it is that you would want to tell the judge about your case, then write it down and don't beat around the bush!

The types of supporting evidence that will be the most useful to your medical claims are medical evaluations, letters from doctors, medical test results, Physical Evaluation Board or PEB findings, and certain medals (such as the Purple Heart), etc.

Other types of great supporting evidence are deployment orders, incident reports, official witness statements (from other service members that were there, that saw what happened, that filed them at the time of the incident), schedule rosters, letters from inside your immediate chain of command (that are relevant), etc.

For example, let's say that a service member sustains injuries during a firefight in Iraq. Only to wake up three days later in a hospital bed with sutures in several areas of their body (from shrapnel wounds). Bandages around their head (from a concussion) and a cast on their right arm. Oh, by the way, did I mention that they have three broken ribs? Ouch!

After they awaken, they are quickly going to realize that their life has changed, but they are not going to realize how, at first, this is pretty common.

The military is going to do everything in its powers to first and foremost make sure that you live. Then at some point shortly thereafter, you will be offered a Purple Heart. Chances are, your commanding officer will have put you in for one. If you know what is good for you, you will take it. Nothing says absolute proof like a Purple Heart.

In most cases, what comes next after healing is exhaustive physical therapy and psychological therapy to try to get you back to the condition that you were in prior to the injury. Although these things will help you tremendously, these injuries can often plague you for the rest of your life though.

Physical Evaluation Board or PEB

Next the military will oftentimes be forced to give you a PEB or Physical Evaluation Board. Doctors will evaluate your injuries and try to determine the level of your disabilities. The board will then review your doctor's statements and evaluations.

Then determine if you are either fit for duty or should be separated with or without pay, then be placed on either the Permanent Disability Retirement List or PDRL (this would be for permanent conditions) or Temporary Disability Retirement List or (TDRL) for temporary medical conditions.

Once the PEB comes back with its determination, you will be assigned a rating. These ratings come in 10 percent increments. Anything 30 percent or over will result in medical retirement, hence retirement pay, with a pretty little retired military ID card. This is explained in detail in chapters 5 and 6.

Painting a Clear Picture to the VA

So now that we understand that, let us resume. You received a Purple Heart for your injuries, which were for a concussion, broken arm, three broken ribs, and shrapnel wounds.

For VA purposes, it is always best to paint as clear a picture as possible. Using your supporting evidence to give them the clearest picture of what is going on with your claims, so here is the supporting evidence you would want to use for your VA health care and disability compensation claims.

Well, to start, you would want to first collect copies of your DD Form 214. This will let them know when you served, where you served, and that you received the Purple Heart. The Purple Heart is very important because it is only awarded to those service personnel who are injured or wounded in combat. Then you will need documentation stating that you were part of the forces that came under attack in that particular battle. This will put you at the scene of the attack at the correct time and date.

By providing documentation through incident reports that are usually made by either those who were there, ordered you to be there, or at least found you there. Which would be filed shortly after the incident occurred. These are all things that will make it evident that you were there. The military has gotten somewhat better over the years about documenting things like this, so it is getting easier to get copies of these types of evidence in most cases. In the event that there was no documentation made for one reason or another. Then at minimum make sure that you get statements from other service members that were there with you, that can attest to what happened.

Medical Documentation as Evidence

Then comes all of the medical documentation, this is the vital part. Get copies of everything, start to finish. Every surgery, MRI, CAT scan, doctor's visits, medical opinions, PEB results, blood draws, anything and everything! All of it tells a story—the story of a soldier that woke up one morning, put on his or her uniform, went to work, then got injured. All of the medical documentation will prove that it happened this way. All of that medical documentation will become evidence to support your VA claims.

By going through the process and getting a VA rating. It will help cover you, even if the rating is 0 percent. This is still an acknowledgment of the injury being service-connected. Oftentimes issues and other disabilities take time to manifest. Just ask any Vietnam veteran. Oftentimes an injury that happens on active duty can stay with you for the rest of your life and get worse over time. Therefore, you can work toward getting that percentage raised.

Take the soldier with the broken arm. What if it doesn't heal correctly? This could be a lifelong problem.

The shrapnel wound could cause any number of issues. Anytime you introduce a foreign object into your body, especially metal on a battlefield. There can be problems such as blood disorders or hepatitis.

As for the broken ribs. This can cause a shortness of breath and impede your ability to remain active. It may or may not heal correctly, causing possible long-term health problems.

Last but not least, you have the concussion. This is often called a traumatic brain injury or TBI for short. This can have lasting effects such as memory loss and migraine headaches that are often permanent.

Secondary Tier Illnesses

Then you have what is often called secondary tier illnesses. That means that because *A* happened, this has caused *B* to now happen.

For example, a person who sustained those types of injuries may show symptoms of PTSD or chronic depression. If you can prove that the PTSD or chronic depression were by-products of your original injuries that are service-connected, they become service-connected as well.

The Assumed Risk of Serving

Listen, everyone that has ever been in the military knows that there is an assumed risk. Our soldiers can and often do get hurt. This is no surprise, but if you have hopes of being taken care of after you finish serving, those are the things you will need to do.

*Remember that with over 23 million veterans, each veteran's situation is different; so as you are reading each section, look for the qualifications that fit your personal situation.

Keeping Track of It All!

I know this may seem obvious, but you really need to keep track of your paperwork, especially if you are filing a claim for disability compensation. Those who are the most organized tend to be the most successful.

The invention of the computer has been a great thing, but it wasn't that long ago that the VA was constantly losing paperwork and files. I cannot tell you how many times my husband came home from a VA appointment ranting that the VA had lost the paperwork in his file again. He would always tell them, "Don't worry. I have plenty more where that came from."

So before you get too far into the process, I suggest that you make a small investment and buy a nice rolling backpack and some file folders with colored tabs. Trust me when I say. You will thank me later. This way you can easily keep track of all your medical documentation, from private doctors, military doctors, and VA doctors.

Remember, even after you get your disability compensation, you will more than likely have appointments in order to keep your benefits from time to time for the rest of your life. This means loads of medical documentation, so if you keep it organized from the very beginning, you will be much better off.

Saving Your Records on Your PC

For those of you that don't like clutter, you can make copies of your records at home. Scan them to your computer, one page at a time. Then copy them to a computer disk. Then you can make as many copies on disk as you need or on a flash drive. It reduces the amount of paper and ink that you use. Just keep the originals. That way, you're not toting everything around with you.

Filing Your Claims

Now that you have soaked up all of this knowledge, it's time to decide which method you wish to use to file your claims. Fill out the proper forms or have a veteran's benefits counselor help you. Include all of your documentation and supporting evidence. Above all else, make sure that you get it right on the first try.

*Keep in mind that delays when dealing with the VA do not take days and weeks; they take months! So be sure before you submit. Now feel free to submit away, but be aware, this can often take a while. These things are often an exercise in patience.

Evaluating Their Evaluations

I also suggest that you have your private doctors regularly evaluate your military and VA medical records. This is a great way to make sure that there are absolutely no inconsistencies in each veteran's medical files. From personal experience, about fifteen years ago, my husband's disability compensation case was held up for over a year, simply due to a doctor's recommendation, when the doctor had never even seen my husband prior to making the evaluation. This happens far more frequently than you may think. It took another doctor having to evaluate his medical file to find the error, so keep in mind, it can happen!

Chapter 3

The Appeals Process

In this chapter, we will be discussing everything that will happen after you file your claims. From C & P exams to navigating those shark-infested waters that they call the VA appeals process. Trust me; you will want to keep your hands and feet inside the boat at all times. Metaphorically speaking!

Now that you have filed your claims, I really hope that you decide to read on prior to receiving your decision letter, which may take a few if not several months to receive. The information in this chapter can be some of the most invaluable knowledge you can possibly receive.

Compensation and Pension Exam or C & P

Now that your claims are pending, you will, more often than not, start receiving correspondence on a regular basis from the VA, asking for supplemental information and things of that nature. Oftentimes the VA will want to give you what is known as a compensation and pension exam or C & P exam for short.

Boy, are these fun, just kidding. C & P exams are the VA's version of bringing your mechanic with you to buy a used car. It gives the VA an opportunity to take a look under the hood. After all, if you are going to file claims with the VA for things like disability compensation or pension. The VA has the right to take a look at the severity of your condition. Anyone who has ever been through one knows that they are not there to administer health care; they are strictly there to observe and report.

Finding Holes in Your Claims

The way that this works is that they will schedule you an appointment with one, if not several doctors, depending on how many medical issues you have that you filed claims for. Once there, the doctors will evaluate your conditions, your VA file, and any other evidence to support your claims. Additionally, they can order any number of tests such as X-rays and MRIs needed to either substantiate or weaken your claims.

Detecting Deception

Listen, if you think that the VA is just going to hand you over a big pile of money, just because they like handing over big piles of money, you're wrong. These doctors are trained in the art of deception to be able to tell if your medical condition is valid or not. If your condition is valid and has merit, you should be fine. If you are trying to pull a fast one, chances are they will catch you!

Using C & P Exams to Strengthen Your Claims

This can be a great opportunity to strengthen your case if you are knowledgeable about your condition.

For example: Nothing can strengthen your case more than offering to submit to an X-ray if you know that you have a herniated disk. By explaining to the doctor how your daily functions are impeded by the pain of this condition, it can often be useful.

C & P doctors' evaluations weigh heavily on your claims. So convincing them can oftentimes go a long way in resolving claims efficiently.

*Remember that even after your case is decided, the VA does reserve the right to have you come in and be evaluated again. Don't worry though. It's usually only every five years or so, to see if your condition has changed. Think of it as a checkup on steroids.

The important part to remember is that even after your claims are resolved, continuing to keep your medical appointments is very important. Many veterans stop being seen shortly after their claims are approved, and oftentimes their disability rating is lowered or completely eliminated following their next C & P exam for failure to continue treatment. So if you work hard to get a disability rating, then you may want to keep this in mind, if you plan to maintain it!

Seeing What the Doc Had to Say

Shortly after your C & P exams are completed. You have the right under the freedom of information act to request a copy of your doctor's notes. Although they can be rather difficult at times to understand. By taking them to a private physician to have them explained, they can give you a pretty good idea of which way the VA is leaning with your case. It can also help with the grounds for your appeal, therefore I suggest requesting a copy of your VA medical records and doctors notes on a regular basis so that you can monitor what your VA medical doctors are saying in your medical file using VA Form 10-5345.

So contact your local veteran's benefits counselor and have them fill out a VA Form 10-5345. This form is the Request for and Authorization to

Release Medical Records or Health Information. Or you can download it yourself. Just go to:
http://www4.va.gov/vaforms/medical/pdf/vha-10-5345-fill.pdf

Once completed, fax the authorization to the facility housing your records, which will typically be the VA regional office or VA medical center that services your area. This information is in appendix A.

Why Veterans Decide to Appeal
The reasons that appeals are filed in VA cases are numerous. After all, when you feel an injustice has occurred, you can't help it.

More often than not, these things tend to start because many veterans feel slighted because your injuries are yours. When the VA puts a number on it like say 30 percent. People often feel that the number is too low. Veterans often think 30 percent, but I feel more like 60 percent. This is how it often begins. As the wife of a severely disabled veteran, I truly understand this feeling.

Proving A Service Connection
The other most common reason is that veterans often have a difficult time proving that their injuries and disabilities are service-connected. Vietnam veterans especially have often been put through the ringer in this respect, often spending years, if not decades, trying to establish a service-connection for the long-term effects that their time over in Vietnam has left them with.

As we go through the rest of this chapter, you may notice that it mostly pertains to medical appeals. Whether it's disability ratings, disability compensation, or pensions, this is because over nine out of every ten appeals fall into this category.

Disability Ratings
You see, many benefits require a minimum disability rating, such as the Chapter 31 Vocational Rehabilitation and Employment Program. You would need a 20 percent rating. If you have less than 20 percent, you wouldn't qualify unless you have a serious employment handicap that stems from a service-connected disability.

Because your disability rating often dictates which benefits are available to you. The higher your disability rating, the more benefits that you and your family can receive. This also dictates how much financial compensation you will receive for your injuries.

Reading Your Rejection Letter Carefully

Claims for benefits that do not fit into either disability ratings, disability compensation, or pensions, rarely need to go through the entire appeals process. Usually, if you meet the qualifications for the other types of benefits yet receive a letter rejecting your claim, the first thing that you should do is carefully read the rejection letter. It should clearly state the grounds that the VA has based your rejection on. Chances are, you will clearly see where the error has occurred which has caused the VA to make the decision they arrived at.

If an Error Occurs in Your Claim

More often than not, there was some sort of an error on either your part or their part. Either way to resolve the matter, you must understand what went wrong. If you are still having trouble understanding why you were denied, contact your local veteran's benefits counselor or VSO. They can help you to understand why your claim was rejected and what your chances are of getting the VA to change their decision.

For example: Let's say that your claim for the new Post-9/11 GI Bill was denied. After all, you separated on July 3, 2001. So you wouldn't qualify for that benefit because the law clearly states that this benefit is for veterans that served on or after September 11, 2001. Therefore, the VA denies your claim because you're not eligible for this benefit.

But wait, that's right, you got recalled for two more years; therefore, you do qualify for the Post-9/11 GI Bill.

Fixing Clerical Errors

So why did the claim get denied? Well, chances are it was just a clerical issue. Will you still have to go all the way through the nightmare of the appeals process?

Well, yes and no. Yes, you will have to start the appeals process. But no, you will probably not have to make it all of the way through it.

Once you have received your rejection letter, you should quickly be able to diagnose the problem, which in this case, would be your dates of service.

So as with all claims that are rejected, you have two options. Either you can walk away or appeal their decision. In this case, it would be a foolish not to appeal this.

Notice of Disagreement or NOD

The first step in the appeals process is to file a Notice of Disagreement, better known as a NOD. Since there is not an actual form for this, what you would have to do is just write down on a sheet of paper that you disagree with their findings. I would also suggest that you clearly state in easy-to-understand terms your reasoning and any additional evidence that will help support your claim.

For example: Notice of Disagreement.
I, Robin, disagree with your decision to reject my claim for the Post-9/11 GI Bill. Although I did separate from active duty on July 3, 2001. I was recalled to active duty on October 1, 2001, and served until October 1, 2003, as shown on my DD Form 214, which I will enclose another copy of [that's why you never send originals]. This would make me eligible to receive this benefit.

See, not so hard. That should do the trick. Now send your Notice of Disagreement off to the VA regional office that denied your claim, with the supporting evidence. Which in this case would be your DD Form 214.

*Remember that you will want to be careful though. You only have one year from the date that the VA regional office mails you its decision to file a NOD in your case. Otherwise, you lose your rights to appeal.

Connecting the Dots

After the VA regional office receives your NOD. They will take another look at your case. In the example that I have been using, because we left them a really nice trail of bread crumbs. They should be able to see the error of their ways. So hopefully, they will see that you do in fact qualify for the benefit and then go ahead and grant it because after all they have the power to grant your claim.

To Dig In or Walk Away

If you do decide to walk away, make sure that the VA is in the right, before you give up. Nothing makes me more upset than seeing a veteran who faithfully served their country, and in many cases sustained an injury, only to give up on the process when they are in the right. These brave warriors who fought with such bravery and heroism often need to dig in and use that same fighting spirit to achieve their goals in receiving their benefits.

To Appeal or Not to Appeal? That Is the Question

For those of you that do decide to appeal, make sure that you are in the right. I promise you this: nothing will make you more upset than to go through all of the appeals process, only to realize later on that you don't qualify and have wasted your time!

Statement of the Case or SOC

Once you have filed your NOD as I stated. The VA regional office will reconsider your claim. Sometimes, they will approve your claim, and you will be on your way.

Although oftentimes, especially with cases involving service-connected disabilities. This oftentimes doesn't work out so well for the veteran. So after you have submitted your NOD, if the VA regional office that is reviewing your case decides that they are not going to overturn their decision, hence another rejection letter. The VA will provide you with a Statement of the Case, better known as a SOC.

A statement of the case is used to inform you that the VA regional office isn't going to change their decision and why. The why is truly what is important here. You see, it can give you a lot of valuable insight as to why your claim continues to get denied.

The SOC will provide you with a summary of the evidence. Then it will explain all of the applicable laws and the regulations governing their decision. The SOC will also include all of the reasons for their decision as well as the statute numbers the VA is quoting should be listed as well. All you need to do is take the statute numbers and do a search on your computer with them. By reading the actual statutes you can start to understand why the VA made the decision they did; furthermore, they will enclose within the SOC your very own VA Form 9. This would be your next step in the appeals process.

Getting Ready for the Long Haul

When you receive your (SOC), this is more of a gut check time. You seriously need to evaluate your position on where you stand. I am not implying by any means that you can't win from this point forward. What I am saying is that it is more often than not going to be a very long and painful process to continue, so you will have to strap yourself in for the long haul.

Having a Loved One's Help

Since those who usually press on from this point tend to be severely disabled veterans that have serious health issues. I recommend that you have either your spouse or a loved one (who is organized) help you, if they haven't been already, from this point forward. In cases that go the distance, there are often numerous time deadlines. If you do not meet these deadlines, you can lose your rights to appeal. Since oftentimes these veterans are in and out of the hospital. They could really use a hand.

For example: While my husband was going through the process of trying to fight his appeal. He was hospitalized on numerous occasions for paralysis. He was also taking a chemo-type drug, lost over a hundred pounds, had several surgeries, and had gangrene in his intestines.

So see, oftentimes they will need your help. So it is better to start helping early in the process. That way, you are not trying to play catch-up and learning as you go. Oftentimes these veterans are simply trying to survive. Fighting their own personal wars. Between trying to survive, fighting with the VA, and often social security as well. They often need help, but are too proud to ask, so don't let them do it alone.

Appeal to the Board of Veterans' Appeals VA Form 9

These types of veterans often have no other recourse but to continue on with the process of trying to receive their benefits. This is why the VA has given us the VA Form 9. Which is the Appeal to the Board of Veterans' Appeals form. If you make a mistake or lose yours, you can print off another one at: http://www4.va.gov/vaforms/va/pdf/VA9.pdf

The Sixty-day Rule

*Keep in mind you only have sixty days to file this form, from the time that the VA regional office mailed you your SOC. Or one year from the date that your claim was originally denied, whichever date is later.

The Board of Veterans' Appeals is located in Washington D.C. This will more than likely add several years onto the time that it takes to settle your claims. This would be the point that I would absolutely be seeking counsel or representation in a hurry.

Counsel

Counsel would be in the form of a lawyer. Sometimes depending on the complexity of your case, it can be necessary. Since most people that have been injured in the service are not doctors or lawyers. They often need someone who is knowledgeable about the laws governing these types of issues.

The downside would be that they are normally going to charge you a fee for their services and expertise. These attorneys usually work on what is known as a contingency. The contingency fee for disability claims is based on the amount of back payment you receive when your claim is settled, plus the administrative fees.

They do this for both VA disability claims and social security disability claims since their fee is contingent on them winning your claim. They will only take your case if they feel that they can win. If you decide to go this route, make sure that the attorney specializes in veterans' legal issues before you hire them!

Some attorneys offer what is known as pro bono services. This means that they take your case for free. Be careful to make sure that they specialize in veterans' legal issues. There is also an independent, nonprofit organization called the National Veterans Legal Services Program. They are located in Washington D.C. They help veterans through the appeals process. They also manage the Veterans Consortium Pro Bono Program.

Veterans Service Organizations (VSO)

As for representation, this would be your VSOs, such as the American Legion, Veterans of Foreign Wars, the Disabled American Veterans or one of the various other organizations that assist veterans. I strongly urge you to join at least one of these VSOs. These groups are great. They can assist you with information having to do with your appeal and can also act as representation for you, free of charge; but the amount of representation is limited due to the amount of resources versus the number of people seeking them. Either way, you will definitely need one or the other.

Appointment of Individual as Claimant's Representative VA Form 21-22A

If you hire an attorney, you will need them to submit a VA Form 21-22A. This is the Appointment of Individual as Claimant's Representative. This is your authorization to have an attorney on your case. You can download this form at: http://www.vba.va.gov/pubs/forms/VBA-21-22A-ARE.pdf

VA Form 21-22

If you decide to go with a VSO, you will need to submit VA Form 21-22 to the VA regional office. This is the Appointment of Veterans Service Organization as Claimant's Representative. This is your authorization to have a VSO as a representative on your case. You can download this form at: http://www.vba.va.gov/pubs/forms/VBA-21-22-ARE.pdf

Getting ready for your appeal

Now it's time to fill out that good ole VA Form 9 so that you can appeal to the Board of Veterans' Appeals. This is the first step in having your appeal go to Washington D.C.

Make sure that you state very clearly which decisions you are appealing. (In some cases, there may be multiple benefits in question.) Then you will want to tell them of any mistakes that you have found within the SOC.

*Remember, you will want to use this as your opportunity to request a hearing with the Board of Veterans' Appeals, more about this later in this chapter.

Submitting New Supplemental Evidence

You will also want to use this as an opportunity to submit any new and relevant evidence into your claim, although you should have submitted any and all evidence already into your claim (when you originally filed the claim). Oftentimes new information comes into play, especially when it comes to disability ratings and such.

For example: "Say that your claim is for an increase in your service-connected disability rating." Although you have already established that your injuries are service-connected because the VA has already granted you a 40 percent disability rating. Which actually seemed fair at the time, but five years later, your condition gets much, much worse, so therefore, you filed for an increase in your disability rating. I mean, after all, you are completely incapacitated now.

You filed your claim for an increase in your disability rating, but it was denied. You then filed your NOD, but they gave you a SOC instead, but with all of the time that has passed since you originally filed your claim to increase your disability rating. You now have a whole new mountain of medical documentation (new evidence) that can be used to strengthen your claim in your ongoing appeal. This is your opportunity to submit it.

Preparing Your VA Form 9

Now put it all in with your VA Form 9 paperwork. Then send it back to your VA regional office. The VA will then reconsider your case based on the new information, such as the errors that you found in the SOC or the new medical documentation that you have provided. It's quite possible that the new medical documentation (hence new medical opinions by your doctors as to the increased severity of your condition and clinical treatment records) can often make the difference.

Supplemental Statement of the Case (SSOC)

After the regional office considers the new evidence, they will either grant your claim or send you a Supplemental Statement of the Case, better known as an SSOC. If you receive an SSOC, it's just like an SOC, but it addresses all of the new evidence and disagreements that have come up since and often by the first SOC.

Now it's time to repeat the process all over. You once again have sixty days to respond as to what you disagree with. I like to look at this as the VA's version of mediation. These SSOCs can often go back and forth several times. Taking up valuable time. In some cases, these issues can get cleared up by going back and forth with SSOCs and NODs, but oftentimes this can be demoralizing with how long it takes.

Why You Should Request a Local Office Hearing
Which is why when you originally file your VA Form 9, you should ask for a local office hearing. This is different than a Board of Veterans' Appeals hearing. It will give you and your counsel or representative (if they can come) the opportunity to speak directly with a hearing officer from the VA regional offices staff.

Chances are your case won't end right here, but it's a great way to pick their brain. If you ask the right questions, you can often figure out how strong your claim is, any other supporting documentation that you will need to support your claim, and which laws you may be needing to overcome to get the proper outcome. So prepare for your hearing ahead of time and write down any relevant questions pertaining to your appeal that way you can ask questions during the hearing. By requesting a local office hearing along with your VA Form 9, and asking direct relevant questions, it will almost assuredly shave off quite a bit of time that it takes to settle your appeal.

*This way, you're not just randomly guessing as to what they might be needing.

Don't Fall into the SOC Hole
This is where veterans often get caught up, every time that you submit new evidence or argue mistakes from the last SSOC. The VA regional office must reevaluate your claim, then decide if they are going to grant the benefit or reject your claim again.

If the regional office still feels that your claim does not have merit, they will send you another SSOC. Then you will have to respond all over again. This can add years alone onto your appeal. By requesting a local office hearing, veterans can easily cut down on the number of SOCs, SSOCs, and NODs because every day that your claim is caught up arguing with the regional office is another day that your case hasn't been docketed in Washington D.C. Therefore, the faster you make it through this part, the better unless you and your attorney/representative feel that you can settle your claim without it going to Washington D.C. In which case, it may be more efficient to handle your case at the regional level.

The Ninety-day Rule

Once you finish going back and forth with the VA regional office. They will send you one final letter stating that you have ninety days from the date that the letter was sent to either send in any additional information (evidence) or to switch counsel or your representative. This is called the ninety-day rule.

After the ninety days, unless you have elected to change counsel/representation or submit new evidence, in which case, you will be waiting on another SSOC. After the ninety days, your appeal will finally be sent to the VA Washington center to be placed on the docket.

Taking Your Case to Washington

Up until this point, you have been going back and forth with the VA regional office that services your area. By docketing your case in Washington D.C., you are taking the decision out of the regional office's hands and placing it squarely in the hands of the Board of Veterans' Appeals or BVA for short. The advantage of your claim going to Washington D.C. is that oftentimes decisions on claims vary from state to state. While one veteran has their claim approved in Alabama, the next veteran may have their claim denied in Georgia. By going to Washington D.C., the BVA can make a more uniformed decision.

The Odds of Your Appeal

This is by no means a guarantee that you will get a different result though. In 2009 the BVA made determinations on 48,804 cases. Of those, 24.0 percent were approved, 36.1 percent were denied, 2.6 percent were other and 37.3 percent were remanded or sent back for further work to be done by the regional office because they were incomplete. If you look carefully you will notice the highest percentage of outcomes were those remanded back to the regional office for more work to be done. In simple terms this means that either the appeal is incomplete and they need more information to make an informed decision. Or that there is not enough documentation to correctly diagnose the severity of your condition. Therefore you will want to be extremely careful not to rush your appeal to quickly through the regional office stage and push it up to Washington D.C. without having your appeal being properly worked on, because they BVA will just send it back to the regional office to have them do more work on it. This will end up adding several months if not longer onto the amount of time it takes to settle your appeal.

Researching Possible Outcomes

One suggestion would be to research online as to if other veterans with the same exact condition or injuries, with the same exact documentation, to see if they were awarded their claims. If you can research and find other veterans that have been through the exact same scenario that you're going through, this can often give you an idea of the possible outcome. The BVA makes uniform decisions. Their decisions don't vary from state to state.

*Remember that if you want a hearing with the BVA, you need to make that request when you submit your VA Form 9. The request is located on line 8 on VA Form 9. These are different than local office hearings because they are with a BVA hearing officer, not a regional hearing officer.

If you are going to request a BVA hearing, make sure that you request it as early in the game as possible. Otherwise, it can delay the process. If you failed to request a hearing on your VA Form 9, you can still ask for one though (prior to the ninety-day rule), by writing the board directly to request one. You need to make your request to:

> Board of Veterans' Appeals (014)
> Department of Veterans Affairs
> 810 Vermont Avenue, NW
> Washington, D.C. 20420

Stating Your Case to the BVA

If your claim is for a disability that is either rare or complicated, I would suggest asking for a hearing, although the BVA bases their decisions on the supporting evidence in your case. A hearing is a good way to clarify any questions that the board may have about your case. You want to give the board the clearest picture possible about your case so that they can make the correct decision.

There are three different ways to have a BVA hearing. You will want to be specific when you request which type you would like on VA Form 9 because you can only choose one.

1. BVA hearing in Washington D.C. This means that you go to Washington D.C. and speak with the board in person. The problem associated with this is that you will be responsible for any and all costs incurred by you and your counsel/representative. Hotels, meals, airline tickets, etc., will be your responsibility if you choose to do it this way.

2. Travel boards. This means that the board will come to your VA regional office. Well, it's better than going to them but the problem with this is that getting the board to come to you can often cause delays. Due to scheduling conflicts such as when they will be coming to your area versus when your case will be decided. Also the amount of travel funds available to the board are limited, which can further cause delays.

3. Videoconference hearings. This is a great alternative because it causes neither party to have to travel, at least very far. They are arranged so that the board can stay in Washington D.C. and you can speak with them via videoconference at your VA regional office. This is the easiest way to get it accomplished.

Remember, the sooner the BVA receives your appeal. The sooner your case gets docketed. They will review your case in the order that it is received, so now the waiting game begins.

The Waiting Game

This would be the bad part. This is why you should exhaust every other alternative prior to requesting that the BVA make a decision on your claim. In 1998, it was taking about two years to receive a decision from the board on each case. From the time that the appeal was placed on the board's docket until the BVA decision was issued. Since the war started in 2001, more and more claims are being filed (hence more appeals). Now it is taking considerably longer. The average time in 2009 was in excess of four years.

Stuck in a Pileup

There really isn't an effective way to speed up the process once your case has been placed on the BVA docket, and you have been given a docket number. The only way that you can have your case decided before the cases that came before yours is to submit a motion to advance on the docket. This is a letter written directly to the board that explains (in detail) why you feel that your case should be decided before other cases, because most appeals tend to have hardships associated with them. The board is not quick to grant them unless you can show convincing proof of exceptional circumstances.

Examples of this would be: terminal illness, danger of bankruptcy or foreclosure, or an error by the VA that has caused a significant delay in the docketing of an appeal. But don't get your hopes up though. Less than 15 percent of requests to advance on the docket are approved, if you would like to submit a motion to advance on the docket. Submit your request to:

> Board of Veterans' Appeals (014)
> Department of Veterans Affairs
> 810 Vermont Avenue, NW
> Washington, D.C. 20420

Checking Up on Your Appeal

This is where veterans often make mistakes. After your appeal is given a docket number. Veterans often feel that nothing is happening fast enough, so they tend to do things like contact their congressman's office. More often than not, all that this tends to do is further slow the process, unless the case has exceptional circumstances.

If you would like to check the status of your appeal, the best way to do this is to contact the VA regional office that has been handling your appeal. You will need your docket number for them to be able to access your case, unless you have received a written notification from your regional office that your claim has been transferred to the BVA in the Washington D.C. center. Up until that point your claim will be at the regional office.

Once the regional office sends your claim off to the BVA, which means that your case will be reviewed within the next three to four months. At this point, if you need to check the status, you will need to contact the board directly by calling (202) 565-5436. The BVA will also notify you in writing when they receive your file.

*Remember that although the appeals process can get pretty frustrating, you will want to refrain from calling them all the time. Being a pain will not speed up your claim at all. Really all it will do is anger the people that control your fate. So being polite and understanding can be helpful here. The fact that hundreds of other disgruntled veterans have already screamed at the VA representative before your call each day, therefore I suggest being polite and engaging then trying to relate to their situation. This really can help when seeking answers to your questions.

BVA Making the Decision

When your appeals docket number finally comes up. Then your appeal is assigned to a board member. The board member is an experienced attorney that has expertise when it comes to veteran's law. This board member acts as a judge when it comes to your appeals claim and makes the final decision. They do have other staff attorneys to help them review your case by reviewing the facts of your appeal and weighing in on all of the evidence and applicable laws.

The board member and a staff attorney will check to see that your file is complete. Then they will review all of your evidence and arguments. They will review all of the SOCs, SSOCs, and NODs. They will then review the transcript of the hearing (if you had one). They will also review any other information included in the claim folder (such as medical evidence).

The staff attorney will also at the direction of the board member. Conduct additional research and prepare recommendations for the board member's review. This is often necessary in severe medical cases.

Then before a decision is reached, the board member will thoroughly examine all of the materials in the claims folder. Along with any recommendations that have been prepared by the staff attorney. Then the board member will issue a decision. Make sure that the VA has your correct mailing address at all times; otherwise, it can cause a substantial delay in contacting you with the outcome of your appeal.

Possible outcomes of your appeal

Once the board has issued a decision on your appeal, they will send your decision in the mail. The board will be deciding to do one of three things.

1. Winning your appeal—If this happens, no other action will need to be taken. The board will notify your regional office that has jurisdiction over your case. Then your benefits will start automatically, and you will be retro-paid for any back payment that may have occurred from the filing date. You will not have to reapply to receive them.

2. Your appeal is remanded—If this happens, your case will be sent back to the regional office that has jurisdiction over your case. To perform additional work on some aspect of your case, this may cause the regional office to issue a new decision, if the regional office changes their decision and approves your claim. Then the appeal is over.

   Depending on why your case was remanded, though, they may issue you another SSOC. Then you will have to send another NOD within sixty days to comment on it.

   If your claim is remanded, and the regional offices decision is still to deny your claim, don't worry. You will not lose your place in line. After the regional office is finished, they will send your claim back to Washington D.C., and your claim will keep its original place on the BVA's docket. It will be reviewed shortly after its return; then, the board will make its determination.

3. Your appeal is denied—If your appeal is denied. Your options really do start to become limited, but there are still three options that you have left.

File a Motion to Reconsider

A motion to reconsider your appeal is used if you can demonstrate that the board made an "obvious error of fact or law in its decision." This is not to be used just because you are unhappy or disagree with the board's decision.

You must show that the board made a mistake, and if that mistake had not occurred, the board's decision would have been different.

If you decide to file a motion to reconsider, I strongly urge you to have your counsel/representative help you with this. You will need to send the motion directly to the board, not your regional office. Just mail it to:

> Board of Veterans' Appeals (014)
> Department of Veterans Affairs
> 810 Vermont Avenue, NW,
> Washington DC. 20420

Reopening Your Appeal

If your claim has "new and material evidence" that was not included in your claims folder when your case was decided. Then the VA regional office *may* decide to reopen your appeal and start the appeals process all over again. The reason that I say "may" is that the VA regional office (yeah, the people that you have been going round and round with), they will decide if the evidence is "new and material."

For example: Say that you have gone through the entire appeals process to raise your disability rating because you lost partial use of both of your legs (which was service-connected). Your condition was bad when you originally filed your claims, but in the four to five years that your claim was stuck in the appeals process, your condition worsened.

Then just as your claim was being reviewed by the board, the doctors decided to amputate. Your claim was too far along to stop the process and add this "new and material evidence" into your claims file, so the board, not knowing this new and material evidence (which would more than likely have affected the cases outcome), decided to deny your claim. This would more than likely qualify as grounds to reopen your appeal.

Appeal to the U.S. Court of Veterans Appeals

This would be your last resort. You must file a notice of appeal to the U.S. Court of Veterans Appeals. Also known as the Court, this is an independent federal court located in Washington D.C. that is not part of the Department of Veterans Affairs. You absolutely positively will need a lawyer if you plan to take your appeal into federal court. Otherwise, you will almost assuredly lose. See the Counsel section earlier in this chapter.

You only have 120 days from the date that the BVA mails its decision to file "an original notice of appeal" with the court. If by chance you filed a motion to reconsider within the 120 days, but the motion was denied. Your 120-day clock starts over from the day that the BVA mails you the letter denying your motion to reconsider.

If you decide to file a notice of appeal with the court, you can fax it to (202) 501-5848. If you decide to fax your notice of appeal, you will have fourteen days to send in the filing fees, or submit a declaration of financial hardship (if you can't afford the fees), or mail your notice of appeal to:

> Clerk of the Court
> U.S. Court of Appeals for Veterans Claims
> 625 Indiana Avenue, NW, Suite 900
> Washington D.C. 20004

You should also file a copy of the notice of appeal with the VA general counsel at:

> Office of the General Counsel (027)
> Department of Veterans Affairs
> 810 Vermont Avenue, NW
> Washington D.C. 20420

*Remember to make sure that when you file your notice of appeal, to include your full name, phone number, current address, date of the BVA decision, and docket number.

The only type of decision that is not allowed to be appealed to the best of my knowledge are decisions concerning the need for either certain types of medical treatments or physician's decisions to either prescribe or not prescribe a particular type of drug. This would need to be taken up with the director of the VA medical center in question.

Section 2

Taking Care of Our Own

In the chapters within this section, we will be discussing all of the issues having to do with how the government is prepared to assist you and your family after your separation from service, from transition counseling to taking care of your injuries through compensation and pensions. Also military retirements for those of you that have completed twenty-plus years of service or that receive medical retirement and how that can affect your disability compensation. Finally, you will learn everything about the VA health care system and medical and dental insurance through TRICARE, CHAMPVA, and the other various programs. So let's get to it. There is a lot to cover!

Chapter 4

Transitioning from the Military

Now that you have a grasp on how the claims and appeals process works. It's time to talk about your life after the military. Although this chapter may not be useful to everybody, there are plenty of soldiers, sailors, and airmen that can use some help in this area because nobody plans to fail, but oftentimes with failure, we have failed to plan!

In this chapter, we will be talking about:

- Transitioning to civilian life.
- Transitioning counseling.
- Coping with PTSD.
- Finding that perfect spot to relocate.
- Choosing a post-military career.
- Keeping our families in mind.

Exiting the military can be quite stressful, to say the least. The challenges that often plague servicemen and women and their families are numerous. While each person's situation and circumstances often vary. There are certain things that each person can do to put themselves in the best situation for success.

If you were to ask one hundred servicemen what they plan to do when they got out of the military. You would more often than not get one hundred different answers. Although certain key components will be recurring (such as they want to go to college or move back home). Each person has different goals that they want to accomplish.

I like to look at getting out of the military as a giant jigsaw puzzle. The more pieces that you have completed prior to getting out, the better off you will be. The things that you really need to factor into your life after the service are the following:

1. What field do I want to work in, and what type of job do I want to pursue?
2. Are there jobs available in that field?
3. Where do I want to live, and can I furnish my new home or apartment?
4. Do I plan to go to college or need retraining?
5. Do I have medical issues that I will need treatment for?
6. What are my finances like? Will I be receiving compensation, pension, or retirement pay?
7. What about my family? Where will my kids go to school?

Things to Consider before Deciding Where to Relocate

Since each person has a different set of circumstances and goals surrounding their separation from the military. It is best to first evaluate your goals as to what you would like to do post-service because this can often dictate where you will want to live.

For example: If you were in the Navy and grew accustomed to sea life and wanted to continue working on or being around boats. Then Montana probably wouldn't be the best place to relocate to.

Your post-military career should always make sense as to where you plan on relocating. In other words, if you worked in the aviation field for the military and plan to work for a commercial airline. Then you should probably plan to locate yourself near an airport. Makes sense, right?

Deciding on a Career Path

One problem that often arises when people decide to separate is that they fail to look at what jobs they are qualified for. Some jobs in the military, as we all know, have very few, if any civilian applications, although you may have learned teamwork and leadership qualities. Those plus fifty cents will typically only buy you a cup of coffee. That is why the VA has all of those educational programs, such as the GI Bill and the Chapter 31 program. We will discuss these in depth in chapters 9 and 10.

On one hand, some jobs within the military can lead to great post-service careers that require little to no retraining in the outside world. By using your educational assistance, you can assuredly still further advance your marketability in private industry.

On the other hand, many jobs in the military can often lead nowhere in the outside world. So oftentimes going back to school can be the best option under these circumstances. So you would want to submit your claims for your educational benefits ahead of time. Then begin applying to schools as explained in chapters 9 and 10. That way, you will know which area you will need to relocate to when your enlistment is up.

Utilizing Transitional Assistance

The transitional assistance program office and the Army Career and Alumni Program Center (for army personnel) can also be an invaluable asset when trying to figure out what to do post-military, if you have already separated from the service. You can also contact your local vet center. They offer transitional as well as PTSD counseling.

The VA offers numerous types of counseling to many veterans after separation from the service. These are explained in detail in chapter 7. Since oftentimes when people separate from the service, the massive change in their life can lead to serious depression, which can affect every aspect of not only the veteran's life, but their family's lives as well.

Coping with PTSD

This is an extremely difficult topic to discuss, but is very necessary, with so many servicemen and servicewomen returning with this life-altering condition that is paralyzing not only for the veteran, but their entire families as well. It's hard to say exactly what to do in these situations because there is no magic spell that can fix our loved ones.

As family members of these veterans, all we can do is love them and be sensitive to their problems. Then work toward fixing them through counseling, in certain cases medicating them, but most importantly showing them that we are there for them.

If you have a veteran that suffers from PTSD in your life, make sure that they are getting the proper help that they need through either a support group or one-on-one counseling. Not a bottle of alcohol or drugs.

In all cases, the thing to remember when dealing with PTSD-related issues is that the only way to get your loved ones back is by dealing with the problems. Do not dismiss them since in most cases the veteran is usually the last person to see the severity of the condition. As family and friends of these veterans, it becomes our job to recognize the problems that exist. By choosing not to deal with the veteran's medical issues or ignoring them hoping they will go away by themselves, their conditions will not get better on their own. In the vast majority of untreated cases it causes a massive strain on the families dynamic. Which frequently ends in divorce. If these problems are ignored, it will more often than not lead to alcoholism, drug addiction, homelessness, or even suicide. If you need help, contact either of the following:

- Your local VA vet center as explained in chapter 7 or the Outreach Center For Psychological Health and Traumatic Brain Injury Info and Resources. This is staffed by the DOD. Their number is (866) 966-1020.
- The National Suicide Prevention hotline at (800) 273-TALK.

PTSD Service Dogs

For veterans that have severe PTSD, there are also several organizations that have been training psychiatric service dogs. These organizations have been growing at an alarming rate due to the amount of returning servicemen and servicewomen that are in need of them. For more information on psychiatric service dogs, visit either: http://www.puppiesbehindbars.org/ or http://www.assistancedogsinternational.org/

Since there is usually quite a long wait, and in most cases, fees that are associated with going this route, if the veteran's PTSD is not severe enough to meet their stringent standards. You may want to look into adopting a regular dog. I have seen many instances of returning soldier's spouses that have adopted a regular pet dog for their veteran, and in many cases, the pet has enriched the veteran's quality of life immensely.

Picking Just the Right Place for Your Entire Family

The trick is to figure out ahead of time what it is that you are trying to accomplish, then when the time is right, move to a place that is most suitable.

For example: My husband was born and raised just outside of Orlando, Florida. He joined the Navy shortly after high school. After a few years into his enlistment, he was severely injured, so he was medically retired from the service.

He knew, growing up in Orlando, that Central Florida has great facilities for veterans. Therefore, in his case, it made perfect sense to come back.

He is now able to enjoy the fact that not only can he live close to his family (which is able to help with his day-to-day life as a disabled veteran). But there is also the Orlando VA Medical Center about thirty minutes away (for VA health care, see Chapter 7).

Then he also is able to shop at the Navy Exchange located fifteen minutes away. Shopping at the exchange is explained in chapter 13.

Also, there is a community college right down the street and a university about thirty minutes away as well. Educational benefits are located in chapters 9 and 10.

Additionally, our VA local office is ten minutes away. We also have access to a full working Air Force base less than an hour away, which rents boats through the MWR program, which is explained in chapter 13.

Also, at the time of his separation, Orlando had a booming job market; so at the time, jobs were plentiful. These were all things that factored into his decision to move back to the Central Florida area.

Although moving to a more rural area may seem like a great idea because it is often less expensive to live. If you're three hours away from a VA hospital or two hours away from your college campus, you will end up paying for a lot of gas.

Also, many disabled veterans have several doctors' appointments each month, each mile farther away from either the hospital or campus. That's a mile there and also a mile back. Trust me, it adds up. Just make sure that the location that you relocate to makes sense with your needs.

Additional Benefits by Each State

Since some states are often more veteran friendly than others for lack of a better term. It's a good idea to research each state's veteran's benefits prior to moving to a particular state. Many veterans plan to move back to the state from which they came from.

While other veterans join the military with the intentions of never going back to where they came from, if you are not sure as to which state you would like to relocate to. You may want to use the state veteran's directory. This is a great little tool available on the Internet. It can help you see each state's additional veteran's benefits. That way, you can make an informed decision as to which state offers the best additional benefits to meet your needs. This great little tool can be found at: http://www. military.com/benefits/veteran-benefits/state-veterans-benefits-directory

Government Jobs versus the Private Sector

For those of you that are looking to jump right into the job market. Take a look at government jobs. The preference points that you will receive because of your military service are often the difference between getting the job or not. This is explained in detail in chapter 11.

For those of you that are tired of working for the man. The SBA has a new program for veterans that can help you get that new small business off the ground. This as well is explained in detail in chapter 11.

Renting versus Owning

Then you will have to decide if you want to either rent or own. Each has its own merits and drawbacks. They are the following:

- Renting has its pros and cons.
Pros—low maintenance, it's often cheaper, easier to qualify, and you can move out easier (if needed).
Cons—you're throwing your money out a window since you have no ownership and the rates often go up every year. You also usually have quite a few neighbors and rules.

- Owning has its pros and cons as well.
Pros—you have ownership. Usually more privacy, and over time it can build you a safety net through equity. Also, you can make alterations to your property if needed.
Cons—if things break, it is your responsibility to fix them, so you will need to have constant upkeep, oftentimes this can be much more expensive.

These are all things that you should consider before you get out of the service. Most service members tend to move several times in the first few years after separating from the service, due to either college, career, or romantic reasons. Since moving can cost you quite a bit of money. The faster you get it right the better. If you're considering owning a home, be sure to read the section on VA home loans in chapter 12. It will be quite helpful to you.

Taking Care of Your Family

For service members that already have families of their own. You really need to consider the impact that your relocation will have on your spouse and children. By moving, your spouse may be forced to change jobs. Your children will often need to change schools. This can especially be a huge shock to your children's systems. That may require extensive counseling, so keeping health insurance on your family is very important. In many cases, you can receive both medical and dental insurance at least temporarily after your separation. This is covered in detail in chapter 8.

Figuring Out Your Finances

Then comes the question of money, will I be receiving VA compensation or a pension for my injuries? If so, how much? All of this is covered extensively in chapter 5.

Also, if you're retiring from the military, you will need to be able to calculate how much your retirement is, to be able to plan for your future. By reading chapter 6, you will be able to calculate your retirement pay.

Just keep all of these factors in mind when deciding if, when, and where to relocate to. Remember that by getting it right the first time, you can save yourself quite a bit of time, energy, and money.

Chapter 5

Disability Compensation and Pensions

In this chapter, we will be discussing everything having to do with financial compensation for your injuries and the VA pension system. You will learn everything from how the physical evaluation board system works. To the importance of proving a service-connection has occurred and all of the ways to prove that a service-connection exists through documentation. Then how the VA determines what your disability rating will be and how to put yourself in the best position to get a fair rating. Next you will learn how the VA combines multiple disability ratings, how to calculate your disability compensation pay, and who qualifies for special monthly compensation and P & T. Finally, we will end this chapter with the rules and amounts of pensions, death pensions, DIC, and Medal-of-Honor pensions.

Learning about VA Compensation

As of June 30, 2010, there were 3.16 million disabled veterans receiving VA disability compensation benefits for their service-connected disabilities. Of that 3.16 million, 289,987 have received a disability rating of 100 percent from the VA. That's just over 9 percent of all disabled veterans that are rated at 100 percent disabled.

Oftentimes, when I speak with disabled veterans, they complain that it's impossible to get a 100 percent disability rating. That's not the case, though, because as the wife of a severely disabled veteran, I have seen that it is possible within my own family. Although the VA isn't jumping up and down to hand out higher disability ratings. It does fall back on the veteran to prove that they meet the eligibility requirements for a higher disability rating under the VA's guidelines.

Why Some Veterans Get a Higher Disability Rating

I often see veterans making the mistake of thinking that they are going to get a really high disability rating for their injuries just because they can prove a service-connection exists. Proving a service-connection will only make the VA acknowledge that your injuries exist and were either caused or aggravated by your military service. That can easily lead to a 0 percent disability rating though.

Why Un-employability Matters So Much

To receive a disability rating higher than 0 percent, you need to be able to prove that your injuries reduce your earning capacity by reducing your ability to get and maintain a decent-paying job. The lower your ability to maintain gainful employment due to your service-connected disability, the higher your disability rating should be through the VA. Often the process to start receiving disability compensation benefits starts prior to separating from the military, through the PEB process.

Physical Evaluation Board or PEB

Oftentimes service members that become either injured or disabled are given what is known as a Physical Evaluation Board or PEB for short. These boards are used by the military to evaluate service members' medical conditions. Then determine if the service member is medically fit to stay in the service branch or not.

What the PEB Does

The PEB is made up of active-duty physicians that are not personally involved in your medical care. These doctors review your entire medical file and make a determination as to if you should be retained, medically separated, or medically retired. The PEB then sends its recommendations to the Central Medical Board (CMB). The CMB will ultimately make the decision whether to send you back to work or to send you home. They base their decision on several criteria:

a. Whether you can perform your military job.
b. The stability of your condition.
c. If your condition will likely worsen by continued military service.
d. Your assigned disability rating.
e. In the case of a preexisting condition, your number of years of active-duty service.

PEB Possible Outcomes

The Central Medical Board will ultimately find that you fit into one of these five groups:

1. Fit for duty—this happens if the board finds that you are reasonably able to perform your job. If they feel that you are unfit to perform your current position, but could reasonably do another job that, from a medical standpoint, would not further aggravate your condition. Then they can put you in for retraining into a different position. This allows you to stay in the service.

2. Separated without severance pay—this happens for several reasons. Such as if you injured yourself through an act of willful misconduct or willful negligence. Such as intentionally breaking your leg to get out of your pending deployment.

    This can also be used if you had a prior service medical condition, if that condition hasn't been permanently aggravated by your military service. This only applies to service members that have less than eight years of active duty though (or an equivalent number of retirement points for reserve and National Guard members). This is where a lot of service members run into problems that have PTSD. After being evaluated by a military psychologist, the doctor merely has to come to a conclusion that the service members psychological issues started prior to their military service and therefore the service member is deemed to have a personality disorder. This absolves the military of responsibility for the injury. If you're a service member that is suffering from PTSD? When speaking with your doctors, make sure that you only discuss your PTSD issues that relate directly to your military service!

3. Separated with severance pay—this happens when a PEB finds you unfit for duty but your injuries are deemed to be less than 30 percent disabling, with less than twenty years of service. They will give you a severance package that will equal two months of basic pay for each year of service. Not to exceed twelve years of service.

Although this may seem like a great deal at the time it is offered. If your injuries seem minor, time often tends to make us look back and regret the decisions we once made, so before you spend that severance money. You will want to seriously consider this first.

Remember that if you receive a severance check often referred to as a lump sum (medical severance package). Then afterward decide to file a claim for disability compensation with the VA. If you are awarded disability compensation benefits, then you *must* pay back the severance money before you can receive any disability compensation.

Oftentimes so many veterans make a huge mistake here. They take ten, twenty, sometimes thirty thousand dollars and often spend it. Not realizing that the VA will just end up garnishing it back from them every month until that money is paid in full, before they can receive one penny of disability compensation. A simple rule to remember is that you will make far more money over time, if you are patient.

4. Temporary Disability Retirement List or TDRL—this would be for service members that receive a disability rating of 30 percent or higher from the board. To qualify, you must also have spent at least eight years in the military *or* your disability must have been incurred in the line of duty. Temporary as the name implies means that if your condition improves, the military reserves the right to find you fit for duty at a later date. The military can reevaluate your condition every eighteen months for up to five years. If they clear you for duty, they can bring you back. If your condition has not improved at the end of the five years. You will be permanently medically retired.

   For example: This is often used for service members with several broken bones or a bad back. Although they are unfit for duty at the time. Three years from now, it may have healed to an acceptable level, so the military may find you fit for duty again.

5. Permanent Disability Retirement List or PDRL—this is often referred to as a permanent medical retirement. This is for injuries that are more permanent in nature. That are over 30 percent disabling, and you have spent at least eight years in the military *or* your disability must have been incurred in the line of duty. If the board feels that your condition will not improve even five years from now. They can place you directly into permanent medical retirement.

   For those placed onto either TDRL or PDRL. Your compensation pay will be calculated based on:

   retired base pay   x   disability rating
   or
   retired base pay   x   2.5%   x   number of years of service

Whichever is higher is the one that will be applied. However, those placed on the TDRL will receive no less than 50 percent of their retired base pay. Another major advantage of being placed onto either the TDRL or PDRL is that you can retain your TRICARE benefits which are explained in chapter 8. This alone can be very helpful when it comes to getting a fair disability rating from the VA because it allows you to be seen by private doctors which can offer unbiased medical opinions.

Reasons to Receive Your Compensation from the VA

You will want to file your claims for disability compensation with the VA as quickly as possible using VA Form 21-526, which was explained in chapter 2. I strongly urge you to contact your local veteran's benefits counselor or VSO to have them help you file the proper paperwork and supporting evidence. The military uses the "Department of Veterans Affairs Schedule for Rating Disabilities" to rate your injuries, which means it is the same schedule that the VA uses.

Why the Ratings Are Different

It is very important to understand that the military rates only conditions determined to be "physically unfitting, compensating for the loss of a military career." As where the VA can rate any service-connected impairments or injuries, therefore compensating for the impact and the loss of civilian employability, huge difference, right!

This is why veterans often receive a PEB and are put on the TDRL with a 40 percent disability rating. Then file a claim with the VA and are offered 50-60 percent. This often happens because the VA looks at it not from the loss of a military career. The VA bases their determination upon the average impairment in earning capacity, which means in layman's terms, how much it affects the average person's ability to secure and maintain a decent-paying job.

Another major reason to file your claim with the VA is that your military disability rating is final upon disposition. As where VA ratings can and often do vary over time. In the event that your medical condition deteriorates over time, your VA disability rating can be raised as the service-connected condition becomes more severe!

The VA, as does the military, rates your disability on a scale from 0 to 100 percent, in 10 percent increments. The more severely your disability impairs your ability to function within society (hence your ability to maintain gainful employment). The higher your disability rating should increase. Also, VA disability compensation is tax free as where DOD compensation is often not in most cases. Unless, you either entered the military prior to September 24, 1975 or your disability rating is for a combat related disability.

How Social Security Fits into Your Disability Claims

If your disability severely impairs your ability to maintain employment, you may want to look into social security disability benefits at this point. Social security has its own hoops to jump through. More often than not though, right around the time one of your cases gets settled. The other one will get settled right behind it.

The Importance of Proving a Service Connection Exists

Although when filing your claim for disability compensation your discharge characterization does become a factor, seeing as to qualify, the VA must determine that your discharge wasn't under dishonorable conditions. See chapter 1.

The most important thing to remember, though, when filing your claim for VA disability compensation is proving a service-connection exists and that the disability is currently affecting your life in an adverse way. This is the key. Oftentimes this may seem difficult to do, but it is imperative to prove your disability or injury is either service-connected or presumptive service-connected.

Making the Service Connection

The trick when it comes to getting disability compensation from the VA is proving that your disability, injury, or illness was either caused or aggravated by your military service. This means that you have to establish that your injuries are connected to your military service. There are a few ways to do this:

1. Incurred during your military service—this means that it happened while serving in the military. This is by far the easiest to prove because there typically will be evidence in either your military medical records or at least an injury report documenting that the injury occurred. To make the service-connection. This is why you need to have each and every injury no matter how large or small checked out and properly documented.

2. Your condition was made worse or aggravated by your military service—this can be quite a bit more difficult to prove that a service-connection exists. Seeing that the VA is not responsible for prior service conditions that get worse over time due to natural progression.

   For example, before joining the service, you had a mild hearing problem from an ear infection that occurred when you were a young child. It was even documented during your entrance screening into the military. Not a big deal, right? Well after ten years in the service, you now have lost complete hearing in one ear and lost 80 percent hearing in the other ear, leaving you legally deaf. So will the VA cover this?

   The VA will consider the places you served, the jobs you did, your medical records, and the circumstances surrounding your military service when determining if your condition was aggravated by your military service.

   If your entire career you sat behind a computer in an office somewhere on a nice quiet base. The VA probably isn't going to conclude that your military service had anything to do with your disability's natural progression, because under normal circumstances, working in an office wouldn't affect your hearing. So the condition unless you can prove otherwise would not have been aggravated.

   If on the other hand you served on the flight deck of an aircraft carrier (which requires regularly scheduled flight deck physicals) or on the battlefields of Iraq. It would be easy to see that your condition was aggravated by your military service.

3. Secondary conditions—these are also referred to as secondary tiers of infection. This means that if you have a service-connected disability, injury, or illness. Then a secondary condition is caused as a by-product of the service-connected disability. If you can prove a link between the two conditions. Then the second condition can be rated as a service-connected disability as well, which can raise your disability rating.

For example, a soldier becomes temporarily paralyzed during a horrible accident during a training exercise, then spends two years in rehabilitation, relearning how to walk again and getting his range of motion back. The problem is that after two years of rehabilitation, he finds himself having some serious side effects, such as arthritis (from being bedridden) and serious depression (from the mental anguish of being paralyzed). In this case, it really wouldn't be stretching to prove either of these things occurred as by-products of the original injury. So the other two secondary injuries could relatively easily be considered service-connected, which, if deemed as a secondary condition, would then be given a disability rating.

Admitting You're Injured

The problem that I see more often than any other is what I call the alpha-male mentality. So often in the military, servicemen and women alike don't want to acknowledge their injuries when they happen, for fear of showing weakness. Only to regret it several years later, often they have lasting effects from their injuries but no documentation to prove that their injuries were service-connected.

It often reminds me of the Black Knight in *Monty Python and the Holy Grail*. After having his arms chopped off, the Black Knight argues that it was merely a flesh wound. This type of mentality more often than not leads to no record of a service-connection for the service member's disabilities. If you know a current service member, please make sure that you tell them this. It can really change the course of their life!

Presumptive Service Connections

Then there are presumptive service-connections. That means that the VA presumes that certain veterans that served in certain places at certain time periods. If they are diagnosed with certain disabilities or illnesses, the VA will presume that the disability or illness was caused "by the unique circumstances of the veteran's military service." Veterans that are diagnosed with disabilities or illnesses that are on the presumptive service-connection list. The VA will presume that the circumstances of their service caused that condition and will award them disability compensation.

Making It on the Presumptive List

These medical conditions do not get there by chance. It often takes a miracle and three to four decades to get these illnesses to become recognized by the VA as presumptive service-connected disabilities. Since these lists tend to be long. I will just give you the highlights. If your medical condition doesn't fall within the lists that I am providing. Check the complete list of presumptive medical conditions, which is in Title 38 of the Code of Federal Regulations, in sections 3.307, 3.308, and 3.309.

Former POW for Any Length of Time

If you were a prisoner of war for any length of time and are diagnosed with any of the following listed disabilities. They are presumed to be service-connected. If they are rated to be at least 10 percent disabling at any time after your military service:

- Psychosis
- Any of the anxiety states
- Any aftereffects of frostbite
- Stroke and its residual aftereffects
- Dysthymic disorder (which is clinical depression)
- Post-traumatic osteoarthritis
- Heart disease and its complications

Former POW for at Least Thirty Days

For prisoners of war that were imprisoned for at least thirty days and are diagnosed with any of the following list of disabilities. They are presumed to be service-connected. If they are rated to be at least 10 percent disabling at any time after your military service:

- Beriberi
- Avitaminosis
- Helminthiasis
- Chronic dysentery
- Irritable bowel syndrome
- Malnutrition, including associated optic atrophy deficiency
- Pellagra and other nutritional deficiencies
- Peptic ulcer disease
- Peripheral neuropathy
- Cirrhosis of the liver

Vietnam and Korea War Veterans Exposed to Agent Orange

Veterans that served in the Republic of Vietnam between January 9, 1962, and May 7, 1975, or Korean War veterans that served at or near the demilitarized zone in Korea between September 1, 1967, and August 31, 1971, are presumed to have been exposed to Agent Orange and other herbicides. Therefore, the VA assumes that a service-connection exists for veterans diagnosed with the following list of medical conditions:

- Prostate cancer
- Diabetes mellitus, type 2
- Chronic lymphocytic leukemia
- Porphyria cutanea tarda (must have occurred within one year of exposure to Agent Orange)
- Chloracne and other acne form diseases similar to chloracne (must have occurred within one year of exposure to Agent Orange)
- Soft tissue sarcoma (other than osteosarcoma, chondrosarcoma, Kaposi's sarcoma, or mesothelioma)
- Hodgkin's disease
- Non-Hodgkin's lymphoma
- Multiple myeloma
- Acute and subacute peripheral neuropathy (must have occurred within one year of exposure to Agent Orange)
- Respiratory cancers (lung, bronchus, trachea, and larynx)
- B cell leukemia
- Parkinson's disease
- Ischemic heart disease
- AL amyloidosis

Agent Orange and Other Herbicides

Oftentimes veterans that have had exposure to herbicides such as Agent Orange have illnesses that are not on this list. That doesn't mean that your illness cannot be service-connected. It just means that it is going to be considerably more difficult. You can still apply for a service-connection. The difference is that you will have to establish a direct service-connection instead of a presumed service-connection. Which although is extremely difficult to do, it can be done in many cases but often requires a private doctors assistance. I say this because over the years, I have seen numerous cases where veterans had overwhelming proof of exposure to Agent

Orange and the VA put them through the ringer to prove they had been exposed. In most cases it took private doctors and often lawyers getting involved to help prove a service-connection existed.

*Remember that there are certain veterans that never even served in Vietnam or Korea that were still exposed to herbicide. Herbicides were used by the U.S. military as far back as the 1950s. So some veterans were exposed to and have had lasting illnesses because of their exposures to these herbicides. To be covered as a service-connected disability. You will need to prove that you were exposed to the herbicide and that there is a nexus or casual relationship between the herbicide and your current disability or illness. This is typically an uphill battle as well because many of these groups of veterans were left off the presumptive illness list as well.

Spina Bifida

Spina bifida is a serious birth defect that has been linked to veterans that were exposed to Agent Orange. Congress has passed laws to provide health care, monthly disability compensation, and vocational rehabilitation to children of veterans that suffer from this birth defect, due to their parents exposure to Agent Orange.

Veterans Exposed to Radiation

Veterans that have participated in "radiation-risk activities" as defined in Title 38 of the code of federal regulations in section 3.309, while on either active duty or active/inactive duty for training, the following list, of conditions are presumed to be service-connected medical conditions:

- All forms of leukemia (except for chronic lymphocytic leukemia)
- Multiple myeloma
- Bronchiolo-alveolar cancer
- Lymphomas (other than Hodgkin's disease)
- Primary liver cancer (except if cirrhosis or hepatitis B is indicated)
- Cancer of the thyroid, pharynx, breast, stomach, esophagus, pancreas, small intestine, bile ducts, salivary gland, gall bladder, urinary tract (kidney/renal, pelvis, ureter, urinary bladder, and urethra), bone, brain, lung, colon, and ovary

Gulf War Veterans

Veterans that have served in the Persian Gulf theater of operations and have been diagnosed with any of the conditions listed (which must be diagnosed on or before December 31, 2011).

Since this War is still going on, the VA is still in the process of determining which conditions are diagnosed versus undiagnosed illnesses. Either way, here is the current list of possible diagnosed/undiagnosed illnesses and their symptoms:

- Fibromyalgia
- Chronic fatigue syndrome (lasting more than six months)
- Irritable bowel syndrome
- Joint pain
- Muscle pain
- Abnormal weight loss
- Headaches
- Menstrual disorders
- Sleep disturbances
- Symptoms involving the respiratory system
- Neurological symptoms
- Neuropsychological symptoms
- Gastrointestinal symptoms
- Cardiovascular symptoms
- Skin symptoms

Evening the Odds at Compensation Claims

Now that you understand the importance of proving a service-connection has occurred and how your employability factors into your disability rating. It's time to strengthen your case for VA disability compensation.

I suggest that if you have the capability to be seen by private physicians through either military or private health insurance. Then you should absolutely take advantage of it. Between TRICARE, which is explained in chapter 8, and health insurance from either a post-service job or your spouse. This gives you an unbiased second opinion as to the severity of your service-connected disability. Private doctors can also monitor your condition and make sure that any errors or inconsistencies that may have occurred in your military and VA medical files are brought to your attention. They can also run their own battery of medical tests that can often counteract what the VA has claimed.

Private physicians can often be more accessible than VA physicians as well. Your private doctors can also give you a different perspective about your disability and are great at answering the questions that may arise prior to your next VA medical appointment. They can also submit their own medical opinions and test results that can show the severity of your disability, which can really help to counteract the VA's claims that your disability is not as severe as you're claiming, which can be quite useful.

Giving the VA a Clear Picture of Your Disabilities

Oftentimes when veterans go to the VA for medical exams and C & P exams, the VA only gets a snapshot of that particular day. Well, the problem is that "what if that day in particular is a good day?" You can't pick which days are going to be good or bad for your injuries. A problem that occurs quite frequently is that when veterans often feel at their worst from their disabilities. They more often than not don't have a VA medical appointment scheduled for that day and may have to wait weeks if not months to get a VA medical appointment. Then by the time that they are seen, oftentimes the worst is over.

Having an accessible private physician at all times can often give the VA a true snapshot of what your day-to-day life really looks like, as a disabled veteran.

If You Can't Afford Private Physicians

If you can't afford to be seen by a private medical physician, at minimum, make appointments regularly at your local VA medical center or VA health care clinic. Then document your appointments and take notes as to what you and your doctor discussed. If you have swelling that is clearly visible to the naked eye. Then take pictures that have dates on them, of your whole body including your face on them.

*Remember that a kneecap that is swollen to the point that it looks like it has a baseball in it can speak volumes as to how bad your injuries really are.

The Importance of Being Knowledgeable

Nobody expects each disabled veteran to have several years of medical school under their belt. This would be a pretty unrealistic thing to ask each veteran. On the other hand, learning everything there is to know about your particular disability is the smartest decision you can make. By becoming an expert on your injuries, over time your VA physicians will come to realize that you are not only knowledgeable about your medical condition, but more importantly they will come to realize that nobody knows your particular disabilities better than you. They will also begin to take your requests for certain medical tests more seriously, which can ultimately help to prove the severity of your particular disabilities and can help keep them from dismissing your claims.

Calling Your Doctor Out

Finally, in some cases, your VA medical doctors may often say something that can greatly help your claims. Such as the words "Although your condition is extremely disabling, and you have been seen by numerous VA doctors. I don't feel that there is anything more that we can do for your service-connected disability at this time. Accept ease the pain through the pain management clinic." In cases like this, don't be afraid to ask for the doctor to document that statement and ask for a copy of it. These things can often make the difference in substantiating a high level of severity, for your disability claims.

A Unique Situation for Reserve and National Guard Members

There is a very popular misconception that National Guard members and reservists cannot receive disability compensation for injuries that were sustained while on active duty for certain call-ups and deployments, while they continue their service in the reserves. Although you will have to be rather careful not to receive a 30 percent disability rating or higher for any single medical issue (because then you will risk receiving a medical discharge). On the other hand, members with valid DD Form 214s can file claims with the VA and may waive an equal portion of their pay for the days that they continue to drill.

This can be a great deal for those that would like to continue drilling and receive disability compensation at the same time. When you consider the fact that the average weekend drilling guard member only receives about two months of full-time pay per year. It typically can be a great deal to accept VA disability compensation while continuing to receive your guard pay as well. Then merely have to waive a few months of VA compensation annually (typically in the beginning of the year) to make up the yearly shortfall. Additionally, if you're called up for another deployment, then you will have to notify the VA and stop payments for the entire amount of your call-up. Because when you're on active duty, you cannot receive both.

Calculating Your Combined Disability Rating

Disabled veterans that have multiple service-connected disabilities often receive several disability ratings, one for each of their medical conditions. In cases that have multiple disability ratings, the VA doesn't just simply add them together.

The reason being is that some veterans would take advantage of the system. If you merely had ten different minor or relatively less significant injuries that were each rated at 10 percent, then you could receive 100 percent disability rating. So to keep that from happening the VA has a combined disability ratings table.

How the Combined Disability Table Works

Here is how the VA combined disability ratings table works. If you have multiple disability ratings, you will need to use the table located on the following page labeled Table 5-1. Although it looks a little complicated, it is actually pretty easy to use.

COMBINED DISABILITY RATING TABLE

Table 5-1

	10	20	30	40	50	60	70	80	90
19	27	35	43	51	60	68	76	84	92
20	28	36	44	52	60	68	76	84	92
21	29	37	45	53	61	68	76	84	92
22	30	38	45	53	61	69	77	84	92
23	31	38	46	54	62	69	77	85	92
24	32	39	47	54	62	70	77	85	92
25	33	40	48	55	63	70	78	85	93
26	33	41	48	56	63	70	78	85	93
27	34	42	49	56	64	71	78	85	93
28	35	42	50	57	64	71	78	86	93
29	36	43	50	57	65	72	79	86	93
30	37	44	51	58	65	72	79	86	93
31	38	45	52	59	66	72	79	86	93
32	39	46	52	59	66	73	80	86	93
33	40	46	53	60	67	73	80	87	93
34	41	47	54	60	67	74	80	87	93
35	42	48	55	61	68	74	81	87	94
36	42	49	55	62	68	74	81	87	94
37	43	50	56	62	69	75	81	87	94
38	44	50	57	63	69	75	81	88	94
39	45	51	57	63	70	76	82	88	94
40	46	52	58	64	70	76	82	88	94
41	47	53	59	65	71	76	82	88	94
42	48	54	59	65	71	77	83	88	94
43	49	54	60	66	72	77	83	89	94
44	50	55	61	66	72	78	83	89	94
45	51	56	62	67	73	78	84	89	95
46	51	57	62	68	73	78	84	89	95
47	52	58	63	68	74	79	84	89	95
48	53	58	64	69	74	79	84	90	95
49	54	59	64	69	75	80	85	90	95
50	55	60	65	70	75	80	85	90	95
51	56	61	66	71	76	80	85	90	95
52	57	62	66	71	76	81	86	90	95
53	58	62	67	72	77	81	86	91	95
54	59	63	68	72	77	82	86	91	95
55	60	64	69	73	78	82	87	91	96
56	60	65	69	74	78	82	87	91	96

Table 5-1 continued

	10	20	30	40	50	60	70	80	90
57	61	66	70	74	79	83	87	91	96
58	62	66	71	75	79	83	87	92	96
59	63	67	71	75	80	84	88	92	96
60	64	68	72	76	80	84	88	92	96
61	65	69	73	77	81	84	88	92	96
62	66	70	73	77	81	85	89	92	96
63	67	70	74	78	82	85	89	93	96
64	68	71	75	78	82	86	89	93	96
65	69	72	76	79	83	86	90	93	97
66	69	73	76	80	83	86	90	93	97
67	70	74	77	80	84	87	90	93	97
68	71	74	78	81	84	87	90	94	97
69	72	75	78	81	85	88	91	94	97
70	73	76	79	82	85	88	91	94	97
71	74	77	80	83	86	88	91	94	97
72	75	78	80	83	86	89	92	94	97
73	76	78	81	84	87	89	92	95	97
74	77	79	82	84	87	90	92	95	97
75	78	80	83	85	88	90	93	95	98
76	78	81	83	86	88	90	93	95	98
77	79	82	84	86	89	91	93	95	98
78	80	82	85	87	89	91	93	96	98
79	81	83	85	87	90	92	94	96	98
80	82	84	86	88	90	92	94	96	98
81	83	85	87	89	91	92	94	96	98
82	84	86	87	89	91	93	95	96	98
83	85	86	88	90	92	93	95	97	98
84	86	87	89	90	92	94	95	97	98
85	87	88	90	91	93	94	96	97	99
86	87	89	90	92	93	94	96	97	99
87	88	90	91	92	94	95	96	97	99
88	89	90	92	93	94	95	96	98	99
89	90	91	92	93	95	96	97	98	99
90	91	92	93	94	95	96	97	98	99
91	92	93	94	95	96	96	97	98	99
92	93	94	94	95	96	97	98	98	99
93	94	94	95	96	97	97	98	99	99
94	95	95	96	96	97	98	98	99	99

Trying Out the Combined Disability Table

1. First take your highest disability rating number, and locate it at the left-hand side of the table.
2. Then take the next highest disability rating number, and locate it at the top of the table.
3. Now find the number that they intersect at.
4. Next take the number that they intersected at, and find the corresponding number on the left hand of the table.
5. Then take the next highest disability rating number and find the corresponding number at the top of the table.
6. Now find the number where they intersect.
7. Repeat as needed until you have used all of your disability ratings.
8. Once you have combined all of your disability ratings. Round that number to the nearest ten. This will be your combined disability rating.

For example, you have been rated at 60 percent for your back, 20 percent for your knee, and 10 percent for hearing.

- Take the highest rating which is 60 percent, and locate it at the left-hand side of the table.
- Then take the next highest rating which is 20 percent, and locate that number at the top table. They intersect at 68.
- Now take the 68, and locate that number at the left-hand side of the table.
- Then take the next highest disability rating which would be 10 percent, and locate that number at the top of the table.
- They intersect at 71.
- Round the 71 to the nearest ten, which in this case would be 70. So the combined disability rating in this case would be 70 percent.

One Hundred Percent Un-employability

In certain cases (like the one that was just used), the VA can determine you to be 100 percent unemployable, without actually being 100 percent disabled. This comes down to the veteran's individual circumstance. Just because they are not rated at 100 percent disabled doesn't always mean that they are capable of keeping a job. If the veteran is deemed to be un-employable by the VA, then the veteran can be awarded compensation equal to 100 percent disabled. This is only done in certain circumstances though. The only reasons that the VA will consider this as an option would be as follows:

1. If the veteran has only one service-connected disability that is rated as 60 percent or more disabling.
2. If in the VA's opinion, the veteran's service-connected disability prevents him or her from getting or staying gainfully employed because of their disability.
3. If a veteran has multiple service-connected disabilities. With at least one of those disabilities being rated at least 40 percent and the combined service-connected disability rating is at least 70 percent or more.

As with the example that was just used. Even though they didn't have a disability rating that was 100 percent.

They may be (if the VA determines them unemployable) able to receive compensation equal to 100 percent. In that example, they would have a great shot at it because not only did they have a combined rating that was 70 percent. They also had one of their disabilities which was rated at 60 percent by itself for a back injury. Back injuries alone can be difficult to overcome by themselves.

Is There Such a Thing as over 100 Percent?

For those of you that are curious as to if you can be rated at over 100 percent disabled? For disability compensation purposes, the highest you can be rated is 100 percent disabled, although my husband has two different service-connected disabilities. One rated at 100 percent and the other at 70 percent. For disability compensation purposes, the combined rating still comes out to 100 percent disabled. So he is paid at the 100 percent level.

Also if you were awarded several disabilities that each amounted to only 10 percent, you would add together the first two sets of 10 percent and come up with 19 percent.

Determining Your Disability Compensation Rate

Now that you have a basic understanding of how disability compensation works. Let's take a look at how much monthly tax-free compensation you can receive. Depending on your disability rating and how many dependents you have. These amounts are based on the 2010 disability compensation rate schedule as shown in Tables 5-2 and Table 5-3 on the following pages. They are adjusted each year for an annual cost of living adjustment better known as COLA on December 1 (if Congress approves a rate increase). Although disability compensation rates cannot go down. Congress can refuse an annual increase if the economy shrinks. They base this off the consumer price index. Since the consumer price index has continued to stay well below the level that it was at in the end of the 2008 fiscal year, which caused a 5.8 percent COLA increase for 2009. This is causing a second consecutive year without an annual COLA increase for 2011. If you would like to make sure that the rates are current. Go to:
http://www.vba.va.gov/bln/21/Rates/comp01.htm

How to Calculate Your Disability Compensation Payments

Keep in mind, if you are 10 percent disabled, your compensation will be $123.00 per month for 2010, and eventually 2011 as well, based on the consumer price index levels.

If you are 20 percent disabled, your compensation will be $243.00 per month for 2010, and eventually 2011 as well. You do not qualify for additional allowances for your dependents unless you are 30 percent disabled or higher.

Dependents are defined as spouses, dependent parents, and children under the age of eighteen. Children over the age of eighteen still qualify if attending college full-time until the age of twenty-three. Also, children that are considered helpless (incapable of caring for themselves medically) do qualify as well, if the child lost their capability of caring for themselves prior to the age of eighteen. Or twenty-three if enrolled in school.

A/A spouse means aid and attendance. For spouses that are seriously disabled that require special aid and medical assistance in the home. There is a special allowance for this.

30% - 100% Without Children
Rates Current as of October 1, 2010

Table 5-2 (part 1)

Dependent Status	30%	40%	50%	60%
Veteran Alone	$376	$541	$770	$974
Veteran with Spouse Only	$421	$601	$845	$1,064
Veteran with Spouse and One Parent	$457	$649	$905	$1,136
Veteran with Spouse and Two Parents	$493	$697	$965	$1,208
Veteran with One Parent	$412	$589	$830	$1,046
Veteran with Two Parents	$448	$637	$890	$1,118
Additional Four A/A Spouse	$40	$54	$68	$81

30% - 100% Without Children
Rates Current as of October 1, 2010

Table 5-2 (part 2)

Dependent Status	70%	80%	90%	100%
Veteran Alone	$1,228	$1,427	$1,604	$2,673
Veteran with Spouse Only	$1,333	$1,547	$1,739	$2,823
Veteran with Spouse and One Parent	$1,417	$1,643	$1,847	$2,943
Veteran with Spouse and Two Parents	$1,501	$1,739	$1,955	$3,063
Veteran with One Parent	$1,312	$1,523	$1,712	$2,793
Veteran with Two Parents	$1,396	$1,619	$1,820	$2,913
Additional Four A/A Spouse	$95	$108	$122	$136

30% - 100% With Children
Rates Current as of October 1, 2010

Table 5-3 (part 1)

Dependent Status	30%	40%	50%	60%
Veteran With Spouse and Child	$453	$644	$899	$1,129
Veteran With Child Only	$406	$581	$820	$1,034
Veteran With Spouse, One Parent and Child	$489	$692	$959	$1,201
Veteran With Spouse, Two Parents and Child	$525	$740	$1,019	$1,273
Veteran With One Parent and Child	$442	$629	$880	$1,106
Veteran With Two Parents and Child	$478	$677	$940	$1,178
Add for Each Additional Child Under Age 18	$22	$30	$37	$45
Each Additonal School Child Over Age 18	$72	$96	$120	$144
Additional for A/A Spouse	$40	$54	$68	$81

30% - 100% With Children
Rates Current as of October 1, 2010

Table 5-3 (part 2)

Dependent Status	70%	80%	90%	100%
Veteran With Spouse and Child	$1,409	$1,634	$1,837	$2,932
Veteran With Child Only	$1,298	$1,507	$1,694	$2,774
Veteran With Spouse, One Parent and Child	$1,493	$1,730	$1,945	$3,052
Veteran With Spouse, Two Parents and Child	$1,577	$1,826	$2,053	$3,172
Veteran With One Parent and Child	$1,382	$1,603	$1,802	$2,894
Veteran With Two Parents and Child	$1,466	$1,699	$1,910	$3,014
Add for Each Additional Child Under Age 18	$52	$60	$67	$75
Each Additonal School Child Over Age 18	$168	$192	$216	$240
Additional for A/A Spouse	$95	$108	$122	$136

One Hundred Percent Permanent and Total Disability

Although you cannot receive over a 100 percent disability rating, you can, on the other hand, receive a 100 percent permanent and total disability rating, otherwise known as 100 percent P & T. If your disability is rated at 100 percent, I strongly urge you to apply for P & T as soon as possible. Otherwise, when you go in for your next C & P exam, the VA can attempt to reduce your disability rating. This often happens to veterans that do not have the 100 percent P & T status.

If your medical condition is permanent and totally disabling in nature. Then you should be fine. If you're medical condition in all likelihood could get better over time. Then you will probably want to wait a few if not several years to apply for this benefit (so that you can show a continued history of illness). If your medical condition could possibly get better but you plan to file for P & T. Wait a few years until your next C & P exam. Shortly after the examination process is complete. If the VA intends to keep you rated at 100 percent disabled. Then file for it, because you will have current C & P evaluations to help back up your claims.

The Advantages of P & T

The advantages of being 100 percent P & T are that depending on where you live, there are often additional benefits that you will qualify for. Such as a tax-free status on your home or free hunting and fishing licenses, although you will still have to pay taxes for household chemical and solid waste. That is considerably less and can take thousands of dollars off your mortgage payment per year. That translates into hundreds of dollars each month that is put back into your pocket. This is explained in detail in chapter 12.

Keep in mind that just because you are 100 percent disabled does not mean that you have the P & T status. You must apply for it. You will need to fill out VA Form 21-526 (see chapter 2) and submit it along with any supporting evidence (such as doctor's medical opinions) to your VA regional office. Or speak with your local veterans' benefits counselor to make sure that you qualify.

Once you receive your notification that you are 100 percent P & T. Take the award letter to your county's tax assessor's office (assuming you own, not rent, your home). They will adjust your taxes for the following year. Since some states do not have housing taxes. They do not recognize this benefit. Also for free hunting and fishing licenses. Take your award letter to your local agency that issues hunting and fishing licenses (this varies from state to state), and they will issue you a free hunting and/or fishing license.

The Disadvantages of P & T

Keep this in mind, though, before you apply for 100 percent P & T. If you receive the P & T status, then decide to go back to work. The VA can decide that your status was fraudulent, and you could end up in trouble. Under USC, Title 38, section 1163. The law states that "if the veteran maintains gainful employment for a period of twelve consecutive months, then their disability may be reduced."

Receiving Special Monthly Compensation

Some severely disabled veterans with specific major medical conditions that have service-connected disabilities that fall under USC, Title 38, section 1114 (3.350-3.362), can qualify for special monthly compensation, also known as SMC, through the VA. This additional monthly compensation is for certain injuries that happened as a result of the veteran's military service.

If your injuries are on this list and they are service-connected. Then talk with your local veterans benefits counselor about the rules governing SMC for your injuries. Since the amount of compensation varies greatly depending on either your injury or combination of injuries. It will require working with both your physicians and veterans benefits counselor to receive this in most cases. The following are the different medical conditions that qualify:

- Blindness in one or both eyes (having only light perception)
- Deafness in both ears (having absence of air and bone conduction)
- Complete organic aphonia (constant inability to communicate by speech)
- For female veterans, loss of at least 25 percent or more of tissue from a single breast or both breasts in combination (including loss by mastectomy or loss following radiation treatment of breast tissue)

- Complete anatomical loss or complete loss of use or amputation of the following:

    1. One or both hands
    2. One or both feet
    3. Both buttocks
    4. One or more reproductive organs

Also, in certain cases where the disabled veteran is rated at 100 percent, and they are permanently bedridden or helpless to the point where they need the aid and attendance of another person on a regular basis to survive. They too can receive SMC. Take a look at the SMC rates on Table 5-4 and Table 5-5. These tables are located on the following pages. These rates are current as of October 1, 2010 and are not projected to receive a COLA increase for 2011 as well.

Special Monthly Compensation - Rates Current as of October 1, 2010
Rates Without Children

Table 5-4 (part 1)

Dependent Status	L	L 1/2	M	M 1/2	N
Veteran Alone	$3,327	$3,499	$3,671	$3,923	$4,176
Veteran With Spouse	$3,477	$3,649	$3,821	$4,073	$4,326
Veteran With Spouse and One Parent	$3,597	$3,769	$3,941	$4,193	$4,446
Veteran With Spouse and Two Parents	$3,717	$3,889	$4,061	$4,313	$4,566
Veteran With One Parent	$3,447	$3,619	$3,791	$4,043	$4,296
Veteran With Two Parents	$3,567	$3,739	$3,911	$4,163	$4,416
Additional A/A Spouse	$136	$136	$136	$136	$136

Table 5-4 (part 2)

Dependent Status	N 1/2	O/P	R.1	R.2	S
Veteran Alone	$4,421	$4,667	$6,669	$7,650	$2,993
Veteran With Spouse	$4,571	$4,817	$6,819	$7,800	$3,143
Veteran With Spouse and One Parent	$4,691	$4,937	$6,939	$7,920	$3,263
Veteran With Spouse and Two Parents	$4,811	$5,057	$7,059	$8,040	$3,383
Veteran With One Parent	$4,541	$4,787	$6,789	$7,770	$3,113
Veteran With Two Parents	$4,661	$4,907	$6,909	$7,890	$3,233
Additional A/A Spouse	$136	$136	$136	$136	$136

Special Monthly Compensation With Children
Rates Current as of October 1, 2010

Table 5-5 (part 1)

Dependent Status	L	L 1/2	M	M 1/2	N
Veteran With Spouse and One Child	$3,586	$3,758	$3,930	$4,182	$4,435
Veteran With One Child	$3,428	$3,600	$3,772	$4,024	$4,277
Veteran With Spouse, One Parent and One Child	$3,706	$3,878	$4,050	$4,302	$4,555
Veteran With Spouse, Two Parents and One Child	$3,826	$3,998	$4,170	$4,422	$4,675
Veteran With One Parent and One Child	$3,548	$3,720	$3,892	$4,144	$4,397
Veteran With Two Parents and One Child	$3,668	$3,840	$4,012	$4,264	$4,517
Add for Each Additonal Child Under Age 18	$75	$75	$75	$75	$75
Each Additional School Child Over Age 18	$240	$240	$240	$240	$240
Additonal A/A Spouse	$136	$136	$136	$136	$136

Table 5-5 (part 2)

Dependent Status	N 1/2	O/P	R.1	R.2	S
Veteran With Spouse and One Child	$4,680	$4,926	$6,928	$7,909	$3,252
Veteran With One Child	$4,522	$4,768	$6,770	$7,751	$3,094
Veteran With Spouse, One Parent and One Child	$4,800	$5,046	$7,048	$8,029	$3,372
Veteran With Spouse, Two Parents and One Child	$4,920	$5,166	$7,168	$8,149	$3,492
Veteran With One Parent and One Child	$4,642	$4,888	$6,890	$7,871	$3,214
Veteran With Two Parents and One Child	$4,762	$5,008	$7,010	$7,991	$3,334
Add for Each Additonal Child Under Age 18	$75	$75	$75	$75	$75
Each Additional School Child Over Age 18	$240	$240	$240	$240	$240
Additonal A/A Spouse	$136	$136	$136	$136	$136

If you look closely at the SMC tables on the previous page, you will notice several categories ranging from SMC (L-S). These different categories represent the different laws concerning each of these injuries and combinations of injuries, if you have one or multiple injuries that were listed. You may wish to look them up at: http://www.warms.vba. va.gov/regs/38CFR/BOOKB/PART3/S3_350.DOC

One other thing to keep in mind is that if you are awarded SMC due to the need for aid and attendance. This additional allowance is subject to reduction from the first day of the second month of admission to hospitals, nursing homes, and domiciliary care at VA expense.

There are two other additional forms of disability compensation as well. They are combat-related special compensation or CRSC, which is for certain twenty-plus-year retirees. This is covered in chapter 6. Also, there is Dependency and Indemnity Compensation or DIC, which is for certain surviving family members. This is covered later in this chapter.

VA Pensions

Nobody is going to argue that military service is difficult, to say the least. It's oftentimes dangerous to the service member and is very stressful for everybody that is in the service member's life. The other side of the coin is that as you are reading this book, try to think of another company that offers the same kinds of benefits as ones like this.

The VA pension system is in place for wartime veterans that are sixty-five years of age or older, that have either very limited or no income. Also, disabled veterans that are permanently and totally disabled (even if your disability wasn't service-connected!) That means if your injuries are service-connected, you can receive VA disability compensation. On the other hand, if they are not service-connected. They may still be covered by VA pension. Pretty cool huh!

They are both tax free, but remember you can only receive one or the other. Not both. The good thing is that as you fill out the paperwork, which is VA Form 21-526 (which is the same form as for compensation). You will notice that the form is called the Veterans Application for Compensation and/or Pension.

That means that if you are unsure as to which you will have to apply for. The VA will determine which one you are qualified to receive (without having to apply twice). Whichever of the two benefits (if you qualify for both) pays more, the VA will pay you the greater of the two. So fill out VA Form 21-526 and bring it to your local VA office or VSO with any supporting evidence such as your DD Form 214, reports from attending physicians (to validate your claims), or records proving you have dependents.

In cases where the veteran is awarded pension and the veteran requires aid and attendance or is homebound. Additional financial assistance is available, but only for one or the other.

Qualifications for VA Pensions
You will want to apply for this benefit if you meet *all* of the following requirements:

- The veteran was discharged from the service under conditions that were considered other than dishonorable (see chapter 1 for details).
- The veteran served for at least ninety days of active military service. At least one day of which was during a wartime period. For those veterans that entered active duty after September 7, 1980, you generally must have served for at least twenty-four months or the full period for which you were called or ordered to active duty (but there are exceptions to this rule).
- The veteran is age sixty-five or older *or* the veteran is permanently and totally disabled (not due to their own willful misconduct).
- Your annual countable family income is below a yearly limit set by Congress. The rates for 2010 are on Table 5-6 and are adjusted on December 1 of each year. These rates as with the VA disability compensation rates are not scheduled to receive a COLA increase for 2011. Due to the negative inflation rate as well. To check the current annual rates, go to: http://www.vba.va.gov/bln/21/Rates/pen01.htm

Improved Disability Benefits Pension Rate Table - Rates Current as of October 1, 2010

Improved Disability Benefits Pension Rate Table
Veteran Alone & With Dependents

Standard Medicare Deduction: $96.40

TABLE 5 - 6

Maximum Annual Pension Rate (MAPR) Category If you are a Veteran . . .	Amount Your yearly income must be less than . . .
Without Spouse or Child	$11,830
	To be deducted, medical expenses must exceed 5% of MAPR, or, $591
With One Dependent	$15,493
	To be deducted, medical expenses must exceed 5% of MAPR, or, $774
Housebound Without Dependents	$14,457
Housebound With One Dependent	$18,120
A & A Without Dependents	$19,736
A & A With One Dependent	$23,396
Add for Each Additional Child to any category above	$2,020

Determining How Much Your VA Pension Will Be
When you look at the maximum countable income table, you will use this table to figure out your pension rates. How you do this is by taking your countable income if any, which is income from the veteran and their family (children also in most cases). This includes earnings, disability and retirement payments, interest and dividends, and net income from farming or businesses that they own.

Then you subtract any deductions that the VA has determined are allowable, that will reduce your countable income, such as public assistance in the form of Social Security Income (SSI) or food stamps. You're also allowed to deduct a portion of your children's educational expenses if they are over eighteen and a portion of un-reimbursed medical expenses such as co-payments.

Finally, after you have subtracted the deductions from your family's countable income, take the amount that is left and subtract that number from the number that is on the table above (for the proper situation), then take the number that is left and divide it by twelve months, and round down to the nearest dollar—that will be your monthly pension rate.

Remember, just take your family's countable income and subtract deductions, then take that number and subtract it from the countable family income limit on the table—that will be your VA annual pension rate—divide by twelve and round down. The number that you have will be your VA pension monthly rate.

*Make sure that you include all sources of income and deductions with proof of them. Since VA pensions are a needs-based program, the VA will determine which incomes and deductions count.

Qualifications for Death Pensions

The VA also has a pension for qualifying surviving widows and their qualifying children known as the improved death pension. This pension is very similar to the regular VA pension. In that it is a needs-based program. You will have to qualify for this benefit by meeting all of the following requirements:

- The deceased veteran was discharged from the service under conditions that were considered other than dishonorable (see chapter 1 for details).
- You are the un-remarried widow (any age) or unmarried child of the deceased veteran. For the purposes of this benefit, unmarried child means "unmarried under the age of eighteen or twenty-three years of age if still in school, or the child has been incapable of self-support prior to the age of eighteen.
- The veteran served for at least ninety days of active military service. At least one day of which was during a wartime period. For those veterans that entered active duty after September 7, 1980, you generally must have served at least twenty-four months or the full period for which you were called or ordered to active duty (but there are exceptions to this rule).

- Your annual countable income is below a yearly limit set by Congress. The rates for 2010 are on the table below and are adjusted on December 1 of each year if Congress decides to change them. These rates as with the VA disability compensation rates are not scheduled to receive a COLA increase for 2011 as well. Due to the negative inflation rate as well. To check the current annual rates, go to: http://www.vba.va.gov/bln/21/Rates/pen02.htm

Improved Death Pension Rate Table - Rates Current as of October 1, 2010

Improved Death Pension Rate Table

Surviving Spouse/Chlld(ren) - Alone or With the Other

Standard Medicare Deduction: $96.40

TABLE 5 - 7

Maximum Annual Pension Rate (MAPR) Category	Amount
MAPR Without Dependent Child	$7,933
To be deducted, medical expenses must exceed 5% of MAPR or	$397
MAPR With One Dependent Child	$10,385
To be deducted, medical expenses must exceed 5% of MAPR or	$520
Housebound Without Dependents	$9,696
Housebound With One Dependent	$12,144
A & A Without Dependents	$12,681
A & A With One Dependent	$15,128
Add for Each Additional Child	$2,020
MAPR FOR CHILD ALONE	$2,020

Calculating Your Death Pension

The way that you calculate death pensions is the same as for regular pensions. You use the same formula for both. Although the income limits are lowered due to the fact that the veteran has passed away. You can use burial expenses (which are covered in chapter 16) as a deduction with this pension.

*Remember that although there is no exact number as to how much the surviving spouses net worth can be when applying for this benefit, between all of their assets such as the value of the widows residence, stocks, bank accounts, etc. On the other hand, since this is a needs-based program, the VA will make a determination as to if the surviving claimant's assets are sufficiently large enough that the claimant could live off these assets for a reasonable period of time. This protects against building up an estate for the benefit of the veteran's heirs.

You will need to fill out VA Form 21-534, which is the "Application for Dependency and Indemnity Compensation Death Pension, and Accrued Benefits by Surviving Spouse or Child form." To download this form, just go to: http://www.vba.va.gov/pubs/forms/VBA-21-534-ARE.pdf

You will also want to submit any evidence such as a death certificate, marriage and children's birth certificates as well. Submit the proper paperwork to the VA regional office that services your area.

Dependency and Indemnity Compensation

While oftentimes the surviving family members will qualify to receive death pension benefits, there is an alternative that typically pays the family considerably more per month, if they meet the stricter guidelines. It's called Dependency and Indemnity Compensation or DIC for short. It is for certain widowed spouses, surviving children, and in certain instances, even the surviving parents of certain deceased veterans and service members. The good thing is that if you're not sure which of the survivor pensions you're eligible to receive, the application is the same for both. You will need to complete and submit a VA Form 21-534. Once submitted, the VA will determine which benefit you're eligible to receive; and if you're eligible for both, they will pay you the higher of the two amounts.

Qualifying for DIC

To qualify for DIC benefits, the veteran / service member must have died from one of the following circumstances:

a. The service member died while on active duty or while on either active or inactive duty for training.
b. The veteran's death resulted from a service-related disease or injury.
c. The veteran's death resulted from a non-service-related disease or injury and who was either receiving or was entitled to receive VA compensation for a service-connected disability that was rated as totally disabling for one of the following time periods:

1. At least ten years immediately before death.
2. Since the veteran's release from active duty and for at least five years immediately before death.
3. At least one year before the veteran's death, if the veteran was a former POW who died after September 30, 1999.

Eligibility for DIC Benefits

The rules as to who is eligible for DIC payments varies depending on if you're the surviving spouse, child, or parent of the deceased. Here is a basic look at the eligibility standards for each. The surviving spouse may be eligible if they meet one of the following conditions:

- Married the veteran prior to January 1, 1957.
- Was married to a service member that died while on active duty or while on either active or inactive duty for training.
- Had married the veteran within fifteen years of discharge from the period of military service in which the injury or disease that caused the veteran's death began or was aggravated.
- Was married to the veteran for at least one year prior to death.
- Had a child with the veteran and resided together until the veteran's death or, if separated, was not at fault for the separation and is currently not remarried.

In the event that the surviving spouse decides to remarry at the age of fifty-seven or thereafter, they are still eligible for DIC payments if the marriage was on or after December 16, 2003.

The surviving children may be eligible for DIC benefits if he/she is one of the following:

- Not included on the surviving spouse's DIC, which in most cases means that the surviving parent has died as well.
- The surviving child is unmarried and under the age of eighteen. This can be extended to age twenty-three if the child is attending school. Additionally, if the child is helpless due to injury or illness, they may be eligible for DIC benefits beyond the age of eighteen, if they became incapable of caring for themselves prior to the age of eighteen and the VA determines them eligible.

In certain instances, the surviving parents of the deceased veteran may be eligible for DIC payments as well. This is only for parents with little to no income and that meet the income and assets guidelines the VA has in place. Since this is an income-based benefit, the more the parents make the less they are eligible to receive.

DIC Payment Amounts
Depending on when the veteran's death occurred will have a direct impact on the amounts you are eligible to receive under DIC. For veterans whose deaths occurred prior to January 1, 1993, the amount is based on the veteran's rank at time of discharge.

Veterans whose deaths occurred on or after January 1, 1993, the basic monthly DIC payment as of October 1, 2010 is $1,154 for the surviving spouse. Then depending on the spouse's situation, they may be eligible for increased monthly payments based on the following:

- For each dependent child, add $286.00.
- If the surviving spouse is homebound, add $135.00.
- If the surviving spouse requires aid and attendance, add $286.00.
- If the veteran was in receipt of or entitled to receive compensation for a service-connected disability that was rated at 100 percent for eight years prior to death, and the spouse was married to the veteran for those same eight years, then add $246.00.

DIC Rates for Qualifying Children
In some instances, in the event that there is no qualifying surviving spouse, the surviving children are eligible for monthly DIC payments

on their own. In this case, the amount available is based on the number of qualifying children. The following DIC monthly rates for children are current as of October 1, 2010:

- $488.00 for one child
- $701.00 for two children
- $915.00 for three children
- $174.00 for each additional child

Survivor Benefits Program (SBP)

Service members that have completed twenty or more years in the military are offered the survivor benefits program while they are processing out of the service for retirement. Unless you elect otherwise, retirees are automatically enrolled into SBP, which is managed by the Department of Defense. By enrolling, the veteran elects to have 6.5 percent of their monthly retirement pay taken out. In exchange, if the veteran dies prior to their spouse, minor child, or designated family member, then the beneficiary will continue to receive 55 percent of the amount of retirement pay the retiree has chosen to ensure.

The bad part is that surviving spouse's SBP payments are reduced by the amount of DIC payments they receive. The good part is that in these cases, the surviving spouse is also eligible for a special survivor indemnity allowance, more commonly known as SSIA. This is a special allowance that is intended to help make up for any offset.

Receiving a Medal of Honor Pension

There are a special group of veterans that receive this special benefit. For those veterans that have earned the Medal of Honor, they will automatically receive a lifelong pension, from the day that they either separate or retire from the military.

This pension rate is $1,194.00 per month as of October 1, 2010 and is not currently scheduled to change in 2011 as well. There are no other qualifications other than receiving the medal itself. This particular pension is paid in addition to any other benefits such as disability compensation or military retirement, which the veteran may be entitled to receive. To check the current rates, go to: http://www.vba.va.gov/bln/21/Rates/special1.htm

Chapter 6

Military Retirement

In this chapter, we will be discussing everything having to do with military retirements. You will learn about each of the different military retirement plans. All of the differences between Final Pay, High 36, the Career Status Bonus / REDUX program, and the National Guard and reservists retirement programs. You will learn how each of these programs works, which ones you qualify for, and exactly how to calculate your retirement and/or medical retirement pay. You will also learn how your military retirement pay works with disability pay, through the CRDP and CRSC programs. Then you will learn how to keep track of where your payments come from. After that, we will discuss all of the ways that having a post-military career can affect your retirement payments and how social security factors into the equation. Finally, we will discuss everything you will need to know about that all important military ID card, as well as who qualifies to retain it after their service has ended and how to properly keep all of your information updated so that you don't have a problem with your benefits.

Number 7,305, any idea of the significance of that number?

That's an important number to any service member that plans to complete twenty years of military service. After all, 7,305 is the number of days in twenty years. On that particular day, which is the twentieth anniversary of the day that you started your journey, you will become eligible for retirement benefits assuming that you meet all of the eligibility criteria for a military retirement, which most notably includes an honorable discharge.

I have never personally met anyone that ever served or any of their family members for that fact, that didn't know that they received retirement pay if they completed twenty or more years of service (seeing as it's a pretty big selling point for the military). On the other hand, there have been a few changes made over the years that have impacted military retirement pay. These changes, if you are not paying pretty close attention to the details, can have a pretty negative impact on your ability to have a comfortable retirement.

Why You Deserve Retirement Pay

Anyone that has ever made it through the challenges that the military hands them on a daily basis for twenty or more years will tell you that they have earned every single penny of that money. After all, even after they leave the service, the military does reserve the right to bring them back, if they want to. To either recall them to duty or to stand trial.

Usually, when they put these recalls out to recently separated or retired personnel, many recently separated service members tend to jump in and volunteer for a voluntary recall. Seeing as they typically have seniority and they often land in a pretty sweet management position with good pay.

The thing to remember here is that if you earned it, you will need to learn how to keep it; and by reading about how the system works, you can ensure that you don't fall into the traps.

The Proper Way to Calculate Each Type of Retirement Pay

First off, for the purposes of calculating your retirement pay, you are only allowed to use your basic pay. That means no subsistence allowances, no hazardous duty pay, bonuses, or anything else for that fact, basic pay only.

For the purposes of determining your twenty-plus-year active-duty retirement pay, there are three different categories:

1. Entered on or before September 7, 1980.
2. Entered on or after September 8, 1980.
3. Those that accepted the Career Status Bonus / REDUX plan.

Active Duty Starting on or before September 7, 1980, Receive Final Pay

Any service members that began serving prior to September 7, 1980. This includes members in the Delayed Entry Program, reservists, ROTC, cadets, and midshipmen that entered into contractual service prior to September 7, 1980 (this is the date that Congress designated for the law to take effect). These veterans receive what is known as final pay. They will need to calculate their retirement pay through the following formula:

basic pay   x   the number of years of active-duty service   x   2.5 percent

If you do the math, you will notice that 2.5 percent x twenty years = 50 percent retirement pay. This is why veterans often say that if you stay past twenty years, you are doing the same work for only half the pay. For each year that you stay beyond the twenty-year mark, you will gain an additional 2.5 percent onto your monthly retirement pay when you eventually decide to retire.

Counting the Final Pay Beans

In essence, if you decide that you enjoy military service, and you decide to complete thirty years, you will receive 75 percent. For forty years of active duty, you will receive 100 percent of your basic pay as monthly retirement pay. Don't get your hopes up too much though; the government is very selective as to how many people they will allow to serve for forty years.

Those that entered into the service prior to September 8, 1980, by far, have received the best retirement pay scale. Seeing as their basic pay (for their final month of service) is the only month that is calculated in the equation, that's a huge difference when you stop and think about it because logically you make your highest basic pay at the very end, which factors in your rank, time in service, and COLA, which will all be at their highest. All of which were a pretty great deal for the veterans that qualified. This retirement pay also receives a Cost of Living Adjustment (COLA) each year assuming Congress approves an increase that is.

Active Duty Starting on or after September 8, 1980, High 36

Any active-duty service members that joined the military on or after September 8, 1980, will need to calculate their retirement pay using this new formula because the military (at Congresses direction) switched over to a new way of doing things.

This is called the High 36, often referred to as the High 3 retirement program because there are thirty-six months in three years. The reason that Congress came up with this new formula was to save some money at the veteran's expense. The government felt that they were giving away far too much in retirement benefits.

They felt that the military's incentives outmatched those in the private sector, so they enacted this change. At the time of this change, many service members were retiring by the age of thirty-eight, then going to work in federal jobs and with government contractors, then having huge multiple retirements by the age of fifty-eight.

Under the High 36 retirement program, you take the average of your highest thirty-six months of basic pay. The key word here; being *average*. You take the average basic pay and multiply that number by the number of years in service. Then multiply that number by 2.5 percent. Take a look at the following formula:

average basic pay x the number of years of active-duty service x 2.5 percent

The Difference between Final Pay and High 36

This may not seem like a big difference, but consider this: if you joined the military anytime after September 8, 1980, for argument's sake, you joined at the age of eighteen, then retired at age thirty-eight. Then went on to live for forty more years until the age of seventy-eight. Assuming that under this new system, your monthly retirement pay was only reduced by $100.00 per month. You would stand to lose $48,000 plus all of the COLA on that money to boot. Pretty big change, right!

Under the High 36 as with the Final Pay system, if you decide to extend your career, you will receive an additional 2.5 percent increase per year onto your monthly retirement pay when you decide to retire. This monthly retirement is also subject to a Cost of Living Adjustment annually.

The Career Status Bonus / REDUX Plan

Then there is the newest and subsequently biggest change to the military retirement system; it's called the Career Status Bonus / REDUX plan.

Congress decided that effective August 1, 1986; anyone that entered the military from that point forward can either take the High 36 or accept the career status bonus along with a reduction in retirement pay.

How this works is that at the fourteen years and six month's mark into your career, the military will inform you of your right to choose either the High 36 or to take the bonus at the fifteen-year mark. At which point you will have to make a choice, assuming that you plan to finish out your twenty years.

*Remember that if you take the bonus, then exit the military without completing twenty years. You will have to pay back the portion that you failed to earn. Just in case you were wondering.

By electing to take the career status bonus (which is $30,000), you will be agreeing to accept a reduction in your retirement percentages by one-half a percent and a reduction in COLA of 1 percent. So the reduction is that instead of receiving 50 percent of your average monthly basic pay for a twenty-year active-duty retirement. You will be agreeing to take 40 percent instead. Then for each year after twenty that you continue to serve, you will receive a 3.5 percent increase (up to thirty years). So if you plan to stay in for thirty years, you can make up the difference. Take a look at Table 6-1. This table shows all of the possible scenarios.

Table 6-1

YEARS OF SERVICE	FINAL PAY MULTIPLIER	HIGH-3 MULTIPLIER	REDUX MULTIPLIER
20	50%	50%	40%
21	52.5%	52.5%	43.5%
22	55%	55%	47%
23	57.5%	57.5%	50.5%
24	60%	60%	54%
25	62.5%	62.5%	57.5%
26	65%	65%	61%
27	67.5%	67.5%	64.5%
28	70%	70%	68%
29	72.5%	72.5%	71.5%
30	75%	75%	75%

So in essence, for a twenty-year active-duty retirement, under REDUX, you will need to calculate your monthly retirement pay using the following formula:

> **average basic pay   x   the number of years of active-duty service   x   2 percent (for the first twenty years) and 3.5 percent (for each year after twenty years up to thirty years)**

Then your annual COLA is also reduced by 1 percent as well. REDUX only allows for a onetime catch-up on COLA at the age of sixty-two.

The Confusing World of REDUX

Confusing, right? Great, then it worked. That is how it was intended to work. As I researched for this section in particular, I realized that the DOD and other government agencies always put REDUX in a positive light. I like to look at REDUX as a game of Three-card Monte with your retirement pay. They confuse you into picking the wrong retirement.

More often than not, those who elect to take REDUX are those who need the money the most. These servicemen and women often have multiple children and are living paycheck to paycheck or not much over that. They are offered a huge sum of money being $30,000 in exchange for only one-half a percent here and one percent there. They fail to see the long-term consequences of that action.

Putting REDUX to the Test

Keep this in mind: I simply borrowed the Office of the Secretary of Defense's calculator for this simple little test. (Not personally of course!) You can use it as well at:
http://www.defenselink.mil/militarypay/retirement/calc/index.html

I simply entered in the exact same sets of circumstances using the High 3 (which is the same as the High 36) and then with CSB/REDUX. Here are the numbers that I used:

- Year of retirement: 2011
- Age of retirement: 38
- Years of service at retirement: 20
- Grade at retirement: E-8
- Inflation rate: 3.5 percent
- Annual active-duty pay raise: 3.5 percent
- Tax rate: 28 percent

The questions were answered identical for each of them. The only difference was with the CSB/REDUX calculator, it asks you to enter the amount in the thrift savings plan and the amount in taxable investments (which implies that you put the bonus into a savings plan). For the vast majority of people that take the $30,000 bonus though, by the end of the five years when they go to retire, it was spent long ago; that's also $30,000 before taxes of course.

The Truth about CSB/REDUX

The Office of the Secretary of Defense's own calculator will give you these exact same results. Keep in mind that these results are from a simple calculation, but the results were. Well, I'll let you decide for yourself.

If you retired at age thirty-eight, after twenty years of service, at E-8 grade. By the time you are seventy-eight years old, you will have received $1,587,849.00 in retirement pay after taxes under the High 3. Under the same exact conditions using the CSB/REDUX plan, you will have received $1,387,409.00 in retirement pay. That's a difference of $200,440.00. That's almost seven times the amount of the $30,000 bonus that you took. Some bonus! The moral of the story is think and research what is right for your particular circumstances before you act.

National Guard and Reserves Retirement Pay

Then comes the National Guard and reserve components' way to calculate military retirement pay, since they obviously work both part time and full time, they have elected a different system because of their members' often unique circumstances. They use a point system instead.

The way it works in the guard and reserves is that you must have twenty qualifying years of service to receive a retirement. To make the year a qualifying year, you must have a minimum of fifty retirement points. These are often referred to as good years.

If you receive less than fifty points in a year, then that year is not a qualifying year for retirement purposes (but it does count toward total time in service). These are referred to as bad years. The more points you have at the end of twenty qualifying years. The higher your retirement pay will be. You can earn points in two different categories:

1. Inactive-duty points
- Inactive-duty time—you typically earn four or five points for each weekend drill (depending if it starts on Friday night or Saturday morning).

- You receive fifteen points each year as membership points for annual training periods.

- One point is received for every three hours of nonresident instruction or correspondence courses that are documented as successfully completed (on your own time, not while on Title 10).

- You also receive one point for each day of performing military funeral honors (but military funeral honors' points do not count against the inactive-duty time limits).

60/75/90 Rule

Keep in mind you can only receive sixty inactive-duty point per year prior to September 23, 1996.

You can receive seventy-five inactive-duty points a year from September 23, 1996, to October 30, 2000.

Then from October 30,2000 to October 30, 2007 you can earn ninety inactive-duty points per year. From October 30, 2007 on you can earn up to 130 points per year.

2. Active-duty points
•   Active-duty time—you earn retirement points for active-duty time as well.

•   You earn one retirement point for each day of active duty up to a maximum of 365 per year or (366 in a leap year).

•   You also earn one point for each day of military training, such as being in military schools for advanced training.

*Each year, members will receive a leave and earnings statement or LES informing them of their total number of retirement points accrued.

Calculating National Guard and Reservist Retirement Pay

After you have reached twenty qualifying years of service, you can retire. To figure out your retirement pay, though, you will first need to convert your retirement points into the equivalent number of active-duty years. This makes it so your retirement is adjusted accordingly with those that served full time.

The formula is simple. You simply take your number of retirement points and divide that number by 360. That number will be your number of total years of service. Then use the Final Pay or the High 36 formula (whichever applies to you).

Total number of retirement points divided by 360 = total years of service.
then
Basic pay   x   total years of service   x   2.5 percent = retirement pay.

Receiving Your Retirement Payments

One of the biggest differences between active duty and National Guard and reservists is when you can start receiving your retirement pay. For active-duty and medically retired personnel, (see chapter 5.) They start receiving their retired pay on the first day of the month after retiring.

National Guard and reservists have to wait until the age of sixty. On the other hand, under the 2008 National Defense Authorization Act, Congress has reduced the age limits for receipt of retirement pay by three months for each ninety days of specified duty (which is either responding to a national emergency or combat duty at the president's request) that is performed in any fiscal year after January 28, 2008. Currently the lowest age that you can receive your retirement pay, though, is age fifty.

Putting Your Military Retirement Pay with Your Disability Compensation

Veterans often get confused with the process of figuring out how their service-connected injuries factor into their military retirement. On one hand, they have completed twenty years of service. They know they qualify for military retirement pay; then, on the other hand, they are not sure how it works in receiving payment for their injuries through the VA. Many veterans know that they can receive both, but are unsure as to *how*.

There are two different laws that have been passed over the last several years that in many cases can allow disabled veterans to receive both retirement pay and disability compensation at the same time. They are called CRDP and CRSC.

Concurrent Retirement Disability Pay Known as CRDP

As of January 1, 2004, Congress has started a ten-year process to phase in your ability to collect both your twenty-year retirement pay and your disability compensation pay at the same time in some cases.

Prior to 2004, retired veterans with VA disability ratings that were receiving disability compensation had to waive an equivalent amount of their retirement pay.

In other words, if they received $2,000 per month for their retirement, then $750 per month for their VA disability, then they had to basically give back $750 from their retirement to be able to receive their disability compensation, which was not a good deal of course, but remember disability compensation is tax free, which in that case would at least make the $9,000 per year in VA disability compensation as nontaxable income.

Under this new law, which is often referred to as concurrent receipt, military retirees that have service-connected disability ratings of 50 percent or more can receive both their retirement payments, as well as their disability payments together.

For those military retirees that have less than 50 percent disability ratings from the VA. You must still waive a portion of your military retirement, but that amount will continually go down each year, until the phase is completed in 2014.

By 2014, the full amount of your military pay will be exempt. These payments will come from the Defense Financing and Accounting Service commonly referred to as DFAS. CRDP payments are taxable and are also subject to collection actions for child support, garnishment, government debt, community property, and alimony as well.

Combat-related Special Compensation Known as CRSC

This form of compensation is similar to CRDP but is for veterans with combat-related injuries. It applies only to retired veterans with injuries that fit into one of the following categories:

1. Armed conflict (gunshot injuries, shrapnel injuries, injures incurred in battle, etc.)
2. Hazardous duty (rappelling injuries, parachuting injuries, etc.)
3. Training that simulates war (injuries that occurred during field training and exercises to simulate battle, etc.)
4. An instrumentality of war (herbicides such as Agent Orange, run over by a tank, etc.)

Congress designed this form of compensation specifically for retired veterans with these types of injuries. It allows veterans with combat-related injuries to receive full concurrent receipt even if their injuries are less than 50 percent, which allows them to receive both retirement pay and disability compensation (equal to that of VA disability compensation) at the same time.

How CRSC Works

The way that it works is that military retirees with VA-rated disabilities that are either combat or combat related are allowed to receive CRSC, through their individual branch of service, not the VA. You will need to provide proper documentation, proving that your injuries were combat related rather than service related. That is the important distinction. You will need to submit DD Form 2860 and the proper documentation to the branch of service that you served in. You can find this form at: http://www.dtic.mil/whs/directives/infomgt/forms/eforms/dd2860.pdf

Choosing CRDP or CRSC

*Remember that you can only receive CRSC or CRDP. Not both. You will want to go with whichever is going to pay you more obviously. This can be a problem if your injuries are a mixture of combat and non-combat-related. Seeing as CRSC will only compensate you for combat-related injuries.

Another factor that comes into deciding which to take is that CRSC payments are tax-exempt, as where CRDP payments are not. This can often influence your decision. The good thing is that either of these programs will either help to reduce or eliminate the offset of income.

Applying for CRDP or CRSC

One thing to remember is that CRDP payments are automatic, so you will not have to apply. On the other hand, the CRSC program you will have to apply for using DD Form 2860 with documentation proving that your injuries were sustained in combat or combat related. Your military branch will notify you of their decision, either approving or denying your application. If approved, they will notify the Defense Financing and Accounting Service better known as DFAS; then, your monthly CRSC payments will begin.

Keeping Track of Where Your Retirement and Disability Compensation Payments Come From

Each veteran has a different set of circumstances, which often dictates where their money comes from; therefore, they will need to keep the proper corresponding agency informed of any changes in address, marital status, allotments, or changes with dependents as well.

Otherwise, you will probably end up owing them someday for a huge overage of some sort, such as being paid for a spouse that you have been divorced from for five years. Then you will have to pay that money back. So just keep them informed.

Money from the VA

The VA handles disability compensation, pensions, special monthly compensation, educational benefits, and any other forms of financial compensation that are applied for and received by the Department of Veterans Affairs.

To keep your information updated, you can simply contact your local veterans benefits office, regional office, or call the number 1-800-827-1000. For the deaf using TTY at number 1-800-829-4833 using your telecommunications device, do not just assume that they will know that you have moved or your status has changed. Even the departments within the VA do not necessarily share this information.

For example: If you are receiving disability compensation and education benefits through the GI Bill. You will need to make sure that they each know about any and all changes to your status. By only telling the people at disability compensation that you have moved, the kind people in the GI Bill department will have no idea that your address has changed. So when they realize that you no longer live at the previous address, they may decide to stop your payments. This confusion will only cause you, the veteran, plenty of hardship and frustration; so make sure that you cover yourself.

Money from DFAS

The other place that both twenty-plus-year retirees and medical retirees that do not receive their medical retirement payments through the VA, also veterans that receive CRSC payments. They will need to notify the Defense Finance and Accounting Service often referred to as DFAS of any changes. You can contact them at 1-800-321-1080. Outside of the US. Call (216)522-5955. Or you can also use myPay at: https://mypay.dfas.mil/mypay.aspx

The Effects of a Second Career on Your Retirement

Whether you decide to retire from the military and just enjoy your retirement or have a second career. Your payments will not be effected. You can work in the private sector and still receive the retirement benefits that you have earned.

Military Retirement and Civil Service Retirement

Then there are many military retirees that go on to other civil service careers working for the local, state, and federal government. These retirees can receive their retirement pay while working in their second government career.

These veterans typically use their preference points which will be discussed in chapter 11 to land a job within the government and tend to work for another twenty years or more, or they work for the National Guard or as a reservist for twenty years while working in a federal position at the same time.

Can You Dual Retire?

Upon retirement from both their federal government position and their military careers after twenty-plus years of service in each, the veteran will most likely want to waive any future military retirement pay. In exchange, many civil service retirement programs will allow you to include your military service into the computation of your big, fat retirement annuity! Which nine times out of ten will be a great deal for all of your hard work.

Usually, veterans that wouldn't want to calculate their retirement pay into the annuity are those that were injured in the military because if you combine the two, you no longer can have your CRDP or CRSC. Other than that, it's usually a great deal.

The Effects of Social Security

This also will not affect your ability to receive social security retirement benefits. Whether a reduced amount at the age of sixty-two or the normal retirement age of sixty-five years old, your ability to receive military retirement payments has absolutely no bearing on your ability to receive social security retirement benefits.

For those that leave the military and have service-connected injuries (see chapter 5), that are receiving VA disability compensation for their injuries. The amount of social security disability payments you receive will not be impacted by your disability compensation payments. The good part is that by receiving VA disability compensation, it can often strengthen your claims for social security benefits.

The Advantages of Qualifying for a Military ID Card

In some cases, veterans and their family members are allowed to retain their military and dependent identification cards even after exiting the military. Uniformed services identification and privilege cards can provide numerous opportunities to those veterans that qualify for them. Such as TRICARE as described in chapter 8, on-base shopping privileges and MWR benefits that are described in chapter 13, Space-A travel, reduced hotel rates, and numerous other discounts that are described throughout this book. While retaining your military ID card is a good thing, different groups of retirees are eligible for different benefits. So you will want to keep that in mind as you read through this book because you will see that not everyone that has a military ID card is eligible for certain retiree benefits.

Who Qualifies to Keep Their ID Cards

To be eligible to either retain or receive a uniformed services identification card after separation from the military, you generally need to meet one of the following criteria:

1. Active-duty retirees with twenty years or more of qualifying service that are eligible to receive retirement pay or would be eligible to receive retirement pay if not for their civil service retirement annuity as described earlier in this chapter.
2. Medical retirees placed onto either TDRL or PDRL as explained in chapter 5. With disabilities that are rated by a physical evaluation board as 30 percent or more disabling.
3. Veterans that have received an honorable discharge, that have been rated as 100 percent disabled by the VA for a service-connected injury. As explained in chapter 5.
4. Veterans that have received the Medal of Honor.
5. Retired National Guard and reserve component members that are eligible to receive military retirement pay, which is described in detail, earlier in this chapter.
6. The qualifying dependents for each type of the above-listed veterans. These include the following:

   - Current spouses.
   - Former spouses that qualify under either the 20/20/20 rule or the 10/20/10 rule that is explained later in

this chapter. As long as they remain unmarried. If the ex-spouse remarries, they lose this benefit, unless they divorce again, in which case they can become eligible to reapply.

- Children (this includes stepchildren and children adopted by the veteran) under the age of twenty-one that are unmarried. This is extended until the age of twenty-three if the child remains a full-time student. Or if the child is severely disabled and incapable of self-care.
- Parents, adopted parents, and in-law parents of the above-mentioned veterans can qualify for identification cards. If the veteran provides at least 50 percent of the relatives support, which would make them dependent on the veteran.

Qualifying for Surviving Family Members' ID Cards

Oftentimes, even after the veteran has passed away, the above-mentioned qualifying family members can still retain their uniformed services identification and privilege cards, with three important additions to the rules:

1. Members that have died while on active-duty orders that were intended to be on active duty for over thirty days.
2. National Guard and reserve component members that have died due to either injuries or illnesses that were either caused or aggravated while on active duty for thirty days or less, or on active or inactive duty for training, or while traveling either to or from the site where they were intended to perform their duty.
3. Dependents of National Guard and reserve component members. If the veteran was retired from the service after twenty or more years of qualifying service, yet ineligible to receive retirement pay. In these cases, the dependents will still qualify for dependent ID cards from the day the veteran would have been eligible. If the veteran would have still been alive.

*Remember that with each of these different ways to qualify for a uniformed services identification and privilege card. That if you are a qualifying spouse and you either divorce or become widowed from the veteran. If you decide to remarry, you will lose your ID card privileges for the entire time that you are remarried, if the second marriage ends in either divorce or death. The spouse will be eligible to receive commissary, exchange, and theater benefits, but will not be eligible for medical benefits if they reapply.

The 20/20/20 and 10/20/10 Rules

Under normal circumstances, when a current or former service member and their spouse divorce, the non-service-member spouse will lose their ID card when the divorce is finalized unless the former spouse qualifies under, one of these two rules:

1. 20/20/20 rule—Under this rule, the former spouse can retain full benefits unless they remarry if they meet all of the following criteria:

   - The spouse was married to the service member for at least twenty years.
   - The service member has completed at least twenty years of qualifying service. As explained earlier in this chapter.
   - The former spouse was married to the service member for at least twenty of those military service years.

2. 10/20/10 rule—This rule is intended for former spouses that have been subjected to domestic abuse. If the service member was discharged from the military for domestic abuse that was documented. The former spouse can retain full benefits if they meet all of the following criteria:

   - The spouse was married to the service member for at least ten years.
   - The service member had completed at least twenty years of qualifying service. As explained earlier in this chapter.
   - The former spouse was married to the service member for at least ten of those military service years.

*Remember that if you qualify under either the 20/20/20 or the 10/20/10 rules, that they are still subject to the same rules if you remarry. In other words, you will lose your ID privileges for as long as you decide to stay remarried.

Enrolling into DEERS

For those veterans that have not had any sort of communication with the military over the last several years. The government has begun to use this enormous computer system to help keep track of current service members, retirees, and their dependents when it comes to eligibility for military benefits.

The Defense Enrollment Eligibility Reporting System better known as DEERS is used to verify each veteran's status for benefits, each service member's information, whether currently serving or veterans that have already separated are already automatically registered into DEERS.

Dependents, on the other hand, are not automatically enrolled into DEERS, so the sponsor being the qualifying veteran or service member will have to bring the proper documentation with each dependent to the closest base, armory, or any other card-issuing facility in order to enroll their dependents into DEERS and receive their dependent ID cards.

*Remember, when enrolling dependents into DEERS, you will need to bring any relevant documentation with you the first time. Such as marriage certificates, birth certificates, retirement orders, DD Form 214, proof of disability status, your expired ID card, or any other pertinent documentation with you. Nothing will ruin your day like a wasted trip.

Receiving Your Identification Card

The good thing is that enrolling into DEERS and receiving your ID card is a one-stop trip, seeing that after dependents are enrolled into DEERS, they are issued an ID card. If you are not sure as to where the closest ID card issuing facility is, all you need to do is use the RAPIDS Web site. This will tell you where the closest facility is. You can find this at: http://www.dmdc.osd.mil/rsl/owa/home

This is a great tool that can save you time in locating the proper facility. If given the choice, you may wish to go to a smaller facility such as a National Guard armory. These smaller facilities tend to be much quicker and often much closer. It also doesn't matter which branch of service you may have served in. They can still enroll you into DEERS and issue ID cards even if you served in a different branch of service.

Once at the ID-card-issuing facility, the veteran will only have to provide proper identification and complete DD Form 1172, which is the Application for Uniformed Services ID Card and/or DEERS Enrollment form. Dependents will need their proper documentation as previously described and complete a DD Form 1173. Which is the dependents' version. I do suggest that you wait until you speak with a person from the ID-card-issuing facility before completing these forms, due to the fact that the rules often vary depending on your sponsor's situation. Either way, if you would like to download this form ahead of time, just go to:
http://www.dtic.mil/whs/directives/infomgt/forms/eforms/dd1172.pdf

Applying for ID Cards without the Sponsor Being Present

I only suggest that you use this as an option if the veteran is incapable of escorting their dependents to enroll into the DEERS system and receiving their ID cards. Qualifying dependents can submit their completed applications with the sponsor's signature already on it, if the sponsor's signature is notarized.

The Importance of Keeping DEERS Updated

Once you are enrolled into the DEERS system, it becomes very easy to update your information when changes occur. It is the veteran's responsibility to keep DEERS informed of any changes that may occur. By not doing this, you will surely end up having problems. Seeing as if your dependents are not properly enrolled into DEERS, you will not receive payment for your dependents. On the other side of the coin, if you divorce and continue to receive compensation for your dependents, you will end up paying it all back when they catch you. So make sure you keep DEERS updated!

Dependents are allowed to make address changes, phone number and e-mail address changes, but only the veteran that is sponsoring the dependents can add or delete family members from the DEERS system. To add family members, the veteran will need either a marriage certificate, birth certificate, or adoption paperwork. To delete an ex-spouse, you will need the divorce decree. To add or delete family members from the system, you will need to either make the request in person, by fax, or through the mail with the supporting documentation. All other changes can be made in several ways:

1. Visit your nearest military personnel office or card-issuing facility.
2. Use the DEERS Web site at:
   https://www.dmdc.osd.mil/appj/deerswebsite/home.do
3. Call the DEERS support office at (800)538-9552.
4. Fax your changes to (831)655-8317.
5. Or you can mail changes to:
   DEERS Support Center
   ATTN: COA, 400 Gigling Road
   Seaside, CA 93955-6771

Chapter 7

Examining VA Health Care

In this chapter, we will be examining (no pun intended) everything having to do with the VA's health care system. From determining who is eligible and how to enroll into the VA healthcare system to figuring out which priority group that you fit into.

Then we will discuss all of the VA's medical benefits and how the extended care programs work, as well as how the VA pharmacy works.

We will close this chapter with all of the financial information. We will help you to figure out if you will have any financial obligations for VA health care and how much they will be. For those veterans with lower incomes, you will really want to pay close attention to the income thresholds that are explained toward the end of this chapter and how, if necessary, to reduce or eliminate co-pays in case of financial emergencies.

The Ever-changing VA Health Care System

Over the last decade or so, the VA health care system has gone through quite a dramatic change. I remember back to a time not so long ago when the conditions were, let's just say, less than acceptable. There were always hundreds of (disgruntled) disabled veterans around every corner. Spending all day there, just trying to get seen for the disabilities that the government promised to take care of. In the interest of being fair, though, it wasn't necessarily the VA employees' fault that it was that way.

The simple fact is that it all starts and ends with funding. In the 2011 VA budget, 41.7 percent of that $125 billion budget will be going to VA health care. That makes the VA health care system, by far, the largest benefit that the VA administers. Between medical care, which has an estimated budget of $51.5 billion, and medical and prosthetic research, which has an estimated budget of $590 million. That is just over $52 billion, in the 2011 budget for VA health care alone.

Compare that with the VA's 2001 total budget, which was only $49 billion. That was their entire budget for all VA benefits and programs combined in 2001. So in a decade alone, the VA's health care budget has risen to more than the entire budget once was. That is a huge difference.

What VA Health Care Manages

As of June 30, 2010. The VA was managing over 1,400 facilities in the United States and its territories to help meet the needs of millions of veterans' health-related needs. With new facilities being added on a regular basis, and older facilities being renovated to stay ahead of the curve, there are:

153 VA medical centers—which are hospitals.

773 VA community-based outpatient clinics—which are the size of clinics and doctors' offices. They are much smaller, and usually closer by, due to the sheer number of them.

260 VA vet centers—these centers are for veterans that have returned after serving in a wartime period. They offer a very broad range of

counseling services, referral services, and outreach programs. They can also help you in filing your claims.

Then there are other various types of facilities as well, such as community-living centers, nursing homes, and domiciliary care facilities. These make up the rest of the VA's health care system.

Who Is Eligible for VA Health Care

Since the VA health care plan is only for veterans. The first step in receiving health care through the VA, as with any benefit, is making sure that you meet the eligibility requirements. Your ability and the amount of medical care you can receive from the VA are based upon several factors.

1. Your discharge characterization—The VA must determine that your discharge wasn't under dishonorable conditions (see chapter 1.) This happens frequently for healthcare eligibility related issues with veterans that have received punitive discharges.

    Such as veterans with service-connected injuries that have a bad conduct discharge. The VA regional office will have to make an administrative decision regarding the veteran's character of service. They may or may not decide to grant you health care benefits.

2. Meeting the minimum service requirements—If you served on active duty either on or prior to September 8, 1980, as an enlisted service member. Or October 17, 1981, as an officer, you are eligible for health care with only one day of active-duty service.

VA Health Care Eligibility Exceptions

If, on the other hand, you served after these dates, you will need twenty-four months of continuous active-duty service. That is unless you meet at least one of the following exceptions:

- The VA determines that you have a service-connected disability. That entitles you to disability compensation (see chapter 5).
- You are only requesting a benefit for or in connection with:

    a. Counseling or treatment for a sexual trauma that occurred while on active military service.

    b. A service-connected disability or medical condition.

    c. Treatment for conditions related to ionizing radiation.

    d. Neck or head cancer that is related to nose or throat radium treatment while in the military.

- You were either discharged or released from active duty because of a disability that either began or was made worse because of your military service (see chapter 5).
- If you were discharged from the military for a reason other than disability. At the time of discharge, though, you had a medical condition that was disabling and, in the opinion of a doctor, your medical condition would have justified a discharge for disability, which was documented in your service records.
- If you are a National Guard member that is called to federal active duty (under Title 10) and has completed the entire term that you were called up for.
- If you are a reservist that is called to active duty and has completed the term that you were called up for.
- If you were discharged as an early-out. This is for those that leave the service due to when the military is downsizing.
- If you left the military for reasons of hardship, and it was properly documented in your military records as such.

Non-enrolled Veterans

Some certain veterans, on the other hand, do not even need to be enrolled in the health care system to be able to receive medical care by the VA (although I do suggest that you go by enrollment anyway and register). These veterans can make appointments for medical care even if they are not enrolled into the VA's health care system. The veterans that are eligible without enrolling are as follows:

- Veterans that have been determined by the VA to be 50 percent or more disabled from a service-connected condition or conditions.
- It has been less than one year since you were discharged for a disability that the military has determined was caused or aggravated by your service, but the VA has not yet rated.
- You are only seeking care for a VA-rated service-connected disability.

- Veterans that are seeking registry examinations for:
  a. Gulf War / Operation Iraqi Freedom.
  b. Agent Orange.
  c. Ionizing radiation.
  d. Depleted uranium.

Now that we know who qualifies for VA health care. Let's take a look at how and where to apply. Then which group you fit into. Because which group you qualify for has everything to do with the following: if you can receive health care, when you can receive health care, and how much that health care will cost you!

Enrolling in the VA Health Care System and Receiving Your ID Card

Enrolling into the VA health care system is easy. Just go to your nearest VA medical center and find the enrollment department. It is usually located right near the front of the hospital, when you first walk in. They will provide you with a VA Form 10-10EZ to fill out, which doesn't take very long. Then they will take your picture.

*Keep in mind, though, that the VA will only issue you a veteran's identification card (once they have verified your eligibility for VA health care). They will then mail you your ID card within seven to ten days and also inform you of which priority group you have been placed into. If you feel that you were placed into the wrong priority group, then you will need to submit proof of eligibility using verifiable evidence (being your decision rating letter, Purple Heart, etc.) that you belong in the higher priority group. You can also download VA Form 10-10EZ at: https://www.1010ez.med.va.gov/sec/vha/1010ez/Form/1010ez.pdf

You can download this form and complete it at home. Even if you decide to mail it to the VA medical center, though, you will still need to go there to have your picture taken for your ID card. So it's usually best to just return the form in person. (It will save you from having any confusion.) Then, once enrolled, if any of your information ever changes, all you will need to do is update your information using VA Form 10-10EZR, which you can download at: http://www4.va.gov/vaforms/medical/pdf/vha-10-10ezr-fill.pdf

*Keep in mind that if you haven't applied for any other VA benefits previously, you will also have to prove eligibility. In other words, bring your DD Form 214, driver's license, and any other special eligibility indicators that can affect which group you will be placed into.

Such as a copy of your Purple Heart award letter or service-connected disability paperwork from your military medical findings. Also, paperwork stating that you were a former POW will help as well to identify your special eligibility circumstances if it applies in your particular case.

Making Medical Appointments

After you have enrolled into the VA's health care system, you can start making appointments immediately pending approval and placement into whichever priority group you qualify for. Then the VA will assign you to either the medical center or outpatient clinic that is closest to where you live. That will be your primary care provider unless you are away from your area on vacation, business, or such. In that case, just locate your nearest VA medical center or medical clinic, seeing as you can be seen at any VA medical facilities.

Also many times, especially for veterans that are seen at smaller facilities, you may have to travel to larger medical centers to be seen for certain types of disabilities, depending on the nature of your injuries. Not all VA medical facilities may be equipped to handle your situation. This has been the case on several occasions with my husband. So if your disabilities are severe in nature, you will probably want to live near a larger VA medical center. You may find the information in chapter 4 helpful in determining where to relocate to.

The Beauty of Patient-driven Scheduling

Whoever came up with this idea should really be given a raise. This was a great idea that seems to be sticking with the VA. Not so long ago, when you were seen at the VA, you had to commit far off in advance to your next appointment. Well, most people have no idea what time and date would be good for their next appointment six months or a year from now, so the VA came up with a great idea. It's called patient-driven scheduling.

By doing this, the people at the VA will send you out a reminder about a month before your doctor asked to see you again. Then all you have to do is check your schedule, then call and make an appointment. This has drastically reduced the number of no-shows.

Keeping Your Medical Appointments

Please keep in mind that if you have an appointment, you will need to keep your appointment. They are hard enough to come by in the first place. If you cannot make your appointment, you need to at least call twenty-four hours in advance so that the VA can allow another veteran to take your slot. Also, not showing up for your medical appointments can seriously harm your case for disability benefits. Because if it's not important to you, I can assure you that it's not important to them.

My husband once got into a car accident on the way to a VA medical appointment. The paramedics wanted to take him to the hospital, yet he insisted on going to his appointment instead. Claiming that he was going to a hospital anyway! If he can make his appointments, so can you.

How the Priority Groups Work

For those of you that qualify for multiple groups. The VA will automatically place you into the highest group that you qualify for. This is a good thing seeing as the higher the priority group, the higher the priority you become and the less time it will take you to be seen!

During the enrollment process, each veteran is placed into one of eight different priority groups. The VA uses this system to help make sure that the more severely injured service-connected injuries are treated before those that are not. Seeing as Congress annually changes the amount of resources that are available to them. This often reflects in the amount of resources available to those in the lower tier groups within the priority group system. To figure out which group you are eligible to be in, use the following guide:

Group 1—Veterans that have service-connected disabilities rated at 50 percent or more disabling by the VA, and veterans that the VA has determined that they are unemployable. Both types are eligible for group 1. (See chapter 5 for details.)

Group 2—Veterans that have service-connected disabilities that are rated at 30 percent, or 40 percent, disabling by the VA, (See chapter 5 for details).

Group 3—Veterans that have service-connected disabilities that are rated at 10 percent, or 20 percent disabling by the VA, (See chapter 5), also included into group 3 are:

- Veterans that were awarded the Purple Heart.
- Veterans that are former prisoners of war (POWs).
- Veterans whose discharge was for a disability that either occurred or was aggravated in the line of duty.
- Veterans that were awarded special eligibility because of a disability incurred in either treatment or participation in a VA vocational rehabilitation program.

Group 4—Veterans that are receiving either aid and attendance benefits, or housebound benefits from the VA, (See chapter 5 for details), also included are veterans that the VA has determined them to be catastrophically disabled.

Group 5—Veterans that are receiving VA pension benefits or that are eligible for Medicaid programs. Also non-service-connected and non-compensable, 0 percent service-connected veterans. Who have a gross annual household income and net worth that falls below the established VA's national income limits, (See later in this chapter for details).

Group 6—This group is for veterans of World War I. Veterans that are seeking care solely for conditions that are associated with being exposed to ionizing radiation during either nuclear testing sites, atmospheric testing, or during the occupation of Hiroshima or Nagasaki.

Additionally, veterans with compensable 0 percent service-connected disabilities fall under this group as well. Veterans that were part of project SHAD (Shipboard Hazard and Defense) also qualify for group 6 as well.

Then there are Vietnam veterans that were exposed to Agent Orange while in Vietnam, that have presumptive service-connections that were explained in chapter 5. These veterans are eligible for group 6 as well, unless they meet the qualifications for a higher priority group.

Veterans of the Persian Gulf War that served between August 2, 1990 and November 11, 1998.

This group is also for veterans that served in combat zones such as Iraq or Afghanistan for at least one day. This applies to veterans that served after November 11, 1998, as follows:

1. Veterans that were discharged from active duty on or after January 28, 2003, who were enrolled into the VA health care system as of January 28, 2008.

2. Veterans that apply for enrollment on or after January 29, 2008. These veterans are automatically placed into group 6 for five years post discharge.

3. Veterans that were discharged from active duty before January 28, 2003, who apply for enrollment into VA health care after January 28, 2008, until January 27, 2011.

Group 7—Veterans whose annual income and/or net worth is above the VA's national income limits, yet falls below the geographic income limits that are established by HUD (as explained later in this chapter), which are determined by where you live. If you land into group 7, you will have to agree to make co-payments.

Group 8—This group is for veterans whose annual income and/or net worth is above the VA's national income limits and is also *above* the geographical income limits (that are established by HUD). These veterans, as do group 7 veterans, must agree to make co-payments as well. Unless they can become eligible for a priority group that is group 6 or lower.

Since January 16, 2003, the VA has not been accepting new enrollments into group 8. If you were already enrolled prior to that date, you are fine as long as you continue to meet the requirements to remain enrolled.

On the other hand, as of June 15, 2009, the VA has relaxed the income restrictions on enrollment for health benefits. Although these new relaxed income restrictions do not remove the consideration of income. It will increase the income threshold in an effort to accept more veterans. So some veterans may become eligible for enrollment under this new provision. The VA is going to review the enrollment applications since January 1, 2009, that were denied, and determine whether these new rules will allow enrollment.

Veterans Returning from OEF/OIF

For the new veterans that are returning from service overseas, first off, I would like to thank you for your service and welcome you back home! If you served in either Operation Enduring Freedom or Operation Iraqi Freedom, I strongly urge you to enroll into the VA's health care system as soon as you become eligible. You only have five years to apply from the day that you separate.

You will automatically be placed into group 6 (unless you meet the criteria for a higher priority grouping). Then you will remain in group 6 for five years post-discharge so that you will be able to receive free VA health care and medications. For any medical conditions that may be related to your combat service.

At the end of the five-year period, the VA will reassess your situation and then decide whether to keep you enrolled in the same group or place you into priority group 7 or 8 (depending on your income level), unless you qualify for a higher priority group that is. This is for combat veterans.

Combat Veterans

The VA in many areas have become better at addressing the needs of our returning heroes. So don't try to do it on your own. Between medical examinations and medical care for any health issues that may arise. To the numerous types of counseling that are being offered by the VA. Give them a chance to help you readjust and let them help you with the medical and psychological issues that you may have from your time over there.

If you are a combat veteran and are applying for this new enhanced eligibility period, you will need to provide the following proof of eligibility when you enroll:

- DD Form 214.
- Proof of receipt of combat pay after November 11, 1998.
- Proof of receipt of at least one of the following medals: Iraq Campaign Medal, Afghanistan Campaign Medal, Global War on Terrorism Expeditionary Medal, Southwest Asia Campaign Medal, Armed Forces Expeditionary Medal, Kosovo Campaign Medal, or Air Force Combat Action Medal.

VA's Health Care Coverage

Now it's time to take a look at what the VA will cover. First, we will cover the standard medical benefits package that all enrolled veterans are eligible to receive. Then we will examine the special and limited medical benefits, which are only offered to certain veterans and to veterans that have special medical situations. Last, we will explain which medical benefits that are excluded from coverage so they will not be covered by the VA.

VA's Standard Medical Benefits

The following medical benefits are covered under the standard medical benefits coverage. They are pretty easy to understand and are available to all enrolled veterans:

- Emergency inpatient and outpatient care in VA medical facilities.
- Inpatient and outpatient medical, mental health, substance-abuse care, and surgical care (surgery includes reconstructive/plastic surgery as a result of a disease or trauma).
- Cosmetic surgery if medically necessary.
- Bereavement counseling.
- Chiropractic care.
- Health care assessments.
- Physical examinations.
- Screening tests.
- Health education programs.
- Immunizations.
- Medical and surgical supplies.
- Prescription and over-the-counter medications that are prescribed by VA physicians (see the Co-payments and Ordering VA Medications section later in this chapter to make sure that you qualify).
- Dental care for certain eligible veterans as described later in this chapter.

Special and Limited Medical Benefits

Then there are special and limited medical benefits, although they fall outside of the standard medical package. You will still be able to receive these benefits if, in your situation, they are medically necessary. You typically will not need to fill out tons of additional forms to receive these medical benefits. Your physician will just refer you as necessary. These benefits are the following:

Maternity Care

The VA does provide maternity care to pregnant veterans. This includes labor and delivery of the baby. After that, though, the VA isn't authorized to provide free services to the child after birth, so the parent must reimburse the VA for any and all services associated with the baby's care after birth.

Female Veteran's Services

Besides shopping and needing more closet space! Us women have certain gender-specific health care needs. Luckily, the VA has the women's program that will provide:

- Gynecological care.
- Breast care.
- Hormone replacement therapy.
- Limited infertility treatment (excludes in vitro fertilization).

Military Sexual Trauma Counseling

The VA does provide treatment and counseling for both male and female veterans. To help them overcome and work past any psychological trauma as a result from any sexual trauma (such as sexual harassment or sexual battery) that occurred while serving on active duty or active duty training for National Guard and reservists. Even if you are currently not enrolled or do not qualify for any other VA health care services, you will still qualify to receive this care at no charge.

Readjustment Counseling

The VA allows any veteran that served on active duty in any war or conflict to apply for counseling to help them readjust back into civilian life. This often entails marital and family counseling, employment counseling, and drug and alcohol assessments as well.

PTSD Counseling

PTSD counseling is available as well for veterans that are having a hard time coping with the after effects of their military service. The VA offers both group and one-on-one counseling for veterans with PTSD. For more information, see chapter 4.

Bereavement Counseling

Bereavement counseling is available to veterans and their family members that are enrolled into the VA health care system. It is also provided to spouses, children, and parents of any service member that dies while on active duty.

Each of these forms of counseling can often be done at either VA medical centers or vet centers. Given the option to pick, Vet centers are usually much more private and more like a private doctor's office and provide a more comfortable atmosphere.

Services for Blind Veterans

Blind veterans may be eligible for additional services at VA medical centers and VA blind rehabilitation centers. You will need to speak with the visual impairment services coordinator that works at your local VA medical facility. They can help you with the following resources:

- Guide dogs (Also included are the expenses of training the veteran to use the dog and the cost of the dog's medical care.) The VA does not pay for the dog's food, grooming, boarding, dog treats, and any other of the routine expenses associated with owning a dog though.
- A total health and benefits review by a VA visual impairment services team.
- Adjustment to blindness training.
- Low-vision aids and teaching you how to use them.
- Electronic and mechanical aids for the blind (This includes adaptive computers, reading machines, and electronic travel aids).
- Talking books and Braille literature.
- Home improvements, structural alterations, and special adaptations to your home (see chapter 12).

Eyeglasses and Hearing Aids

This is kind of a "whichever side of the fence you fall on one". The VA will give free hearing and vision exams to anyone that is enrolled. They will not give hearing aids and prescription eyeglasses to all veterans though. This is due to the fact that vision and hearing both tend to diminish over time on their own. To qualify for free hearing aids or eyeglasses, you must meet one of the following criteria:

- Be a former prisoner of war (POW).
- Have received a Purple Heart.
- Be receiving disability compensation for a service-connected disability.
- Have a vision or hearing disability that is service-connected and rated at 0 percent, in which case, hearing aids are only to be provided on an as-needed basis.
- Be receiving an increased pension based on the fact that you are either permanently housebound or in need of regular aid and attendance (see chapter 5).
- Have significant functional or a cognitive impairment that severely impairs their ability to perform the activities of daily living.
- If your physicians feel that your vision and/or hearing impairments are severe enough that it interferes with the VA's ability to administer your medical treatment.

Prosthetic and Durable Medical Equipment

Veterans that are enrolled into the VA health care system that need any type of medically necessary prosthetic equipment, appliances, or devices for any medical condition that their VA doctor feels they medically need may receive them through the VA. This includes artificial limbs, orthopedic braces and shoes, CPAP sleep machines, crutches, canes, wheelchairs, and other durable medical equipment and supplies. Lately, some of the VA medical centers have even been issuing out Palm Treos to service disabled veterans with traumatic brain Injuries to help them remain organized (for those veterans that have short-term-memory loss). This helps to make life a bit easier. Veterans that qualify are still responsible for their monthly charges.

Veterans that are not enrolled into the VA health care system may still receive these prosthetic items. If they need them for a service-connected disability and also veterans rated at 50 percent disabled or more by the VA.

Annual Clothing Allowances

Certain veterans are also entitled to an annual clothing allowance from the VA. These are veterans that are receiving disability compensation for service-connected disabilities that use prosthetic or orthopedic appliances (including wheelchairs) or that use medications (for skin conditions) that damages their outer garments.

These disabled veterans are entitled to an annual clothing allowance, which is paid between September 1 and October 31 of each year as long as their application is submitted prior to August 1 of that year. The current rates for 2011 are $716 per year. To apply, you will need to download and complete VA Form 10-8678. Then return your completed application to the Prosthetic and Sensory Aids Service department at the closest VA medical center. To download this form, go to: http://www4.va.gov/vaforms/medical/pdf/10-8678-fill%204-08.pdf

Adapting Your Automobile

Veterans that need assistance modifying their vehicle to accommodate their disability may qualify to receive a one-time payment of not more than $11,000 toward the purchase of an automobile or other vehicle. The VA pays for the adaptive equipment and for its repair. Replacement or reinstallation required because of your disability is also covered. To qualify, you must have one of the following medical conditions to be eligible:

- Entitlement to disability compensation for ankylosis (which is immobility) of one or both knees or one or both hips.
- A service-connected loss or a permanent loss of use of one or both feet or hands.
- A permanent impairment of vision of both eyes to a certain degree.

Adapting Your Residence

In addition to adapting your vehicle to accommodate your disability, the VA can also help you with adapting your residence to help make life a little less complicated. Although these grants will not fix your medical condition, they can help in fixing how we live with them! There are three different grants that you may be eligible for. These include:

- The specially adapted housing grant (SAH).

- The special home adaptation grant (SHA).
- The home improvements and structural alterations grant (HISA).

Although these grants are not exactly part of the health plan. They are often an important piece of the puzzle in how to deal with major medical disabilities. These grants are explained in detail in chapter 12.

Dental Benefits

To be eligible for dental benefits through the VA, you must fit into one of the following categories that are described in Table 7-1:

Dental Care

Table 7-1

If you:	You are eligible for:
Have a service-connected compensable dental disability or condition.	Any needed dental care.
Are a former prisoner of war.	Any needed dental care.
Have service-connected disabilities rated 100% disabling or are unemployable due to service-connected conditions. Please read the additional eligibility information located beneath the table.	Any needed dental care.
Are participating in a VA vocational rehabilitation program.	Dental care needed to complete the program.
Have a service connected and/or noncompensable dental condition or disability that existed at the time of discharge or release from a period of active duty of 90 days or more during the Persian Gulf War era.	One-time dental care if you apply for dental care within 180 days of separation from active duty and your certificate of discharge does not indicate that all appropriate dental treatment had been rendered prior to discharge.
Have a service-connected noncompensable dental condition or disability resulting from combat wounds or service trauma.	You are eligible for needed care for the service-connected condition (s).
You have a dental condition clinically determined by the VA to be currently aggravating a service-connected medical condition.	You are eligible for dental care to resolve the problem.
You are receiving outpatient care or scheduled for inpatient care and require dental care for a condition complicating a medical condition currently under treatment.	You are eligible for dental care to resolve the problem.
Certain veterans enrolled in a VA Homeless Program for 60 consecutive days or more.	May receive certain medically necessary outpatient dental services.

* An important note: Veterans awarded a **temporary total disability** rating by the VA are NOT eligible for comprehensive outpatient dental services.

As where veterans with disabilities rated at 100% by scheduler evaluation with NO future exams scheduled are considered permanent and the veteran would be eligible for comprehensive outpatient dental services.

Receiving Extended Care

These are all of the different types of care that are offered outside of the traditional hospital type setting. There are numerous types of extended care programs that veterans (depending on their medical needs) may qualify for.

Since most of these programs do require co-payments depending on either your financial situation or which priority group that you fit into. That is if you are in priority groups 4-8. You will need to read the Accepting Financial Responsibility for Your Health Care section later in this chapter. To help you figure out how much you are financially liable to pay for these types of care.

Additionally, you will need to apply for extended care programs separately by completing VA Form 10-10EC. This is the "Application for Extended Care Services." You can download this at: http://www4.va.gov/vaforms/medical/pdf/vha-10-10EC-fill.pdf

You may want to have a VA social worker assist you with completing this application process, which includes questions about your financial situation.

Nursing Home Programs

First off, there are three different types of nursing home programs that are offered to eligible veterans depending on their eligibility, medical conditions, priority group, and in some cases, financial means. Please realize that the VA will need to assess your situation and determine if you are eligible or not to receive these types of benefits.

Keep in mind that to be admitted to any of the nursing home programs, you must be medically and psychiatrically stable. Also, you will need to be assessed by an appropriate medical provider, and they must agree that you are in need of institutional nursing home care. Additionally, you will need to meet any eligibility criteria that each facility may have.

VA Community Living Center

Community living centers are usually located at VA medical centers. They are in place to provide veterans with short-term care, restorative and rehabilitative care for up to one hundred days, and longer term care for veterans who either meet the eligibility requirements or that require care at the end of their life.

Community living centers were tailored to meet the needs of veterans with chronic stable conditions that include dementia, rehabilitation, and short-term specialized services such as intravenous therapy or respite care. The goal of these centers is to restore their residents to maximum function, prevent further decline, and work toward maximizing the residents' independence.

I was actually pleasantly surprised the first time that I visited one of these community living centers. There always seems to be a bunch of older veterans sitting around specially adapted tables talking and playing spades and other card games in good spirits. They were all enjoying themselves and were very appreciative of the staff!

State Homes for Veterans

These are homes that are owned and operated by the state. Since they are run by the individual states, the services offered often vary by which state you live in. They provide care for eligible veterans that are disabled by age, disease, or otherwise, that are incapable of earning a living due to their disability.

State homes often offer services for veterans in need of nursing home care, domiciliary care, and adult day health care. The VA helps by paying a percentage of the construction or renovation costs and a per diem cost to the state. In exchange, the state will allow at least 75 percent of the bed occupants to be veterans. The VA medical center that services the area that the state home is in will conduct annual inspections, audits, and reconciliation of records, to make sure that the VA's standards are being met.

Contract Community Nursing Homes

These are nursing homes that are owned and operated within the private sector. The local VA medical centers establish contracts with these businesses in order to help meet the nursing-home needs of enrolled veterans that meet the eligibility requirements, that are in need of long-term care. By doing this, it allows veterans to remain close to their families by remaining in their communities.

The VA's nursing home program contracts with over 2,500 community nursing homes. This includes VA-operated nursing home care units, state homes, and contract community nursing homes.

Eligibility for Nursing Homes

To be eligible for VA nursing home care, you must meet one of the following conditions (you may want to reference chapter 5 to answer any questions you may have):

- Veterans with combined service-connected disability ratings of 70 percent or more.
- Veterans with a service-connected disability that is rated at 60 percent and is unemployable or that has an official rating of permanent and total disability.
- Any veteran whose service-connected disability is clinically determined to require nursing home care.
- Veterans rated at 0 percent service-connected and non-service-connected veterans who require nursing home care for any non-service-connected disability. With income and assets that fall below the VA's national income limits and the geographical income limit established by HUD. As explained later in this chapter.
- If space and resources are still available. Other veterans will be accepted on a case by case basis, with priority given to veterans with service-connected disabilities and those who need care for rehabilitation, respite, hospice, geriatric evaluation and management, or spinal cord injuries.

Domiciliary Care

Domiciliary care falls under extended care as well. These are both short-term and long-term health maintenance programs for veterans that require minimal medical care as they recover from psychiatric, psychological, and medical problems. Examples of this would be residential drug and alcohol treatment programs or psychiatric residential rehabilitation programs.

Other Extended Care Programs

Then there are several other services that the VA offers as extended care programs. These programs are the following:

- Hospice/palliative care—provides comfort and supportive services in the advanced stages of incurable diseases that are terminal.
- Geriatric Evaluation and Management (GEM)—this is a program that evaluates and manages older veterans with multiple medical, functional, or psychiatric problems, and veterans with particular geriatric problems. These veterans can receive assessment and treatment from an interdisciplinary team of VA health care professionals.
- Community residential care—this program provides room and board, limited personal care, and supervision to veterans that do not require hospital or nursing home care yet are incapable of living independently because of either psychiatric or medical conditions, that have no family to provide care for them.
- Respite care—is used to temporarily relieve the spouse or other caregiver from the burden of constantly having to care for chronically ill or disabled veterans at home.
- Home health care—this provides chronically ill veterans with long-term primary medical care in their own homes. Under the coordinated care of an interdisciplinary treatment team.
- Homemaker / home health aide services—this is for service-connected veterans needing nursing home care. The VA provides health-related services from public and private agencies under a case management system provided by the VA medical staff.
- Adult day health care—this provides veterans with health maintenance and rehabilitative services in a group setting during daytime hours.

What the VA Will Not Cover

By now, you must be thinking that there is nothing left, seeing as the VA's health care system covers just about everything. There are a handful of things that the VA will not cover though. They are as follows:

- Health club or spa memberships.
- Gender alterations.
- Abortions and abortion counseling.
- In vitro fertilization.
- Special private duty nursing.

- Cosmetic surgery except when the VA has determined that it is medically necessary for reconstructive or psychiatric care.
- Services not ordered and provided by licensed or accredited professionals.
- Drugs, biologicals, and medical devices that are not approved by the FDA unless the treating medical facility is conducting a formal clinical trial under an investigational device exemption, investigational new drug application, or it is prescribed under a compassionate use exemption.
- Hospital and outpatient care for veterans that are either patients or inmates in institutions of another government agency (such as jails and prisons), if the other agency is required to provide the care or services.

Receiving Emergency Medical Care in Non-VA Medical Facilities

Although being enrolled into the VA health care program does have many advantages. It doesn't necessarily mean that you can just walk into any non-VA medical facility and expect to be covered by your VA health care plan. I strongly urge you to carry additional health insurance if you have the capability (see chapter 8 for more information).

With health care costs being the way that they are, it only takes one hospitalization to end up paying for it for the rest of your life. As someone who has seen firsthand exactly what a multimillion dollar hospital stay looks like when it comes to a disabled veteran. With health insurance, it's nice to know that you will only have to make a co-payment.

Unless you have health insurance or plan to pay for the services out of your own pocket, you will want to avoid being seen by any non-VA medical facilities unless it is an emergency. To reimburse you for outside emergency care from the VA, you must meet all of the following criteria:

- The emergency medical services were either for a service-connected condition or you are enrolled in the VA health care system and you have been provided care by a VA health care provider within the last twenty-four months.

- No other VA medical facilities or other federal facilities (such as military hospitals) were readily available at the time of the emergency.
- That delaying medical attention would have endangered your life or health.
- You are not covered by any other forms of health care insurance.
- No other third party is liable for your emergency care (such as car insurance if in a car accident or an accident in your home which would be covered by your home owners insurance). If a third party is either responsible or liable for some if not all of the medical bill. You will need to seek payment from them instead.

*Remember that if you are seen for emergency care in an emergency room or admitted to a non-VA hospital. The veteran or a family member will need to notify the medical facility that they are being seen at, and the VA medical center that is closest to where the veteran is admitted as well.

So that once the veteran's medical condition has been stabilized, the VA can move them to a VA medical facility, because if the veteran decides to stay in the non-VA medical facility beyond the point that the VA feels that the veteran is stable for transport. At that point, the veteran will become liable for any medical expenses that are incurred from that point forward, if they decide to stay where they are at, instead of being transported to a VA medical facility.

Accepting Financial Responsibility for Your VA Health Care

With the ever-changing, and always-rising cost of health care. You will really want to take a close look at these numbers for health care costs. Since nothing I could find really compares out in the private sector. You will more than likely want to at least seriously consider using the VA's resources if you qualify before you try doing it on your own. Especially seeing as there are no enrollment or monthly fees just to be enrolled. You only pay a portion called a co-pay for the services that you need.

*Remember that if you have additional health care insurance, you will want to keep it. Since depending on which priority group that you qualify for, you may still have to make co-pays. Additionally, these benefits only cover the veteran, not family members, and only if the care and medications are obtained through the VA. Additionally, private physician's medical opinions can help to strengthen your disability compensation case, as explained in chapter 5.

Determining If You Will Have Co-pays By Priority Groups

The following is a general guideline as to what you may or may not be obligated to pay for services for each priority group. Since the rules are subject to change at any time and often do. You will want to keep up on any policy changes that occur within the VA health care system.

Veterans in priority groups 1 and 4. Veterans in this group receive inpatient, outpatient, and extended care along with their medications for free and require no co-pays, if treatment is through the VA. Assuming that you continue to stay enrolled in the same priority group and, if placed into group 4, remain under the applicable pension levels.

Veterans in priority groups 2 and 3. The only thing that you will have to pay for in this group is medications. That is if the medication is not for treatment of a service-connected disability or if you are an ex-prisoner of war. In which case, medications would be free and require no co-pays as well. In this priority group, inpatient, outpatient, and extended care are all free as well when obtained through the VA.

Veterans in priority group 5. Veterans in this group are not required to make co-payments for inpatient or outpatient care received through the VA. You will, on the other hand, have to make co-payments for medications and extended care services that are obtained through the VA. Unless you are either receiving a VA pension or your income level falls below the VA national income threshold, which is explained in Table 7-2. Then you would not have to make co-payments.

Veterans in priority group 6. Veterans that are in this group can receive free medications, inpatient, outpatient, and extended care that is received through the VA. This applies only if the medical treatment or care that you are receiving is for a service-connected medical condition (see chapter 5) or disability that resulted in your being placed into priority group 6.

If the medical treatment is not in connection with your military service or related to your being placed into group 6, you will be required to pay the full co-payment amount for either the service or medication that you are requesting.

Veterans in priority group 7. Veterans enrolled into priority group 7 will have to make co-payments to the VA for outpatient and inpatient care, as well as extended care and medications that are received from the VA.

Due to the fact that these veterans' income and/or net worth is above the VA's national income limit. Yet fall below the geographic income limit (as explained later in this chapter). These veterans only have to pay 20 percent of the co-payments for inpatient care.

For example: The VA's inpatient co-pay for 2010 is $1,100.00 for the first ninety days of care, with a $10.00 per diem charge per day of care.

Those enrolled into priority group 7 would only have to pay 20 percent of the inpatient co-payment charges, that would only be $220.00 for the first ninety days of care, with a $2.00 per diem charge per day of care.

Veterans in priority group 8. These veterans are required to make the full co-payments for all medical services and medications that they receive from the VA.

Figuring Out Your Co-payments

Depending on which priority group you are in, you may need to make co-payments. The co-payments for inpatient care, outpatient care, and medications are all on a co-pay schedule. If you have a VA pension or a VA-rated service-connected disability, the percentage that you are rated at has a lot to do with if you will be obligated to make co-pays.

If you do not have a service-connected disability or a VA pension, then your financial assessment will have a great impact on which priority group that you will qualify for. By providing the VA with information about your gross annual household income and your net worth, this will absolutely work to your advantage if your income is below the income limits.

The VA will match the numbers that you provide during your annual financial assessment with the financial information at the IRS and Social Security Administration, so be honest. Veterans that either exceed the income limits or choose not to complete the financial assessment will have to agree to pay the required co-pays to become eligible for VA's health care services.

If you have private health insurance, the VA will bill the insurance company for any medical care, prescriptions, and supplies that they provided for non-service-connected conditions. Keep in mind, though, that the VA cannot bill Medicare, but they can bill Medicare supplemental health insurance for covered services.

Additional Services That Are Exempt from Co-pays
Some additional services do not require co-payments as well. These are:

- Immunizations.
- Care that is part of a VA-approved research project.
- Preventative screenings.
- Laboratory services (such as flat film radiology and electro-cardiograms).
- Publicly announced VA health initiatives such as health fairs.

VA Outpatient and Inpatient Co-pay Rates
The following are the co-pay rates for VA health care as of July 1, 2010, although they are subject to change. You can look up the current rates at: http://www4.va.gov/healtheligibility/Library/pubs/CopayRates/CopayRates.pdf

- Co-pay for outpatient services—$15
- Co-pay for specialty care services—$50
  Specialty care services are those that are provided by a clinical specialist. Such as a radiologist, cardiologist, surgeon, audiologist, and optometrist. This is also the cost of specialty tests such as CAT scans, MRIs, and nuclear medicine studies.

- Co-pay for the first ninety days of inpatient care during a 365-day period—$1,100.00.
- Co-pay for each additional ninety days of inpatient care during a 365-day period—$550.00.
- Inpatient care also carries a per diem charge of $10 per day.

VA Prescription Co-payments and Ordering Information

The co-pay for medications from the VA for the treatment of non-service-connected conditions is $8.00 for each thirty-day or less supply, if your in priority groups 2-6. Veterans in priority groups 7 and 8 are charged $9.00 for each thirty-day or less supply of medications for the treatment of non-service-connected conditions. There is also an annual cap as to how much the VA can charge you for medications in a year's time. Except for veterans in priority groups 7 and 8. The annual co-payment cap for medications for veterans in groups 2-6 is $960.

When your VA doctor prescribes you medications, they will usually offer to have your first original prescription filled that day. Then all you have to do is reorder your refills either through the routine refill program, or you can reorder you refills online through My Health e Vet. Both of these refill programs have made it extremely simple to refill your medications.

The Routine Refill Program

When the pharmacy fills your original prescription, they will provide you with a refill notice. If you sign the refill notice and mail it back to the VA's pharmacy about fifteen to twenty days prior to running out of medication. The VA will send your refills right to your mailbox. With the following months refill notice. It's very convenient and will save you from constantly having to make trips to the VA medical centers.

Ordering Prescription Refills Online

Veterans can also refill their prescriptions over the Internet by registering with My Health e Vet. You will have to register of course, but it can save you loads of time if you decide to go this route. Once registered, you will just need to sign in, and then you can order your refills. To register, you will need to go to: http://www.myhealth.va.gov/

VA doctors are only obligated to prescribe the medications that they feel are right for your treatment. They are under no obligation to prescribe a medication at your private doctor's request.

*Remember that if you have private physicians in addition to the VA's care. Then be open with your VA doctors. Even though the VA's doctors do not have to prescribe the medications that your private doctors prescribe (so you would have to get them filled by a non-VA pharmacy, which can cost significantly more). By being open with the VA physician, they oftentimes agree with the treatment and can prescribe the same medications, which can often save you some money!

The Cost of Extended Care

Extended care co-pays are based off your income and assets. They determine this by the information that you provide on the VA Form 10-10EC. This form asks extensive questions about your financial situation. Since there is no set rate for extended care, the VA will determine your co-payments based off your income and assets. So co-pays will vary from veteran to veteran depending on their financial means.

The good part is that the first twenty-one days of long-term care services are free during any twelve-month period. The VA only starts charging you co-pays on the twenty-second day of care.

The maximum that the VA can charge you for extended care benefits are as follows:

- Inpatient care—these are nursing homes, respite care, geriatric evaluation centers, etc. $97.00 per day is the maximum the VA can charge.
- Outpatient care—these are adult day health care, outpatient respite care, and outpatient geriatric evaluation, etc. $15.00 per day is the maximum the VA can charge.
- Domiciliary care is $5.00 per day is the maximum the VA can charge.

Figuring Out the VA's Income Thresholds

Unless you have a service-connected disability, the VA will base their determinations as to which priority group and your co-payments off your income and assets. They use two different limits when determining which priority group to place you into. They are the national income threshold and the geographical income threshold.

What Is the National Income Threshold

The national income threshold basically compares your gross household income and total assets against the national average.

Your household income consists of any incomes that are from you, your spouse, or any other dependents that still reside with you. This includes social security, workers compensation, paychecks, even interest and dividends, and any other forms of income.

Your total assets must also be worth less than $80,000. These assets include stocks, bonds, savings accounts, cash deposits, retirement funds, rental properties, etc. Your primary residence is not counted though.

The VA will add up your total assets and gross household income, then compare that number to the national income threshold which are in Table 7-2 which is located on the next page:

VA National Income Thresholds
Financial Test for Year 2010

Table 7-2

Veteran with	Free VA Prescriptions and travel benefits (maximum allowable rate):	Free VA Health Care: (0% service connected {noncompensable} and nonservice-connected veterans only)	Medical expenses deduction (5% of maximum allowable pension rate from previous year):
0 dependents	$11,830 or less	$29,402 or less	$592
1 dependent	$15,493 or less	$35,284 or less	$775
2 dependents	$17,513 or less	$37,304 or less	$876
3 dependents	$19,533 or less	$39,324 or less	$977
4 dependents	$21,553 or less	$41,344 or less	$1,078
For each additional dependent add:	$2,020	$2,020	5% of maximum allowable pension rate
Medicare Deductible: $1,100		Income & Asset Net Worth $80,000	

If you look closely at the free VA prescriptions and travel benefits column, the numbers mirror those of VA pensions, which were explained in chapter 5.

These amounts change regularly. The rates in the table above were current as of October 1, 2010. If you would like to check the current VA income thresholds, just go to: http://www4.va.gov/healtheligibility/ Library/pubs/VAIncomeThresholds/VAIncomeThresholds.pdf

What Are the Geographical Income Thresholds
The VA, realizing that the cost of living varies greatly from one area of the country to the next, puts in this other income threshold based on your geographic location.

This basically applies to veterans in groups 7 and 8. If you do not qualify for priority group 7 by meeting the national income threshold, you can still qualify for priority group 7 if your income is below the geographical income threshold. This is calculated on a county by county basis by HUD. Since adding each county's figures into this book would add an additional 125 or so pages, that really isn't feasible. You can, on the other

hand, see this information at: http://www4.va.gov/healtheligibility/
Library/pubs/GMTIncomeThresholds/

Receiving Co-pay Refunds

Oftentimes veterans need to be seen at VA medical facilities and end up
paying co-pays for their visits due to the fact that at the time they were in
a lower priority group. Yet they have a case open for a service-connected
disability or for a VA pension. If you are awarded your claim, you will
want to contact your enrollment coordinator at your VA medical center.
By being awarded your claim, this can often reduce or eliminate any
future co-payments. You may also be eligible for a refund of previously
paid co-pay charges based on this decision.

Three Things to Do If You Are Unable to Make the Co-pay Charges

In certain instances, even co-pays can get to a point that veterans cannot
afford to pay them. In this case, there are three things that you can do:

1. Hardship determination—This can prevent future billing. If
   allowed, this can prevent you from having to make co-pays for
   a determined period of time. These need to be requested in
   writing through the enrollment coordinator at the VA medical
   center that you are being seen at.

2. Waiver of debt—This can eliminate past debts that are owed.
   This is granted only when there has been a significant change
   in income and the veteran has experienced significant expenses
   for either medical care for the veteran or their family members,
   funeral arrangements, or veteran educational expenses.

   You will need to submit a completed VA Form 5655. It can be
   downloaded at:
   http://www4.va.gov/vaforms/va/pdf/VA5655blank.pdf

   *Remember that you only have 180 days to submit this form
   (from the date on the bill). Although there is no limit on the
   amount that you can request to be waived, you will need to
   specify as to which co-pays you are asking to be waived. This
   also does not prevent you from any future charges for future

services. You will need to contact the revenue coordinator at the VA health care facility where you were seen.

3. Offer in compromise—is basically a settlement with the VA for past co-pay debts. By requesting this using a VA Form 5655, you are requesting to make a settlement with the VA. Usually by offering a lump sum that is payable within thirty days from the date that the VA accepts your offer. You will need to contact the Revenue office at the VA medical facility where you were seen to initiate this process.

Travel Reimbursement

In certain instances, the VA will pay you to come to them. The VA will reimburse you for your travel expenses at a rate of 41.5 cents per mile when traveling for approved medical care. This is subject to a $3.00 deductible each way, up to $18.00 per month. Unless your visit is for either a C & P exam or if you require a special mode of transportation to your appointment, then the deductible is waived. You are eligible for travel reimbursement if you meet one of the following criteria:

- Veterans that have service-connected disabilities that are rated at 30 percent or more.
- Veterans that are receiving a VA pension.
- If you're traveling for treatment of a service-connected condition.
- If your income does not exceed the maximum annual pension rate.
- You are traveling for a scheduled compensation and pension exam, that requires either an EKG, X-ray, or deficiency lab in relation to the C & P exam.
- Veterans that can present clear evidence that they are unable to afford the cost of travel to their appointments.

Veterans that qualify for travel reimbursement payments need only to stop by the travel reimbursement window at the medical facility they have been seen at to request payment after their medical appointment.

Receiving Special Transportation

Additionally, you may receive travel reimbursement for special transportation such as ambulances or wheelchair vans. That is, if you are authorized by the VA ahead of time, except for C & P exams.

Chapter 8

Health Insurance

In this chapter, we will be discussing everything having to do with medical and dental insurance. You will want to keep in mind that we will be limiting the information within this chapter to veteran's needs and which plans that veterans qualify for. Since I could easily write an entire second book just on health and dental insurance coverage, we will only be covering the basics as it applies to veterans and their families. We will discuss each type of coverage, who qualifies, how to use each type of coverage effectively, prescription medications, applying for each type of coverage, and the associated costs for each type of insurance. We will cover each of the following:

- TRICARE Prime/Extra/Standard
- TRICARE for Life
- CHAMPVA
- Using Medicare with each
- TAMP
- CHCBP
- TRDP through Delta Dental

When it comes to health and dental insurance, many veterans and their families are offered several options for really good health and dental insurance coverage plans depending on their healthcare needs through the following health insurance programs:

- TRICARE Prime
- TRICARE Extra
- TRICARE Standard
- TRICARE for Life
- TAMP
- CHCBP
- CHAMPVA
- TRICARE Retiree Dental Program known as TRDP

Becoming Part of the TRICARE Family

TRICARE in any of its forms is the health insurance for active-duty service members, retirees, and their qualifying dependents. It is run by the Department of Defense, not the Department of Veterans Affairs, which is an important distinction.

With over 9 million current service members, retired veterans, and dependents that qualify for TRICARE benefits. The massive TRICARE health insurance program has been broken down into three geographical regions for post-service members and their families. These are the North Region, South Region, and the West Region. For post-service veterans' purposes, each different region handles the veterans that are TRICARE members within that particular portion of the United States.

Eligibility for TRICARE

To be eligible for TRICARE benefits even after your military service has ended. You will need to fall into at least one of the following categories to be eligible to enroll into the TRICARE system:

- Retired active-duty service members. This is explained in chapter 6.
- Retired National Guard and reserve component members that are eligible for retirement benefits. As described in chapter 6.
- Medically retired service members that are either on the TDRL or PDRL with disability ratings of 30 percent or higher from the military. Not the VA. This is explained in chapter 5.

- Medal of Honor recipients.
- The spouse and children of each of the above-mentioned veterans. In the cases of children, each child will remain eligible for TRICARE if they meet one of the following:

  1. The child is under the age of twenty-one and unmarried.
  2. This is extended until the age of twenty-three if the child remains in college or an approved institution of higher learning, and the sponsor continues to provide at least 50 percent of the child's financial support.
  3. If the child either was or becomes severely disabled within the first two time periods.
  4. Children born outside of wedlock that have a qualifying veteran as a parent.

In the event that the child is an adopted stepchild, the child will remain covered even if the parents divorce. On the other hand, if the stepchild was not adopted. The child will lose eligibility for TRICARE benefits on the day that the divorce is finalized.

TRICARE Eligible Former Spouses and Widows

Certain former spouses and widowed spouses may also be eligible for TRICARE benefits as well if the former spouse meets one of these qualifying categories:

- If the spouse was married to the former service member for at least twenty years, and at least twenty of those same years overlapped the service member's military service. Then the spouse remains eligible for TRICARE benefits unless the spouse remarries as explained in chapter 6.
- If the spouse was married to a former service member for at least twenty years, and the service member was in the military for at least fifteen of those married years, but less than twenty years of overlapping military service and marriage. Then the ex-spouse is entitled to TRICARE benefits for one year from the date that the divorce is finalized unless the ex-spouse remarries before the year is over.
- Widowed spouses of military service members that die while on active duty. If this happens, the surviving spouse and qualifying

children are eligible to receive TRICARE benefits, for three years, at the active-duty rates, from the time that the military service member passed away. After the three-year transitional period is over, the surviving family members can continue to receive TRICARE Prime/Extra/Standard benefits at the retired family member rates.

Why Not to Remarry If You Have TRICARE Benefits

Remember that if a qualifying ex-spouse remarries. Then they lose their eligibility for TRICARE benefits permanently. Even if they become divorced again, they are still no longer eligible for TRICARE benefits.

Determining Which TRICARE Plan Is Right for Your Family's Needs

Now that we know who is eligible for TRICARE benefits, let's take a look at each of the TRICARE health insurance plans. Many veterans and their families already know about TRICARE coverage, seeing as when they were serving in the military they used one of the several TRICARE options.

One of the key differences after you exit the military, though, is that you may be required to pay an annual enrollment fee as well as higher co-pays / cost shares, depending on which TRICARE plan you decide to enroll into. After all, they are not going to pay for everything. Also, if you were enrolled into the TRICARE system while in the military, you will still need to re-enroll each family member into the TRICARE system after your separation from the service.

*Remember that when you're picking out a TRICARE health insurance plan. You will want to pick a plan that makes sense to your family's medical needs.

Also, these medical plans are independent from the VA's health care benefits that were described in chapter 7. So keep this in mind because the vast majority of veterans are only covered for their service-connected medical issues through the VA.

So if you qualify for TRICARE benefits, you will still want to take advantage of one of these insurance plans. That way, if and when you become ill, you will not end up losing everything that you own over some extremely expensive medical bills.

TRICARE coverage can also, in many cases, be used to help offset the costs associated with being seen at the VA for non-service-connected medical care, so it's pretty much a win-win situation.

TRICARE Prime Coverage

This is the health insurance plan that active-duty service members and their families typically use while on active duty for the military. Active-duty service members receive this coverage with no annual enrollment fees. After separation, though, veterans will have to pay $230.00 per year as a single veteran or $460.00 per year for their whole family as an enrollment fee to stay on TRICARE Prime.

If you think about it, that's less than a dollar a day for unmarried veterans, and only $1.26 per day for veterans with families, that $1.26 per day will cover not only you, the veteran, but your spouse and all of your children as well, that's a deal no matter how you look at it, and its good coverage to boot.

You can also elect to have this taken directly out of your retirement checks through direct deposit. That way, you never even miss it, because if you fail to make your payments on time, this will cause your regional contractor to un-enroll you from the program. If that happens, you are subject to a twelve-month lockout from TRICARE Prime benefits. So the best thing to do is just ask your TRICARE regional contractor to set up an allotment through direct deposit; it's that simple.

As the author of this book, I can personally attest that TRICARE Prime is a great program. My family has used this benefit for close to ten years. With no complaints whatsoever and we will continue to use it in the future!

The thought process that went into our picking this plan was that although you have to pay an extremely minimal annual enrollment fee, versus TRICARE Standard or TRICARE Extra, which have no annual enrollment fees. The difference is that by being willing to pay the annual enrollment fees, when you need the medical services, your costs will be a very reasonable flat rate fee for each type of service that you need.

The other two plans are great if you never plan to get sick or rarely ever need medical care. There are plenty of veterans out there, though, that rarely ever do get sick, that only need minimal amounts of health insurance coverage. Then there are also veterans that have secondary insurance from either a post-military career or through their spouses, or that only wish to be seen by a specific physician that is not covered under the TRICARE Prime plan. These veterans are probably best suited for TRICARE Standard. The difference is that it's going to cost you significantly more money when you need medical services, as you can clearly see in Table 8-1.

Using TRICARE Prime Effectively

The trick to using TRICARE Prime effectively after you have separated from the military is all about finding a good primary care manager. These are often referred to as a PCM. You will need to find one that is accepting new patients and that is within the TRICARE network. To find out which PCMs are accepting new patients, all you need to do is contact your TRICARE regional contractor (which is located in the end of this chapter) and ask for a provider directory or you can find it online through whichever TRICARE regional contractors Web site that corresponds with where you live.

Once you have located all of the available PCMs within your area, I do suggest that you do some research and find the best PCM for your health care needs. A good relationship with a private doctor that is within the TRICARE network can be invaluable. This can also help strengthen your claims for disability compensation that were discussed in chapters 2, 3, and 5. Starting to make sense now, right!

Because your PCM will be responsible for the majority of your needs and can help you with referrals to any specialists that you may need to be seen by. This is very important especially if you're having a difficult time proving an increased severity for your service-connected injuries to the VA. A good private doctor can help you with the referrals to specialists that can make a huge difference in your case. Remember that a little planning in the beginning stages of using TRICARE Prime (being finding the right provider for your needs), can go a long way when it comes to maintaining a good cost-effective health care plan.

Enrolling into TRICARE Prime

Once you have decided on a primary care manager and checked to make sure that they are accepting new enrollments. You will need to enroll into TRICARE Prime through your regional contractor. (This information is at the end of this chapter.) When doing this, you will want to specify which PCM you desire. This will save you from having to change doctors. Then your regional contractor will mail you an enrollment card, which you will need to present to your physician to receive care.

Changing Your Primary Care Manager

I strongly urge you to consider the implications of switching your primary care manager before you switch. One of the keys to having successful health care is consistency. Although, sometimes, these things are often unavoidable or out of your control. Seeing as some members may need to move or are not satisfied with their physicians. Then other times the provider may even stop accepting TRICARE all together. These things may often be unavoidable. Given the opportunity, though, I strongly suggest that you carefully weigh the options before you act if you intend to switch providers for a minor reason.

*Remember that a physician that has been seeing you regularly and consistently for several years for your medical issues can carry far more weight than ten different doctors that have only seen you once or twice each. It will also save you loads of time and energy when it comes to collecting medical evidence for your disability claims with the VA. Because when it comes to disability compensation claims that were discussed in chapters 2, 3, and 5 consistency is imperative.

If you do need to switch PCMs, all you need to do is contact your TRICARE regional contractor and ask to switch your PCM. Then complete a TRICARE Prime Enrollment and PCM change form that includes the new PCM's name and address on it. If your regional contractor receives your completed form prior to the twentieth of that month. They can usually accommodate your request by the first day of the following month.

Changing TRICARE When You Move

If you decide to move, you will first need to update your new address into DEERS, which was covered in chapter 6. Then depending on where you have moved to will dictate what your next step will be because not all areas offer TRICARE Prime.

Staying Within a TRICARE Prime Service Area

These are called prime service areas or PSAs for short. If you plan to use TRICARE Prime, you will definitely want to factor this information into your decision-making process while deciding on where to relocate to.

PSAs are geographical areas that are usually either around military bases or that have high concentrations of either military personnel or military retirees and their families. If you decide to move to an area that is not a PSA, you will have to un-enroll from TRICARE Prime and will automatically be enrolled into either TRICARE Standard or TRICARE Extra. This can be very useful information that can affect your eligibility for TRICARE Prime.

- If you move locally, you typically will only need to update DEERS and notify your regional contractor. If you plan to continue using the same PCM.
- If you decide to move to a different PSA within the same TRICARE region. All you will need to do is update DEERS and then contact your regional contractor to switch your PCM.
- If you decide to move to a different TRICARE region all together, you will need to update DEERS and contact the new regional contractor as well. This information is located at the end of this chapter. The new regional contractor will then have you submit an enrollment application. Then once they have received the application. The contractor will transfer your enrollment to the new region.
- Veterans and their family members that decide to move overseas are only eligible for TRICARE Standard benefits. (See the TRICARE Standard section later in this chapter.)

Split Enrollment

This is used primarily for families that either have college students that live out of state or veterans that are separated from their families. Even if the sponsor lives in a different region than their family, you can use the split enrollment option. This will allow the veteran's family to remain enrolled even if they live in a different TRICARE region. All the veteran needs to do is contact the regional contractor for each family member and establish one designated payer for the enrollment fees. This can be a great tool if and when it comes time to send the children off to college.

How TRICARE Prime Works with Military Hospitals and Clinics

Some veterans prefer to use their TRICARE Prime at military hospitals and clinics. If you live near a military treatment facility often referred to as a MTF, you can, under TRICARE Prime, have the MTF as your primary care manager. Often, veterans that decide to stay within a community that they were stationed at, due to the fact that they have become part of that community, decide to use this option. Oftentimes these veterans have met their spouses there and have decided to stay within that community after their time in the service is over. By utilizing this option, they can have easy access to health care through the base for their entire families even after their time in the military has ended.

Vision Coverage

*Remember that when deciding on a TRICARE plan, *only* TRICARE Prime allows for eye examinations. Under Prime, you can receive one eye exam every two years, unless they are diabetic. Then it's once per year.

Additionally, under each TRICARE plan, you can receive either eyeglasses or contact lenses if you have one of the following conditions:

- Keratoconus.
- Infantile Glaucoma.
- Corneal or scleral lenses to reduce corneal irregularities other than astigmatism.
- Dry eyes.
- Eyeglasses or contact lenses for the loss of human lens function, resulting from eye surgery, injury, or congenital absence.

In each case, if you are eligible to receive eyeglasses. TRICARE will *not* cover cleanings, adjustments, or repairs to your eyeglasses. So take good care of them.

How TRICARE Standard and Extra Works

TRICARE Standard and Extra are quite different than TRICARE Prime. If you decide not to enroll into TRICARE Prime, you will automatically be enrolled into these two options (if you are TRICARE eligible, see earlier in this chapter). So you will need to do nothing to apply for this benefit. All you will need to do when using either TRICARE Extra or Standard is show your military or dependents' ID card. This acts as your insurance card for the provider. The reason that you will have both Standard and Extra is because they are interchangeable, depending on the provider that you are being seen by.

Using TRICARE Extra

With TRICARE Extra, you can be seen by any providers within the TRICARE network. By using providers that are within the TRICARE network, you will pay less out of pocket than if you use a non-network provider. Another advantage of using a network provider is that network providers have a signed agreement with TRICARE to provide services at a rate that has been predetermined between the regional contractor and the provider. This means that they cannot just tack on additional charges, which is a good thing.

Network providers also have agreed to file your claims and handle all of the paperwork for you, directly through your TRICARE regional contractor. That alone is reason enough to use a network provider because otherwise, you will need to pay for the entire visit out of pocket then have to file a claim for reimbursement (which can take quite a while).

Using TRICARE Standard

This should be your option of last resort if at all possible. Using TRICARE Standard means that you have decided to use a TRICARE non-network provider for your medical care. Although this provides you with the most freedom in deciding where to be seen at, the thing that all prior servicemen and servicewomen know about freedom is that freedom *is never free*! So it's going to cost you the most. These non-network providers are broken down into two different categories:

1. Participating providers—this means that the provider has agreed to accept their payment directly from TRICARE. This is a good

thing seeing, as by doing this, the provider is agreeing to a set charge, this can more or less lock in your cost share amount. By doing this, the provider is also agreeing to file your claims for you so that all you will have to be responsible for is your percentage of the bill. So if you decide to go this route, you will definitely need to ask if they are a participating provider.

2. Nonparticipating provider—this means that the provider has not agreed to accept the TRICARE allowable charges. They may also charge up to 15 percent over the TRICARE allowable charges, which means that, you will be responsible for that charge, in addition to your cost share amount, which is already higher than if you went to a network provider. Starting to feel really expensive, right?

Additionally, you will have to file the claims yourself. Which means that you will have to pay the entire cost out of pocket up front, then file for reimbursement from TRICARE using DD Form 2642. This is the patient's request for military payment form. You can download this form at: http://www.tricare.mil/mybenefit/Download/Forms/dd2642.pdf

Comparing the TRICARE Costs

Here is where the rubber hits the road. Take a close look at each of the TRICARE options. Keep in mind that these are the rates for TRICARE members that are no longer in the service. The rates for 2011 are in Table 8-1 on the following page. These rates took effect on October 1, 2010. To check the current TRICARE rates, just go to: http://www.tricare.mil/tricarecost.cfm

TRICARE Rates for Retirees, Their Family Members, and Others

Table 8-1

	TRICARE Prime	TRICARE Extra	TRICARE Standard
Annual Deductible	None	$150/individual or $300/family	$150/individual or $300/family
Annual Enrollment Fee	$230/individual $460/family	None	None
Civilian Outpatient Visits	$12	20% of negotiated fee	25% of allowable charges for covered service
Emergency Care	$30	20% of negotiated fee	25% of allowable charges for covered service
Outpatient Behavioral Health Visit	$25 (individual) $17 (group)	20% of negotiated fee	25% of allowable charges for covered service
Civilian Inpatient Cost Share	$11/day (minimum $25 charge per admission); no separate co-payment for separately billed professional charges.	Lesser of $250/day or 25% of negotiated charges plus 20% of negotiated Professional fees	Lesser of $535/day or 25% of billed charges plus 25% of allowable Professional fees
Civilian Inpatient Skilled Nursing Facility Care	$11/day (minimum $25 charge per admission)	$250 per diem cost share or 20% cost share of total charges, whichever is less, institutional services, plus 20% cost share of separately billed professional charges	25% cost share of allowable charges for institutional services, plus 25% cost share of allowable for separately billed professional charges.
Civilian Inpatient Behavioral Health	$40 per day; no charge for separately billed professional charges	20% of total charge. Plus, 20% of the allowable charge for separately billed professional services	High Volume Hospitals- 25% hospital specific per diem, plus 25% of the allowable charge for separately billed professional services; Low Volume Hospitals- $202 per day or 25% of the billed charges, whichever is lower, plus 25% of the allowable charge for separately billed services.

Putting TRICARE to the Test

Pay close attention to the fact that although TRICARE Prime may have an annual enrollment fee, TRICARE Extra and TRICARE Standard have annual deductibles. The other important part that you will have to factor in is the percentages.

For example, let's use an inpatient hospitalization. Under TRICARE Prime, for retirees and their family members, a two-week stay in a hospital for inpatient care at a rate of $11.00 per day. That works out to $154.00 for the entire hospitalization. That seems very reasonable, right?

Under TRICARE Extra, you would end up paying $250 or 25 percent of the negotiated charges (whichever is less). Well, figuring that hospital stays can easily cost $1,000 a day just to be admitted. So let us just stick to the $250 per day charge. After two weeks, that is $3,500.00 as your portion of the hospitalization.

Then there is the little problem of the 20 percent that you are responsible for that is your share of the negotiated professional fees. This will depend on what you were hospitalized for. For argument's sake, let's just say that it was a surgery that required another $10,000's worth of professional fees. At 20 percent, that's another $2,000.

Which brings your total two-week cost share up to $5,500.00, this will be your cost share for the surgery. Remember, under TRICARE Prime, the same stay only cost the veteran $154.00 out of pocket. Then if you used a non-network provider under TRICARE Standard, the costs will assuredly be even higher. The moral of the story here is that if you ever plan to get sick. Make sure that you have prime health care coverage!

Catastrophic Caps

This is a cap that is put into place by TRICARE to ensure that if you have a severe medical condition. There will be a limit in place that once you meet that limit for the fiscal year (being from October 1 to September 30), you will no longer be liable for your portion of your medical bills. Once you meet the catastrophic cap, TRICARE will continue paying your portion of the charges for the rest of the fiscal year.

This includes outpatient and inpatient cost shares, annual deductibles, pharmacy co-pays, and any other costs that are based on TRICARE's allowable charges. The current catastrophic cap for retirees and their families is $3,000 per fiscal year.

How TRICARE and Medicare Benefits Work Together

Veterans that qualify for Medicare benefits and TRICARE benefits often find themselves in a unique situation. Since Medicare benefits are typically given to veterans that are either over the age of sixty-five or that are disabled and qualify for social security benefits. So due to the fact that both of these types of veterans are going to need some serious health care, here is how they can get it:

TRICARE for Life

Veterans and their spouses that qualify for TRICARE benefits can only use their current TRICARE coverage until they become sixty-five years of age. At the age of sixty-five, they become eligible for TRICARE for Life. Then Medicare becomes your primary health care insurer, and TRICARE will become your secondary health insurer, leaving TRICARE to pick up the co-pays.

The way this works is that you will need to enroll into Medicare Part B, although there is a monthly cost for this coverage, which is $96.40 per month for most veterans in 2010. By doing this, you will be eligible for free TRICARE benefits with no annual enrollment fees. That is after you have met your annual deductible for the year of course, which is $150 for one person or $300 per family for the year. Once you have met your annual deductibles, everything else is paid for by Medicare and TRICARE as long as the medical service is covered by both (hence free health care).

Then there are disabled veterans that qualify for both TRICARE and Medicare Part B benefits. These veterans need to make their choices based on their medical needs. By keeping both Medicare and TRICARE benefits, although they will be paying enrollment fees, this can also lead to Medicare and TRICARE covering your medical costs when you need them the most. In these cases, Medicare will be your primary insurer and TRICARE will cover the co-payments.

Medicare Costs

When it comes to Medicare Part B premiums as of 2010, your premium rates will be based on several factors as it relates to veterans. While most veterans will continue to pay the same $96.40 per month rate, new members and those with incomes of over $85,000 as a single member or over $170,000 as a married couple will have to pay $110.50 per month. These rates will more than likely stay the same in 2011 as well.

Using Medicare with TRICARE Effectively

When picking your provider (see the Using TRICARE Prime Effectively section) earlier in this chapter. The trick is that when setting up your coverage to make sure that your provider accepts both Medicare and TRICARE. This will save you quite a bit of frustration. Since most physicians accept both, this isn't that hard to do; but by doing this, you can ensure that your plan works for you instead of the other way around.

In certain instances, if either Medicare or TRICARE will not cover a medical procedure or service. In these cases, you will be subject to the co-payment for the medical service of the accepting provider. So, in other words, if Medicare covers the service and TRICARE will not. Then you will be subject to the Medicare co-pay. This happens from time to time, but is not the norm.

Services That TRICARE Will Not Cover

As a TRICARE member that has personally used and researched what TRICARE will and will not cover. I can sum it up pretty simply for you. If what you are asking for from TRICARE is medically necessary and considered medically proven. Then it will probably be approved by TRICARE. The representatives that work for TRICARE seem to be very reasonable from my past experiences. So if you can justify why it is medically necessary, then the chances of having your medical needs approved are pretty good.

Getting a Referral to a Specialist

Some medical services under TRICARE that do not require emergency care will require prior authorization depending on which TRICARE plan you are covered under. Without prior authorization, it can end up costing you quite a bit of money. These authorizations usually require nothing more than a phone call to your TRICARE regional contractor. To request specialists, behavioral health providers, and things of that nature.

During the authorization process, they can even give you the contact information for several physicians that practice in the field that you are requesting authorization for and that accept TRICARE and are network providers. This can save you quite a bit of time and energy.

Having TRICARE Help Pay for Your Medications

When deciding on which plan to use and which health care provider you plan to be seen by. You will also want to figure out how you plan to receive your medications. An efficient system should not only be convenient but cost-effective as well.

Although sometimes, emergencies arise and you may be limited in your choices in having a prescription filled. If you have ever needed a prescription filled at three o'clock in the morning, you know what I mean. When it comes to non-emergency prescriptions, though, by planning ahead for your prescriptions, you can really save quite a bit of money. So here are a few options and their pros and cons:

Using the Mail-order Pharmacy

This is a great option for long-term medications if you are going to be using a medication for an extended period. By utilizing this plan, you can have your medications delivered right to your home. The companies name is Express Scripts Inc. They will mail you up to a ninety-day supply of your medications instead of the traditional thirty-day supply, at a rate of $9.00 for name-brand medications or $3.00 for the generic equivalent. That is a very inexpensive and convenient choice, if you're not in a hurry.

The trick to using this system is ordering your refills two to three weeks before running out of your medication. Because it takes an average of fourteen days from the time that you reorder your refills for your medications to arrive. Another trick is to register ahead of time so that your physician can call in or fax your prescriptions. To register with Express Scripts, you can either register by phone, mail, or online. To register by phone, call 1(866)363-8667.

To register online, go to:
http://www.express-scripts.com/TRICARE/

To register by mail, go to: http://www.express-scripts.com/TRICARE/
and download the form. Then mail the completed registration form to:

Express Scripts Inc.
P.O. Box 52150
Phoenix, AZ. 85072-9954

Using Military-base Pharmacies

Depending on if you live near a military base that has a military treatment
facility and the size of the military hospital or clinic. This can be a really
good option. Since most smaller bases have smaller medical facilities,
oftentimes the smaller bases may not have the medications that you
have been prescribed. The good thing about using military treatment
facilities is that their pharmacies can prescribe up to a ninety-day supply
for most medications. With no co-pays, as long as the medication is
on the MTF formulary, which means that they have the medication in
stock.

Using the TRICARE Retail Pharmacy Network

This is using traditional pharmacies that are located all around towns and
cities throughout the United States. This is usually the most convenient
way in most cases to get your prescriptions filled since the pharmacy can
usually fill your prescriptions after a short wait.

The vast majority of pharmacies and drugstores located throughout the
United States accept TRICARE, so you will not have to file any claims
as long as they are a TRICARE network pharmacy. All you will need
to do is ask if they accept TRICARE. If they are a TRICARE network
pharmacy, then you will only have to make a $9 co-pay for name-brand
medications, or $3 for the generic equivalent.

Using a Non-network Pharmacy

This is not an advisable route. If you just inquire with a few pharmacies
ahead of time and find several pharmacy chains that accept TRICARE.
You will probably never need to go this route. If you ever do choose a
non-network pharmacy, though, you will need to pay the entire cost to

fill your prescription then submit a claim through Express Scripts Inc. Using a DD Form 2642 (as explained earlier in this chapter), even then you are only entitled to be reimbursed up to 20 percent of the authorized cost of the medication. So try to only use network pharmacies unless you plan to pay!

Generic or Name-brand Medications

The DOD has a policy in place that if there is a generic equivalent, then the doctor that prescribes the medication needs to justify their reasoning for using the name-brand version of the medication. If there is no reasoning for using the name-brand medication, but you still insist on using it. Then you will be responsible for the entire cost of the prescription out of your own pocket. So keep that in mind.

Qualifying for TAMP

TAMP is the Transitional Assistance Management Program. This program provides transitional health care benefits to certain veterans. Once qualified, these veterans will receive TRICARE Prime (if they live in a PSA). If not, they will be covered under TRICARE Standard/Extra for a period of 180 days after separation at the active-duty rates. This also applies not only for the veteran, but their family members as well. To qualify for this coverage, you must meet the following:

- If you are separating from active duty, following a voluntary agreement to stay on active duty for less than one year, in support of a contingency operation.
- If you are involuntarily separating from active duty under honorable conditions.
- If you are separating from active duty, following involuntary retention, in support of a contingency operation.
- If you are a member of either the National Guard or a reserve component that is separating after a period of active duty that lasted more than thirty consecutive days, in support of a contingency operation.

Qualifying for CHCBP

CHCBP stands for Continued Health Care Benefit Program. This is for veterans that have not secured health insurance after your TRICARE or TAMP benefits run out. This is a premium-based health care program, so you will have to pay premiums to be able to participate. Veterans are eligible for this coverage for eighteen to thirty-six months, but must apply within sixty days of losing TRICARE or TAMP eligibility.

This coverage is comparable to TRICARE standard benefits and is administered through Humana Military Healthcare Services Inc. To apply for this coverage, all you need to do is contact Humana at 1(800)444-5445. Or you can inquire about CHCBP online at: http://www.humana-military.com/

Understanding CHAMPVA Eligibility

CHAMPVA is the Civilian Health and Medical Program of the Department of Veterans Affairs. This program is very similar to TRICARE, but is for certain qualifying spouses, widows, and children that are not eligible for TRICARE benefits under the DOD's guidelines. So this is run by the VA. To be eligible for CHAMPVA benefits, you must be the spouse, widow, or children of one of the following types of veterans:

- A veteran that has been rated by the VA as permanently and totally disabled due to a service-connected disability (This is explained in chapter 5, see the P & T section).
- A veteran that had a permanent and total disability rating for a service-connected disability at the time of death.
- A veteran that has died from a service-connected disability that was rated by the VA.
- A veteran that has died in the line of duty, that was not due to misconduct (If this happens, the family is usually eligible for TRICARE benefits. This is just a backup in the event that the family is not eligible for TRICARE benefits).

CHAMPVA Rules for Spouses, Widows, and Children

In the event that a spouse terminates their marriage through either a divorce or annulment, the spouse is no longer eligible for CHAMPVA benefits.

Widowers, on the other hand, will continue to be eligible for this benefit. That is unless they remarry before the age of fifty-five. On the other hand, if the widower's new marriage ends, they will become eligible again and can re-establish CHAMPVA benefits the month following the termination of their new marriage.

When it comes to children that are eligible for CHAMPVA benefits, the child's eligibility ends if any of the following occurs:

a. The child turns eighteen years of age. Unless the child is enrolled as a full-time student in an accredited school.
b. The child is a full-time student. On their twenty-third birthday.
c. Stepchildren that no longer live in the household of the veteran.
d. If the child marries. In this case, the child is no longer eligible as of midnight on their marriage date.

Enrolling into CHAMPVA

To enroll, eligible members will need to submit a completed VA Form 10-10d. Which is the Application for CHAMPVA Benefits form. Along with any copies of supporting evidence such as:

- The veterans VA rating decision.
- Birth certificates (for children).
- Adoption court order (for adopted children).
- A casualty report (if the veteran is deceased).
- A school certification (if the child is in college).

The VA Form 10-10d can be downloaded at:
http://www4.va.gov/vaforms/medical/pdf/vha-10-10d-fill.pdf

Once you have filled out the form and collected the proper documentation. You will need to mail it to:

CHAMPVA Eligibility
P.O. Box 469028
Denver, CO. 80246-9028

*Remember that it normally takes forty-five days to process your application from the date that CHAMPVA receives it. At which point, you will receive an insurance card. Also, if you would like more information, you can call CHAMPVA directly at 1(800)733-8387.

Taking a Look at CHAMPVA Coverage

For dependents that qualify for CHAMPVA coverage. The thing to remember is that with CHAMPVA health care coverage, in most cases, if the medical services and health care supplies are either medically or psychologically necessary. Then you will typically not have a problem with coverage in most cases. Here is a basic look at what you are covered for, keeping in mind that CHAMPVA will typically pay 75 percent of these costs after the deductible has been met:

- ambulatory surgery
- inpatient services
- outpatient services
- mental health services
- professional services
- hospice care
- durable medical equipment
- pharmacy services
- certain dental services
- skilled nursing care
- family planning and maternity services
- ambulance services

What CHAMPVA Will Not Cover

Some things, on the other hand, are not covered by CHAMPVA for one reason or another. Here is a list of several things that CHAMPVA will not cover. Keeping in mind that they reserve the right to change this list and add to it at any time they feel it is necessary:

- abortion counseling
- services obtained at a health fair
- experimental/investigational or unproven procedures or treatments
- cosmetic surgeries and cosmetic drugs
- eyeglasses
- employment screening physicals

Using CHAMPVA Effectively

This can really be a great program if used effectively. The first thing that you will need to do is find a provider that accepts CHAMPVA as payment. You may need to read the Using TRICARE Prime Effectively section earlier in this chapter for assistance. Although there is no actual all-inclusive list of providers that accepts CHAMPVA benefits, you will find that most providers that accept either Medicare or TRICARE as payment also accept CHAMPVA, so just inquire ahead of time.

*Remember that just as with TRICARE benefits. You will want to use a CHAMPVA network service provider because by accepting CHAMPVA, the provider has agreed to an allowable charge for their services. That way, they cannot inflate their charges. This also means that they have agreed to submit your claims for you, which means that you are only responsible for your portion of the medical bill.

Using Non-CHAMPVA Providers and Pharmacies

This is not advisable just as with TRICARE Standard, seeing as you will have to pay the entire amount of the visit or prescription up front. Then submit a VA Form 10-7959a, which is the CHAMPVA Claim form. Just to get back, the 75 percent of the allowable costs for medical services and medications that you paid up front. You can download this form at: http://www4.va.gov/vaforms/medical/pdf/vha-10-7959a-fill_110308.pdf

*Remember that you only have one year from the date that you were either seen or discharged to file your claims. Once you have completed the claims, you can send them to:

VA Health Administration Center
CHAMPVA Claims
P.O. Box 469064
Denver, CO. 80246-9064

Utilizing the CITI Option

This is the CHAMPVA In-house Treatment Initiative or CITI for short. This is a great option if you live near a VA hospital that uses the CITI program. Although not all VA hospitals are part of this program, over one hundred medical treatment facilities are.

The reason that not all VA medical centers utilize this program is that many medical centers do not have the capacity. This program is intended to offer access to VA medical benefits through VA facilities, *after* the VA has met the needs of the veteran population, if there are resources still available. If you contact your nearest VA medical center, you can inquire as to if they are part of the CITI program or not. Just call and ask for either the CHAMPVA or CITI coordinator that works within the medical center.

The Advantages of Using CITI

This is for CHAMPVA members that do not qualify for Medicare benefits. This allows the qualifying dependents to be seen at participating VA medical centers free of charge. They can also receive their prescription medications for free through the VA pharmacy. If you are being seen by a VA physician. That's a great deal, right?

Using Your CHAMPVA Pharmacy Benefits

When it comes to getting your prescriptions filled through CHAMPVA, you will probably notice that it is very similar to TRICARE benefits. You will have several options:

- Using the CITI option. This was explained earlier in this chapter. This is a free way to get your prescription medications filled.
- Using the Meds by Mail option. This option is free as well and very convenient for your non-emergency medications. This option is not available to CHAMPVA members that have secondary insurance though (such as Medicare Part D). Also, since Meds by Mail is broken up into two different regions, it is best to just call CHAMPVA at 1(800)733-8387. To request a Meds by Mail order form and patient profile. This is a VA Form 10-0426. You can download this form yourself at: http://www4.va.gov/vaforms/medical/pdf/VHA-10-0426-fill.pdf

Once completed, you will want to determine if you will need to mail the form to either the eastern region or western region, which that information is on page 1 of the form. Once you get this system set up, though, it is a very simple process and free as well.

Using a CHAMPVA Network Pharmacy

This is, in most cases, the most convenient way to get your prescriptions filled. Seeing as you can go to any pharmacy that is within the SXC

Health Solutions Inc. network, which works in conjunction with CHAMPVA. By using a network pharmacy, CHAMPVA will take 75 percent of the allowable cost of each prescription medication plus a $3 dispensing fee. The easiest way to find pharmacies within the network is to check online at:

https://vah.rxportal.sxc.com/rxclaim/portal/memberLogin

CHAMPVA Costs and Catastrophic Caps

Although CHAMPVA has no annual enrollment fees, there is an annual deductible for those enrolled. Do not get too scared, though, the annual deductibles are only $50 per family member, up to $100 for the entire family. Not bad, right? At that point, once the deductible has been met, CHAMPVA will pay 75 percent of the allowable costs.

Another advantage with CHAMPVA is that there is no deductible for inpatient services, ambulatory surgery facility services, hospice services, psychiatric day programs, CITI services provided at VA medical facilities, and the Meds by Mail program.

*Remember that CHAMPVA has a catastrophic cap of $3,000 per family for each calendar year. This is January 1 through December 31.

Dental Insurance

Veterans that qualify for TRICARE benefits are also eligible to participate in the TRICARE Retiree Dental Program known as TRDP. This program is run by a company called Delta Dental of California. They have a contract with the DOD, so it's basically like being part of a massive group plan. Since they have over one hundred thousand dental offices within their network, it really isn't very hard to find a desirable dentist that accepts Delta Dental. To find dentists that are within the TRDP network, just go to: http://www.trdpnetwork.org/

Using a Non-network Dentist

Be careful if you decide to go with a non-network dentist, because Delta will only pay a percentage of their allowable costs for each procedure. Leaving you to pay the rest, and that can be quite a bit since there are no negotiated fees. Also, by using a non-network dentist, you will have to file the claims yourself, which means that you can plan to pull quite a bit of money out of your own pocket up front. To download claim forms, go to: http://www.deltadentalins.com/forms/claimform_ca.pdf

Figuring Out If TRDP Is Right for You

Since this program is not like the other TRICARE benefits, in that they have set enrollment rates for all eligible members. You will want to figure out if this program meets your needs. Delta Dental determines your monthly premiums based on where you live through your zip code and the number of family members that will be enrolling. Since the monthly premiums are based on either as a single person or they are doubled if you have a family. If you have a larger-sized family with multiple children, this tends to be a better deal under the family rate because they only charge you double the single-member rate no matter how large your family is. Although this coverage may not be a good deal for some families, in other instances depending on how much dental work you may need it can be a pretty good deal. To check the rates within your area, you can either call (888)838-8737. Or go to: http://www.trdp.org/pro/premiumSrch.html

*Remember that TRDP can be used overseas as well, through the Enhanced Overseas Program.

Looking at the Coverage

Here is a basic look at the coverage. You will want to pay close attention to the amount of time that you must be enrolled before certain services become available and the annual deductibles before making your decisions. Take a look at Table 8-2 on the following page, it explains each of the covered services and the percentages that Delta Dental will pay.

TRICARE Retiree Dental Program Coverage

Table 8-2

Benefits available during the first 12 months of enrollment:	Delta Dental Pays:
Diagnostic services (such as exams)	100%
Preventive services (such as cleanings)	100%
Basic Restorative services (such as fillings, including tooth-colored fillings on back teeth)	80%
Endodontics (such as root canals)	60%
Periodontics (such as gum treatments)	60%
Oral Surgery (such as extractions)	60%
Emergency (such as treatment for minor pain)	80%
Dental Accident Coverage	100%

Additional services available after 12 months of continuous enrollment or if enrolled within four months after retirement:	
Cast Crowns, Onlays & Bridges	50%
Partial/Full Dentures	50%
Dental Implant Services	50%
Orthodontics	50%

Deductibles & Maximums *Benefit Year is defined as October 1 to September 30	
Annual Deductible (per person, $150 cap per family, per benefit year)	$50
Annual Maximum (per person, per benefit year)	$1,200
Orthodontic Maximum (per person, per lifetime)	$1,500
Dental Accident Maximum (per person, per benefit year)	$1,000

Enrolling into TRDP

The simplest way to enroll into the program is by calling Delta Dental directly at: (888)838-8737 and speak with a customer service representative. It only takes about fifteen minutes, and you can enroll over the phone if you prepay your first two months of coverage.

I also suggest, if you decide to enroll, to request direct deposit. That way, it automatically comes out of your retirement pay. Also, if you decide to enroll into TRDP, you must understand that once enrolled, you only have thirty days to change your mind and cancel the coverage. Otherwise, you must remain enrolled for one year, unless you lose your eligibility for TRICARE benefits.

Contacting Your TRICARE Regional Contractor

Listed below are the contact information for each of the TRICARE regions (regional contractors):

TRICARE North Region—1(877)874-2273.
For behavioral health care, contact 1(877)747-9579.
Or email at: https://www.healthnetfederalservices.com

TRICARE South Region—1(800)444-5445.
For behavioral health care, contact 1(877)298-3514.
Or email at: http://www.humana-military.com/

TRICARE West Region—1(888)874-9378.
For behavioral health care, contact 1(866)651-4970.
Or email at: http://www.triwest.com/

Section 3

Educational Benefits

The chapters within this section will explain all of the educational benefits that veterans and, in many cases, their families can qualify for as well. With all of the educational programs that are available to veterans and their family members, you will definitely want to take advantage of the educational opportunities that your military service has afforded you with. With so many programs that are out there, though, you will really want to pay close attention to which educational program best suits your needs because choosing the wrong plan can be rather costly.

Chapter 9

The GI Bills

In this chapter, we will be explaining everything having to do with each of the different GI Bills and how they work. By reading this chapter, you will realize that you need to be paying very close attention to the decisions that you are making in regard to your educational benefits. Otherwise, it can seriously end up costing you in the long run. You will learn about:

- The Active Duty Montgomery GI Bill (ADMGIB).
- Montgomery GI Bill Selected Reserve (MGIBSR).
- Reserve Educational Assistance Program (REAP).
- The $600 buy-up program and college kickers.
- The new Post-9/11 GI Bill.
- How to transfer your educational benefits.
- The Yellow Ribbon Program.

Anyone that has ever even considered joining any branch of the military knows that the educational benefits alone are reason enough to join the military. After all, this is probably the biggest selling point that the military has and why the vast majority of people decide to join in the first place.

The problem is that with all of the educational benefits that are out there, most veterans not only will need to figure out which benefits they qualify for, but more importantly which benefits will best suit their educational needs. Depending on what your post-military educational goals are, under the new Post-9/11 GI Bill, they may not end up being covered in many instances.

Picking an Educational Plan

Since each veteran has a different set of circumstances surrounding their educational goals, versus which programs that they may qualify for. You will want to carefully evaluate this information based on your personal circumstances. Oftentimes veterans can and often do qualify for multiple educational programs depending on several variables. Such as when and how long they served for, if they were active-duty or a reservist, and based on if they received an educational kicker or if they participated in the $600 Buy-up Program or not.

First and foremost, you will want to remember that to qualify for these benefits, veterans that are no longer serving will need an honorable discharge. If you have anything less than an honorable discharge, you will not qualify unless you can have your discharge upgraded as explained in chapter 1.

In the event that the veteran had a break from service with one period that was categorized as honorable, and another period that was considered anything less than a fully honorable on their DD Form 214. They may still be able to qualify for educational benefits in most cases.

Determining Which Educational Plan Works for You

When determining your educational goals, you will want to be very careful to weigh your options before committing yourself to an educational plan because oftentimes, when you accept one program, you are permanently relinquishing your rights to another. Therefore, I strongly urge you to contact either:

An educational case manager with the VA by calling 1(800)827-1000. A VA education benefits specialist by calling 1(888)442-4551.

To help pick the best course of action to meet your educational goals, these workers help veterans to pick out just the right educational plan for their individual needs. Since these benefits can get rather tricky depending on what your educational goals are. I suggest utilizing them before deciding because making mistakes will assuredly cost you. When the VA says the words irrevocable choice that means no second chances!

Educational and Vocational Counseling

Another option that current service members, post-military veterans, and their dependents that qualify for educational benefits are eligible for is the educational and vocational counseling services. This is a free service that can be of great assistance when it comes to choosing a civilian occupation and planning a proper course of action to get there.

Utilizing these free services can really help you chart a course that is headed for success. These professional counselors are there to help you along the way. They can often see problems that may arise well in advance so that you can prepare and navigate through the system.

To qualify, you will need to submit a completed VA Form 28-8832, which is the Application for Educational/Vocational Counseling, to your VA local office. You can download this form at: http://www.vba.va.gov/pubs/forms/VBA-28-8832-ARE.pdf

Daytime Classes or Nighttime Classes

Another factor to consider before deciding on an educational plan is determining whether to attend courses during the daytime or at night. Although oftentimes, this may seem insignificant or your options may be dictated by things such as your job or family life, deciding between day or night courses is still something that is a relevant decision.

Oftentimes many veterans have a difficult time going to traditional daytime courses. After all, a few years in the military will mature just about anyone. Since daytime classes tend to be for kids straight out of high school. Many times veterans have a harder time adjusting to this, seeing as you have worked so hard to get there in the first place. In most colleges and universities, night school tends to be more for career-oriented people. The average age of night-school students tends to be several years older. It's often a bit more relaxed, and the students are typically much more professional.

Taking on More Courses than You Can Handle

Another aspect that you must consider prior to enrolling into an educational program is how many courses can you realistically handle because the ADMGIB doesn't pay for college courses, tests or certifications that you fail, or license renewals as well. So don't get in over your head.

Before Deciding to Use Your GI Bill Benefits while Serving

In the event that you're currently serving on either active duty or in a reserve component, you will need to meet your individual branch's eligibility and minimum service requirements in order to use your educational benefits. I strongly suggest that you also inquire with your educational assistance officer before using your GI Bill benefits, because each branch of service has a tuition assistance program, which pays 100 percent of tuition for college courses that are taken by military service members that are on active duty. Up to $4,500 per fiscal year, this does not count against your GI Bill benefits, so it would be foolish to waste these benefits when they are willing to pay them for you.

Especially seeing that each of the different GI Bill's will only cover thirty-six months as a full-time student, and a bachelor's degree takes four years of full-time schooling. Therefore, it's best to attempt completing at least a year or more of college while still in the service. Many veterans have learned to utilize these programs effectively and essentially paid for their undergraduate degrees while barely even using their GI Bills, saving them for their postgraduate studies.

Dual GI Bill Benefits

In some cases, certain veterans can qualify for multiple GI Bills as well. These are typically veterans that have completed their initial obligation, then separated from the service, then decided to enter the military a second time. In many cases, these veterans initially spent time on active duty then, after separation, decide to join a reserve component such as the National Guard.

In these cases, veterans with multiple GI Bills are not entitled to both full GI Bills. Instead, the VA will allow full-time educational entitlement benefits for forty-eight months, which can still be a pretty good deal when you think about it.

A Closer Look at the Various GI Bills

Congress has enacted several laws over the years that have dramatically changed the GI Bill programs, although this has been a great thing for most veterans in the fact that it has provided much more financial assistance for those seeking a college degree and relaxed the amount of time in service needed to use these benefits. The downside is that it has put more limitations on the programs that GI Bills can be used for. Let's take a look at each of the programs.

The Active Duty Montgomery GI Bill, Chapter 30, Known as ADMGIB

This is quickly becoming a thing of the past. Seeing that as of August 1, 2009, people entering the service will no longer be able to enroll into the Active Duty Montgomery GI Bill. Instead, they will be enrolling into the new Post-9/11 GI Bill. Veterans that started prior to this date, though, were eligible to enroll by having their pay reduced by $100 each month, for their first twelve months of service. In exchange, they received up to $51,336 this is the rate for 2011, (which is adjusted annually) for college then divided over a thirty-six-month period at the full-time rate.

Which Programs Are Accepted under the ADMGIB, MGIBSR, and REAP

One reason that many veterans are reluctant to switch over to the new Post-9/11 GI Bill is that under the new GI Bill, you are substantially limited in which programs you can choose. Under the ADMGIB, MGIBSR, and REAP, you have a higher level of flexibility in choosing a program that best suits your post-military objectives. Under the old version of the GI Bills, you could choose from the following:

- Undergraduate and graduate degree programs from degree granting institutions (being colleges and universities).
- Non-college degree programs offered at institutions of higher learning.
- Online and correspondence courses.
- Flight training.
- Apprenticeships and on-the-job training.
- Technical and vocational schools.
- Entrepreneurship training and co-op training.
- Work-study programs.
- National testing programs.
- Licensing and certifications up to $2,000 per test or certification.

Meeting the Requirements for ADMGIB

To be eligible to receive the full amount of benefits under the ADMGIB, you will need to have served for at least three years of continuous active duty. For those veterans that have served for less than three years on active duty, there is a reduced rate. This rate is only for veterans that have enlisted for less than three years of active-duty service.

That is unless you were separated early for one of the following reasons. In which case, you are eligible for one month of ADMGIB benefits for each month that you served on active duty. To qualify, you must meet one of the following circumstances:

A. A service-connected disability (This was explained in chapter 5. In many cases, you may instead qualify for the Chapter 31 program, which is explained in chapter 10.)
B. A previous existing medical condition.
C. Any other medical condition that has caused the veteran to separate from military service.
E. A hardship separation.
F. Veterans that qualify for the Sole Survivor Program.

Then there are veterans that have separated for the convenience of the government, due to pregnancy, parenthood, and things of that nature. In these cases, the veteran can retain their full thirty-six months of ADMGIB benefits if they meet one of the following conditions:

1. The veteran served for at least thirty months of continuous active duty, on a three-or-more-year contract.
2. The veteran served for at least twenty months of continuous active duty, on a contract that was less than three years.

Counting Your ADMGIB College Money

Depending on your educational goals and needs, some veterans often choose to go into college at less than full time. Many veterans (my husband included) often elect to start out slow and ease their way back into learning mode. Because jumping back into school as a full-time student can be quite overwhelming. Luckily, your GI Bill benefits can be broken down to fit your needs. Here's how it works.

A full-time student in college typically takes four courses per semester. Each of which is a three-credit-hour course, so a full-time student in college takes twelve credit hours per semester. A three-quarter-time student takes three courses or nine credit hours, and a half-time (better known as part-time) student takes two courses or six credit hours per semester.

If your GI Bill has thirty-six months of entitlement, that means you're entitled to thirty-six months as a full-time student. If you decide to enroll into school at the half-time rate, then you will only receive half of the full-time amount and only be charged for half of each month of entitlement. So if you have thirty-six months of full-time entitlement, then as a half-time student, you will have seventy-two months of entitlement because 36 x 2 = 72.

Take a look at the ADMGIB rates for 2011 in Tables 9-1A and 9-1B on the following page. These are the rates for institutional training in colleges and universities. These rates are adjusted annually. The current rates can be found at:
http://www.gibill.va.gov/resources/benefits-resources/rates-tables.html

Montgomery GI Bill - Active Duty (MGIB-AD / Chapter 30)
(The following rates apply to those completing an enlistment of 3 years or more. This is an important distinction. These rates are effective October 1, 2010)

TABLE 9 - 1A

Institutional Training	
Training Time	Monthly Rate
Full time	$1,426.00
3/4 time	$1,069.50
1/2 time	$713.00
Less than 1/2 time, more than 1/4 time	$713.00 **
1/4 time or less	$356.50 **

Correspondence and Flight - Entitlement charged at the rate of one month for each $1,426.00 paid

Cooperative - $1,426.00

** Tuition and fees ONLY. Payment cannot exceed the listed amount.

(The following rates apply to those completing an enlistment of less than 3 years.)

TABLE 9 - 1B

Institutional Training	
Training Time	Monthly Rate
Full time	$1,158.00
3/4 time	$868.50
1/2 time	$579.00
Less than 1/2 time, more than 1/4 time	$579.00 **
1/4 time or less	$289.50 **

Correspondence and Flight - Entitlement charged at the rate of one month for each $1,158.00 paid

Cooperative - $1,158.00

** Tuition and fees ONLY. Payment cannot exceed the listed amount.

Apprenticeship and OJT Rates

Many veterans have educational goals that fall outside of the traditional classroom setting because many hands-on careers require far more field training than classroom experience. Under the new Post-9/11 GI Bill, apprenticeship and on-the-job training courses typically are not covered, yet under the ADMGIB, MGIBSR, and REAP, they are. Therefore, think before you transfer your benefits.

The rates for these programs are considerably lower than traditional classroom training, but can still be quite helpful if you desire to work in a field that requires either an apprenticeship period or on-the-job training period. Take a look below at Tables 9-2A and 9-2B, which are the ADMGIB rates for 2011 for apprenticeship and on-the-job training. These rates are adjusted annually. Current rates can be found at: http://www.gibill.va.gov/resources/benefits-resources/rates-tables.html

(The following rates apply to those completing an enlistment of more than 3 years.)

TABLE 9 - 2A

Apprenticeship and On-the-Job Training	
Training Period	Monthly Rate
First six months of training	$1,069.50
Second six months of training	$784.30
Remaining pursuit of training	$499.10

(The following rates apply to those completing an enlistment of less than 3 years.)

TABLE 9 - 2B

Apprenticeship and On-the-Job Training	
Training Period	Monthly Rate
First six months of training	$868.50
Second six months of training	$636.90
Remaining pursuit of training	$405.30

*Remember that if you decide to use your ADMGIB or MGIBSR benefits for flight training. The ADMGIB and MGIBSR will only help pay for 60 percent of the approved charges, assuming that you have the necessary ADMGIB or MGIBSR entitlement needed to enroll into the courses. Also, these benefits can only be used for training beyond the private pilot's licensing. So you will need to already have a private pilot's license to qualify, then your rates will be determined by which GI Bill you qualify for.

Expiration of ADMGIB Benefits

Typically, your ADMGIB benefits will expire ten years from the date of your last discharge or separation from active duty. This can be extended, though, under certain circumstances. Examples of this would include the following:

- If you are a disabled veteran and your medical condition (that was service related) makes you incapable of going to school. In this case, all you would need to do is submit a letter from your physician, asking that your benefits be extended by the amount of time that you were medically incapable of attending school.

- If you re-enter the service on active duty for ninety days or more. Then your eligibility period starts over again. That is unless your reentering was for training purposes only.

Leftover GI Bill Money

In the event that your GI Bill benefits expire and you do not qualify for an extension of benefits while you are still in school. The VA can only extend your benefits to the end of the semester that they expired in. In the event that you are in a work-study program, co-op training, or any other type of training that doesn't go on a traditional term system. If you have completed over half of the educational program, then the VA can extend your benefits for a period of twelve weeks from the time that your benefits expired.

The Montgomery GI Bill Selected Reserve, Chapter 1606, Known as MGIBSR

This version of the GI Bill is for veterans and members of the selected reserves, which are:

- The Army and Air National Guards.
- The Army, Navy, Air Force, Marine Corps, and the Coast Guard reserves.

The selected reserve version of the GI Bill is very similar to the ADMGIB, with only a few minor differences. These include the following:

- The amount of money that you are entitled to under the MGIBSR is considerably less than under the ADMGIB. After all, though, this is supposed to be a part-time position.

- To be eligible for MGIBSR benefits, you will only need to have completed your initial active-duty for training. Once this training is completed, your reserve/guard component will "code" your eligibility into the DOD's personnel system and give you a DD Form 2384-1, which is a notice of basic eligibility, when you become eligible for your MGIBSR benefits. This form is very important because it verifies to the VA that you are eligible for benefits because members of the guard/reserves have their service component determine eligibility for this benefit, *not* the VA. Then all you will need to do is follow the procedures for applying for GI Bill benefits that are explained later in this chapter.

*Remember that although guard/reserve members are not required to serve for three years to become eligible for benefits. You must still fulfill the obligations of your service contract. If you decide to stop drilling or quit, they can cancel your entitlement, and the service component can hold you responsible for violating your contract. On the other hand, the guard/reserve component can restore your entitlement eligibility if they determine that you have been participating in a satisfactory manner.

- To be eligible for MGIBSR benefits, you must also have entered into a six-year contractual obligation. That is if you joined after June 30, 1985.

- Members of the guard/reserves are also not required to pay $100 per month for their first twelve months of service to be eligible for MGIBSR benefits.

- Additionally, your MGIBSR benefits become suspended if you are activated under an AGR status, which is active-guard and reserve status. Veterans that have their MGIBSR suspended can resume their schooling after their AGR ends.

- The last important difference is that MGIBSR eligibility expires fourteen years from the date that you either became eligible for this program or the day that you leave the selected service (if your eligibility for this program began on or after October 1, 1992).

- For veterans that became eligible for MGIBSR benefits prior to October 1, 1992, their benefits expire ten years from the date they became eligible or the day they leave the selected reserve.

One exception to this rule is for veterans that are mobilized under Title 10 authority. In this event, your benefits are extended for the entire amount that you are mobilized plus an additional four months.

Counting Your MGIBSR College Money

This works the same way as the active-duty GI Bill. The biggest difference is in the amounts, though, seeing as they are greatly reduced. Take a look at Tables 9-3A and 9-3B below which are the current rates for 2011. To check the current rates for MGIBSR, go to: http://www.gibill.va.gov/resources/benefits-resources/rates-tables.html

Montgomery GI Bill - Selected Reserve (MGIB-SR / Chapter 1606)
These rates are effective October 1, 2010

TABLE 9 - 3A

Institutional Training	
Training Time	Monthly Rate
Full time	$337.00
3/4 time	$252.00
1/2 time	$167.00
Less than 1/2 time	$84.25

These rates are effective October 1, 2010

TABLE 9 - 3B

Apprenticeship and On-the-Job Training	
Training Period	Monthly Rate
First six months of training	$252.75
Second six months of training	$185.35
Remaining pursuit of training	$117.95

Correspondence and Flight - Entitlement charged at the rate of one month for each $337.00 paid

Cooperative - $337.00

Correspondence Payments - 55% of the approved charges

Flight Payments - 60% of the approved charges

Additionally, under the MGIBSR, you can be reimbursed for the cost of certification tests and professional licenses up to $2,000 per test. Even if you fail the test, it's covered. It also covers the cost of renewing your certifications or licenses.

Reserve Educational Assistance Program (REAP), Chapter 1607

This is a program for guard/reserve members that have answered the bell when their country needed them the most since September 11, 2001. For reservists that have been called up under USC Title 10 or guard members that have been called up under Title 32 for at least ninety consecutive days for a contingency operation that is authorized by the President or Secretary of Defense in response to either a war or a national emergency that is supported by federal funds.

This can be a pretty good deal for reservists and guardsmen that have served on active duty, if they want more money than under the MGIBSR, yet want to pursue a program that is not covered under the new Post-9/11 GI Bill, such as flight training, vocational/technical training, correspondence training, OJT and apprenticeship training. These are all things that are typically not covered under the new Post-9/11 GI Bill, yet are covered under REAP.

How REAP Works

Depending on the amount of time that you have completed on active duty during qualifying call-ups will determine not only if you qualify for REAP, but how much you qualify for as well. By qualifying, guard/reservists can receive the following percentages of the ADMGIB for their thirty-six months of educational eligibility. This can easily end up being several hundred dollars more per month toward your college education, seeing as these benefits are based off the ADMGIB rates instead of the MGIBSR rates. Qualifying members are as follows:

- Members that either served for over ninety days but less than one year and members that are injured or have an illness or disease that was either incurred or aggravated in the line of duty. These members will receive 40 percent of the ADMGIB rates.

- Members that served for over one year consecutively but less than two years. These members will receive 60 percent of the ADMGIB rates.

- Members that have served either two continuous years on active service or three years total active service combined. These members will receive 80 percent of the ADMGIB rates.

Counting Your REAP Money

The following is a list of the different monthly rates available for 2011 to qualifying REAP participants. Based on your length of active-duty call-ups. Take a look at the following rates in Tables 9-4 through 9-8 which are the current rates for the REAP program. To check the current rates, just go to:
http://www.gibill.va.gov/resources/benefits-resources/rates-tables.html

Reserve Educational Assistance Program - (REAP / Chapter 1607)
All rates are effective October 1, 2010

TABLE 9 - 4

Institutional Training			
Training Time	Consecutive service of 90 days but less than 1 year	Consecutive service of 1 year +	Consecutive service of 2 years +
Full time	$570.40	$855.60	$1,140.80
3/4 time	$427.80	$641.70	$855.60
1/2 time	$285.20	$427.80	$570.40
Less than 1/2 time; more than 1/4 time	$285.20 **	$427.80 **	$570.40 **
1/4 time or less	$142.60	$213.90	$285.20

TABLE 9 - 5

Correspondence Training	
40% level	22% of the approved cost of course
60% level	33% of the approved cost of course
80% level	44% of the approved cost of course

*Entitlement is charged based on the rate of one month for a benefit amount equal to the full-time institutional rate.

TABLE 9 - 6

Flight Training	
40% level	24% of the approved cost of course
60% level	36% of the approved cost of course
80% level	48% of the approved cost of course

*Entitlement is charged based on the rate of one month for a benefit amount equal to the full-time institutional rate.

TABLE 9 - 7

Cooperative Training			
Training Time	Consecutive service of 90 days but less than 1 year	Consecutive service of 1 year +	Consecutive service of 2 years +
Monthly Rates	$570.40	$855.60	$1,140.80

TABLE 9 - 8

Apprenticeship and On-the-Job Training			
Training Period	Consecutive service of 90 days but less than 1 year	Consecutive service of 1 year +	Consecutive service of 2 years +
1st 6 months of Training	$427.80	$641.70	$855.60
2nd 6 months of Training	$313.72	$470.58	$627.44
Remaining pursuit of Training	$199.64	$299.46	$399.28

* Remember that members of the guard/reserves that have met the requirements for this program will lose their eligibility for REAP, if they transfer to the Individual Ready Reserve (IRR) or the Inactive National Guard (ING). So be careful.

Understanding College Kickers

As an incentive to help attract qualified applicants into critically undermanned occupations, the military frequently offers college funds better known as kickers as an incentive. These typically range from $5,000 to $50,000 for college in addition to the standard GI Bills. The payments just as GI Bills are divided up over the course of your GI Bill entitlement and added to your monthly GI Bill payments. These payments can be added to any of the various types of GI Bills.

The $600 Buy-up Program

Another great program that is available to active-duty service members that plan to participate in either ADMGIB or REAP is the $600 Buy-up. This allows service members to contribute up to an additional $600 to their ADMGIB or REAP. With each $20 you contribute into the program, you will receive an additional $5 onto your monthly ADMGIB monthly rates. Therefore, if you're eligible for thirty-six months of ADMGIB benefits, by contributing the full $600, your total benefit will be $5,400.

This $5,400 is then divided into thirty-six monthly payments and added to your ADMGIB monthly payments. If you participated in the $600 Buy-up Program, you will not be able to receive the additional benefit under the Post-9/11 GI Bill. So be very careful.

*Remember that you are not limited to picking one benefit or the other. Veterans can participate in both the college fund and the $600 Buy-up Program. If you decide not to use your entitlement, though, or lose your eligibility, then you will lose your money.

The Post-9/11 GI Bill, Chapter 33

This new version of the GI Bill really makes the other versions obsolete in many ways, primarily if you plan to use it for a degree program. With so many people in society that are unemployed and that have limited opportunities these days due to the economy. This program can really elevate each veteran's chances of being successful in their post-military careers.

I truly feel that over the last few generations, our country has been losing its competitive edge. I also feel that this program is exactly what our country needs to produce the types of college graduates that can lead our country well into the future. After all, who are better at running our country and its businesses, than those who have defended it and know the meaning of hard work!

Qualifying for the Post-9/11 GI Bill

The Post-9/11 GI Bill is for those that have served on active duty for at least ninety days total or were discharged with a service-connected disability after at least thirty days of continuous service after September 11, 2001.

As with most benefits, there are a few exceptions to the rules though. You can still qualify for the Post-9/11 GI Bill if you were discharged for one of the following reasons as long as your discharge was honorable, of course:

    a. Hardship.
    b. A medical condition that was existing prior to service.
    c. A condition interfering with your duty.

The Importance of August 1, 2009

Although the new Post-9/11 GI Bill benefits are available to all qualifying veterans with military service after September 11, 2001, the Post-9/11 GI Bill benefits did not become available for use until August 1, 2009. While many veterans opted to wait until after August 1, 2009 to enroll into colleges so that they can use these enhanced benefits all the way through college. Many others simply changed over to the new GI Bill for the additional funds. While yet others are using these new rules to transfer their benefits to their spouses and children, which will be explained later in this chapter.

Switching Over to the Post-9/11 GI Bill

Veterans that are eligible for the ADMGIB or the MGIBSR can begin to switch over to the new Post-9/11 GI Bill as of August 1, 2009. The thing to remember is that when doing so, you are making an irrevocable choice, so make sure that your educational goals are going to be met prior to switching. By converting over to the new GI Bill, you will also not be required to pay the $100 per month for twelve months to become eligible for these educational benefits.

*Remember that if you have already paid in your contribution, then decide to switch over to the new GI Bill, a proportional amount of the basic $1,200 contribution will be included with the last monthly BAH payment when your Post-9/11 GI Bill entitlement is exhausted.

Why the New Post-9/11 GI Bill Is Better

Unlike the ADMGIB, MGIBSR, and the REAP programs where you only received a monthly check that was to help pay for the cost of your education, as we have already explained earlier in this chapter.

Under the new Post-9/11 GI Bill, the vast majority of veterans that qualify for this benefit can receive quite a bit of additional money to help them through their college years. That is, if they play their cards correctly. The new GI Bill can provide the following financial resources for those that qualify:

- Tuition and fees—these are paid directly to the school. That way, you are not having to scramble around, making sure that you have the finances to pay for classes, then having to wait for reimbursement. The amount cannot exceed the maximum in-state undergraduate tuition and fees at a public college or university though.

  *Remember that before applying for benefits, I strongly urge you to research the cost of tuition and fees for the institution that you are planning to attend prior to applying for your benefits. After you determine the cost of tuition and fees that are needed for the program that you would like to attend, compare the numbers with the maximum rates that the Post-9/11 GI Bill will allow for that state. You can compare these rates at: http://www.gibill.va.gov/ GI_Bill_Info/CH33/Tuition_and_fees.htm

- Books and supplies stipend—this is paid directly to the student annually to help cover the cost of books and supplies for their schooling. Students can receive up to $1,000 annually based proportionately on the amount of courses taken for each semester during their enrollment.

- A monthly housing allowance—this as well is paid directly to the student on a monthly basis. The amount is equal to the basic allowance for housing better known as BAH for an E-5 with dependents. The amount is based on the zip code for the location of the school that you are attending. To determine the current rates for the school that you plan to attend, go to: http://www.defensetravel.dod.mil/perdiem/bah.html

  You will want to keep in mind that if you plan to attend a school outside of the United States. The BAH rate is fixed at $1,333.00 per month for 2010. You can check the current rates at the Web page listed above.

- A relocation payment—students can additionally receive a one time payment of $500.00 if they reside in a county with six persons or less per square mile (this is determined by the most recent decennial census) and they:

  a. Physically relocated at least five hundred miles to attend an educational institution.
  b. Relocated by air to attend an educational institution (if no other land-based transportation exists).

*Remember that there are several rules that can have a great impact on exactly which parts of the Post-9/11 GI Bill that you are eligible to use, depending on your personal situation. This can impact if and when you decide to use your benefits. These are the following:

- Service members that are on active duty and the spouses of active-duty members cannot receive the monthly housing allowance or the books and supplies stipend.

- Individuals that are enrolled exclusively into online training or distance learning courses will not be eligible to receive the monthly housing allowance unless they are enrolled into at least one course per semester on campus.

- Individuals that are enrolled at half-time or less are not entitled to the housing allowance as well.

A Look at Which Programs Are Allowed under the Post-9/11 GI Bill

One factor to consider before switching over to the new Post-9/11 GI Bill is that you are somewhat limited in which programs you can use these benefits for. Under the Post-9/11 GI Bill, you are only allowed to use these benefits if enrolled into any of the following:

- An institution of higher learning. (These are community colleges, four-year universities, and advanced degree programs).

- Distance and Internet training from an institute of higher learning.

- Licensing and certifications (These are limited to one test).

- Work-study programs that are offered at institutions of higher learning.

*Correspondence courses, flight training, national testing programs, entrepreneurship training, and co-op training that are offered at an institution of higher learning, may or may not be eligible under the Post-9/11 GI Bill, depending on if the VA approves the courses at the institution of higher learning.

Why Your Active-duty Time Counts

Although the Post-9/11 GI Bill program will provide you with thirty-six months of full-time educational benefits, the percentage of the maximum amount payable is directly related to the amount of time that you spent on active duty after September 10, 2001. The more time spent on active duty, the higher the percentage will be of the maximum rates payable for your particular state. The percentage that you qualify for is determined by completing the following benchmarks of active-duty service:

100   percent for thirty or more continuous days on active duty (with a service-connected disability discharge)

100   percent for thirty-six or more months

90   percent for thirty months

80   percent for twenty-four months

70   percent for eighteen months

60   percent for twelve months
50   percent for six months
40   percent for ninety or more total days

Transferring Your Educational Benefits to a Family Member

Another highly anticipated advantage of the new Post-9/11 GI Bill is that you can transfer entitlement for educational benefits to either the spouse or children of the qualifying veteran in many cases. Oftentimes veterans that have decided to make the military their career or that have been provided with the necessary skills to maintain steady post-military employment without needing to use their educational benefits can assign these benefits over to their spouse or children under the new GI Bill. After all, if you've earned them, you should be able to use them in the most effective way to meet your family's needs.

Determining Eligibility to Transfer Educational Benefits

As with all benefits, there are certain eligibility requirements in order to use this option though the rules as to who qualifies and when they can elect to transfer their benefits can become very confusing. Largely due to the fact that this is a new program and it was implemented to help retain qualified service members for a longer period of time, so you will want to closely evaluate your family's educational needs before you elect this option. Because in most cases, you will be required to serve additional time in the armed forces to become eligible to transfer your educational benefits.

To be eligible to transfer your educational benefits, veterans must first meet the requirements for the Post-9/11 GI Bill as explained earlier in this chapter. Additionally, there are time requirements involved with transferring your Post-9/11 GI Bill educational benefits. Seeing as this option is intended to help retain qualified officers/enlisted personnel within the armed forces. The basic length of service guidelines for active duty and select reserve members are as follows:

- If the member has at least six years of service in the armed forces on the date of election and agrees to serve four additional years in the armed forces from the date that they elect to transfer their benefits.

- If the individual has at least ten years of service in the armed forces (whether on active duty and/or selected reserve) on the date of election. If the individual is prevented or it is otherwise impossible by either standard policy or by law that the individual is not allowed to commit to four additional years. Then the individual must agree to serve for the maximum amount of time allowed by such policy or law.

In the event that the individual becomes retirement eligible (see chapter 6) during the period from August 1, 2009, through August 1, 2013. The following rules apply:

- If the member becomes eligible for retirement on August 1, 2009, then no additional service is required.

- If the individual has an approved retirement date after August 1, 2009, but before July 1, 2010. Then no additional service is required if they have an approved retirement date.

- If the individual is eligible for retirement after August 1, 2009, but before August 1, 2010. Then one year of additional service after approval of transfer is required.

- If the individual is eligible for retirement on or after August 1, 2010, but before August 1, 2011. Then two years of additional service after approval of transfer is required.

- If the individual is eligible for retirement on or after August 1, 2011, but before August 1, 2012. Then three years of additional service after approval of transfer is required.

Who Can Receive Your Transferred Educational Benefits?

Once you have elected to transfer your Post-9/11 GI Bill benefits, veterans can elect to transfer either some or all of their unused educational benefits (up to thirty-six months worth) to their spouse or children in any combination that the veteran desires. The service member also retains the right to revoke or modify the transfer of the educational benefits to the spouse or children at anytime.

Determining When Transferred Educational Benefits Will Expire

Spouses may start using their benefits immediately after the service member has elected to transfer their educational benefits, even if the member remains in the armed forces. Spouses will have fifteen years from the service member's last separation date from active duty to use them.

*Remember that spouses are not eligible for the monthly BAH (basic allowance housing) or the books and supplies stipend while the service member is serving on active duty.

Children that are receiving transferred GI Bill benefits may only start using their educational benefits after the service member that is making the transfer has completed at least ten years of armed forces service, and the child has either received their high school diploma, high school equivalency, or reached the age of eighteen.

*Remember that children are entitled to receive the monthly BAH payments and the books and supplies stipend, even if the parent is still on active duty. The rules for children are also different in the fact that their transferred GI Bill benefits expire when the child turns twenty-six years of age, instead of fifteen years after the service member separates.

How to Transfer Your GI Bill Benefits

The first step in transferring your educational benefits is having the service member/sponsor go to:
https://www.dmdc.osd.mil/TEB/

Once logged into the system using your CAC card or your DFAS pin, you will want to log on to the Transferability of Education Benefits Web page. Once logged in, the service member can change and track their requests for their educational benefits to be transferred. After approval, the family member will only need to submit a VA Form 22-1990e. This can be completed online at:
http://www.vabenefits.vba.va.gov/vonapp/main.asp

After completing these forms. You will receive a certificate of eligibility from the VA, then all the family member will need to do is provide the school with the certificate of eligibility from the VA and have the school certify your enrollment.

The Yellow Ribbon Program

This is a really great new program that is a provision of the Post-9/11 GI Bill, so it can only be used by individuals that are eligible under this new version of the GI Bill that are entitled at the 100 percent level, whether as a veteran or the dependent of a veteran.

This program works with the degree-granting institutions (being colleges and universities) that are located throughout the United States, and allows them to voluntarily enter into an agreement with the VA to help fund the tuition and expenses that exceed the "highest public in-state undergraduate tuition rate."

These participating colleges and universities will match the VA on a dollar-for-dollar basis to help cover the shortfall that is often created by going to either an out-of-state college, private college, or even using your Post-9/11 GI Bill benefits for graduate school. By entering into this agreement with the VA, these colleges and universities must guaranty to:

- State the dollar amounts they will be contributing toward each person that will be participating for the academic year.

- Provide these contributions during each of the academic years in which the college or university is participating in the Yellow Ribbon Program, providing that the student maintains satisfactory progress, attendance, and conduct.

- Make their contributions toward the program on behalf of the enrolled individuals in the form of a scholarship, grant, etc.

- Provide contributions to the qualifying applicants on a first-come-first-served basis, regardless of the rate at which the applicant is pursuing training for any given academic year.

- State how many people they will make contributions for in any academic year.

*Remember that since this is a new and voluntary program, not all colleges and universities have chosen to participate at this time. To find a current list of participating schools, the number of students that are being accepted, and the amounts of the contributions. Just go to: http://www.gibill.va.gov/GI_Bill_Info/CH33/YRP/YRP_List_2010.htm

By using this program effectively, you can greatly reduce or, in many cases, completely eliminate any costs associated with attending many great schools. I was surprised with how many schools that are participating in the Yellow Ribbon Program already.

To apply for this benefit, all you will need to do is submit your application for the Post-9/11 GI Bill benefits. If you meet all of the eligibility criteria for the Yellow Ribbon Program, you will receive notification along with your certificate of eligibility. Then all you will need to do is take the certificate of eligibility to your school and have them certify your enrollment to the VA to include Yellow Ribbon because your school must report this information on your enrollment certification.

Things to Remember before Picking a GI Bill
In some cases, you may actually be better off using either the ADMGIB, MGIBSR, or REAP, instead of the new Post-9/11 GI Bill. Some of the things that you will want to consider before switching over to the new Post-9/11 GI Bill are the following:

1. Your educational goals. Seeing as the Post-9/11 GI Bill *cannot* be used for several educational goals such as:

    a. Flight training.
    b. Co-op training.
    c. Correspondence courses.
    d. Entrepreneurship training.
    e. National testing programs.
    f. On-the-job training and apprenticeship training.
    g. Non-college degree programs (that are not at an institution of higher learning or a degree-granting institution).

2. The financial aspects. In most cases, the new Post-9/11 GI Bill is a better deal financially. In certain cases, though, you may be better off sticking with one of the old GI Bills.

    For example, if your state offers free tuition to veterans at selected state colleges, in which case, under the new Post-9/11 GI Bill, all you would be eligible to receive is the monthly housing benefit and the book stipend. This could be a lesser amount than if you had not switched. As where under the other GI Bills, you would be able to collect the entire amounts.

3. Then there are those service members that want to use their Post-9/11 GI Bill benefits either while on active duty or that want to transfer their benefits to their spouses or children (this is explained in the Post-9/11 GI Bill section earlier in this chapter). One of the rules to keep in mind is that under the new Post-9/11 GI Bill, you cannot receive the monthly housing allowance or the books and supplies stipend while you are either on active duty or are the spouse of an active-duty member. (Children that are using this benefit are exempt). This rule could very easily end up costing you thousands of dollars each year, if you're not paying close attention.

*Another thing to remember is veterans that decide to enroll into educational programs at either half-time or less do not qualify for the monthly housing allowance under the Post-9/11 GI Bill program. Therefore, the ADMGIB may very well end up paying significantly more per month.

The Disadvantages of Using the ADMGIB, MGIBSR, or REAP

Although there are some advantages to using the older educational benefits instead of the new Post-9/11 GI Bill, there are several key disadvantages as well. You will want to factor in these disadvantages before making your decision:

1. By keeping the old GI Bills, you are only entitled to a fixed rate per month depending on your amount of active duty time that you completed and your branch of service. This amount

is adjusted annually and is based on the average undergraduate tuition. That is determined by the National Center for Education Statistics.

That may not seem like a big deal, right? But consider this. If you're being paid the average amount, then all you will probably be able to afford is an average education. If you're accepted to either a better college or an out-of-state university (which are typically more expensive), then you will be liable to pay the difference unless you qualify for additional funding through scholarships and such. Since these costs can be huge, you will really want to do some research before you act.

2. Then there is the Yellow Ribbon Program. This program can help to further offset the costs of tuition at participating colleges and universities. This program is only for those enrolled under the new Post-9/11 GI Bill at the 100 percent level.

Applying for Your GI Bill Benefits

This is pretty simple once you have decided on an educational plan. To apply for GI Bill benefits, all you will have to do is download and complete VA Form 22-1990. Then mail the completed form to the corresponding regional office that is listed on the form. There are several ways to do this:

- To download the VA form 22-1990, go to: http://www.vba.va.gov/pubs/forms/VBA-22-1990-ARE.pdf
- Call 1-888-GI BILL-1, and request a VA form 22-1990 be mailed to you.
- Go onto VONAPP online on the VA's Web site.

Once you have completed the proper forms with the VA. You may wish to start speaking directly with the schools administration, financial aid, and admissions offices about the process of certifying your enrollment, once your eligibility has been granted.

Also, you may want to inquire about acceptance into the Yellow Ribbon Program. Although these offices cannot make decisions about your GI Bill benefits entitlement. They can definitely help you through the process.

Chapter 10

Additional Education Benefits

In this chapter, we will be explaining the additional educational benefits that certain disabled veterans and in some cases, even severely disabled veteran's families and surviving family members can qualify for by reading this chapter, you will also learn about how to make the most of these programs and not only who qualifies for them, but more importantly how to utilize them effectively. In this chapter, we will be discussing:

- The Chapter 31 Vocational Rehabilitation and Employment Program.
- The Chapter 35 Dependents' Educational Assistance Program.
- Other scholarship opportunities.

It amazes me that oftentimes, some of the best programs that the VA has to offer are so frequently underutilized. In the 2009 fiscal year, only 59,829 veterans were training in the Chapter 31 vocational rehabilitation and employment program. When you compare that number against the over three million veterans that are currently receiving disability compensation for their service-connected disabilities.

It really makes you wonder why more veterans are not requesting this benefit. After all, most veterans that have received benefits under Chapter 31 have nothing but great things to say about the program. Even my husband used this program for college and swears by it along with every other person that I have interviewed that have used this program, so let's take a closer look.

The Chapter 31 vocational rehabilitation and employment program, which is often referred to as Chapter 31 or VR&E, was enacted to help disabled veterans in several ways to overcome their disabilities and become employable again, or, at minimum, make them capable of achieving the goal of independent living again.

Qualifying for Chapter 31 Benefits

These benefits are for disabled veterans that meet the following criteria. Keep in mind that since you can apply for these benefits while you are still on active duty, that the VA will allow you to apply for these benefits, only if you are anticipating to meet each of the requirements necessary for Chapter 31. These requirements are as follows:

1. Your service characterization—To qualify for Chapter 31 benefits, you will need a discharge characterization on your DD Form 214 that the VA does not determine dishonorable. This was explained in chapter 1.

    *Oftentimes, service members that are applying for this benefit prior to separation are anticipating an honorable discharge. Only to receive a lesser discharge due to lowered evaluations that stem directly from their disability in the first place. In these cases, I strongly encourage you to explain the circumstances surrounding your discharge.

2. Your disability rating—To qualify for Chapter 31 benefits, oftentimes, veterans become confused by the disability rating requirements, to qualify for entitlement to VR&E services under Chapter 31, you must have either of the following:

   a. A service-connected disability rating that is 20 percent or higher and an employment handicap. This is for veterans that are within the twelve-year basic period of eligibility from the time of being awarded 20 percent or higher for a service-connected disability by the VA.

      *The VA defines an *employment handicap* as "an impairment of a veteran's ability to prepare for, obtain, or retain employment consistent with his or her abilities, aptitudes, and interests. The impairment must result in large part from a service-connected disability."

   b. Then there are veterans that have service-connected disability ratings that are only rated at 10 percent or that are beyond their twelve years of basic period of eligibility. These veterans can still qualify for entitlement to VR&E services if they have a serious employment handicap.

      *The VA defines a *serious employment handicap* as "a significant impairment of a veteran's ability to prepare for, obtain, or retain employment consistent with his or her abilities, aptitudes, and interests." The serious employment handicap must result in large part from a service-connected disability.

Determining Eligibility for VR&E

When it comes to determining the severity of your employment handicaps or serious employment handicaps and which VR&E benefits that you qualify to use, it really comes down to your vocational rehabilitation counselor's or VRC's determinations. You see, after applying for Chapter 31 benefits, which will be explained later in this chapter, you will be assigned to a VRC.

The counselor will administer a comprehensive evaluation to help determine if you are entitled to VR&E services. If your counselor determines that the veteran has an employment handicap that exists as a result of a service-connected disability. Then the veteran is entitled to services. This evaluation includes:

1. An assessment as to whether or not your service-connected disabilities impair your ability to find and/or hold a job using the occupational skills that you already have.

2. An assessment of your interests, aptitudes, and abilities.

3. An exploration into which jobs, careers, and professions that may be best suited for you, as well as goal development.

*Remember that it is best to put some serious thought into these things prior to applying for Chapter 31 benefits because having realistic goals that work with not against your disability, and at least a basic knowledge of your primary objective, is very important. Otherwise, you will end up squandering away a great opportunity.

For example: An engineer for the army injures his back while working on a construction site. He separates from the army and receives a 40 percent disability rating from the VA. Then he blindly decides to apply for the Chapter 31 program, and during his comprehensive evaluation, he continually requests for retraining as an automobile mechanic.

Here's the problem with this scenario. If you have a back injury, then chances are that being a mechanic will probably re-aggravate your injuries, so chances are your requests will be denied. Since this benefit is intended to help you overcome your disabilities and become employable again. By planning ahead, you can save everyone involved quite a bit of aggravation. If this veteran had expressed an interest in, let's say, architecture or a field that would not almost assuredly aggravate his injuries, he more often than not would have been fine.

Making the Most of Your Educational Opportunities

Veterans that walk in with a solid plan tend to get quite a bit further. Oftentimes, these vocational rehabilitation counselors are contracted employees that are occupational therapists. In the private sector, these counselors charge quite a bit of money, and civilians pay hundreds if not thousands of dollars just to make the same appointments. So pick their brains and utilize them to formulate a good viable plan.

Formulating a Rehabilitation Plan

Assuming that your VRC feels that you are entitled to benefits under the Chapter 31 program. You will then begin to formulate a rehabilitation plan designed to either achieve suitable employment or independent living. Once your rehabilitation plan is developed, both the veteran and counselor will sign it. Then work toward achieving the goals outlined within the plan. This plan is also reviewed annually to determine whether any changes may be needed.

I can tell you firsthand that once you have committed to a rehabilitation plan, your counselor / case manager has the power to make it happen. These case managers are typically very committed to helping you achieve your goals, although my husband was not able to complete his rehabilitation plan due to medical problems. While he was on the rehabilitation plan, his case manager was able to remove any barriers that came along.

Case managers have the ability to coordinate different services such as tutorial assistance, removing time restraints on tests, providing any special needs within a classroom setting, adjustment counseling, training in job-seeking skills, medical and dental referrals, facilitating your payment of training allowance, and helping with most other services that are required to achieve your rehabilitation program. By speaking openly and honestly with your case manager about your disability and limitations, more often than not, you can resolve just about any problems that may arise concerning your rehabilitation program.

What Is Covered under Chapter 31

One of the most important things to consider before applying for Chapter 31 benefits is that unlike the GI Bills, which were covered in chapter 9. These benefits are much more tailored to meet the individual needs of each qualifying disabled veteran to help them overcome their personal disabilities, depending on the rehabilitation goals and needs that are outlined within your plan. As you read the following section on what can be covered under Chapter 31, pay close attention to how different this program is from the GI Bills. Veterans will start their journey down one of the following five tracks of services. These are as follows:

1. Rapid access to employment—this option is designed for disabled veterans that already possess the majority of the skills necessary to compete for suitable employment opportunities. This option is great for veterans that wish to obtain employment as soon as possible.

   The services provided under this option may include short-term training, licensure, certifications, resume development, job search assistance, job readiness preparation, job accommodations, and post-employment follow-up.

2. Self-employment—this option is designed for disabled veterans that have limited access to traditional employment, that need either a flexible work schedule or a more accommodating work environment due to their disabling condition or other life circumstances.

   The services provided under this option may include the analysis and viability of your business concept, development of a business plan, training, in the operation of a small business, marketing and financial assistance, and also guidance on obtaining adequate resources through the SBA as explained in chapter 11 to implement the plan.

3. Reemployment with previous employer—this option is designed for disabled veterans that wish to return to work with a former employer.

   The services provided under this option may include short-term training, job modifications, job accommodations, work adjustment services, advice about reemployment rights, consultation with the employer, licensure and certifications.

4. Independent living services—this option is for veterans whose disabilities are so severe in nature that they are currently unable to pursue an employment goal. These veterans often may need rehabilitation services to live more independently and to increase their potential to return to work.

The services provided under this option may include independent living skills training, services at special rehabilitation facilities, assistive technology, and connection to community-based support services.

5. Employment through long-term services—this would be the most widely used part of the Chapter 31 program. Veterans that qualify for this option can receive specialized training and/or education to obtain and maintain suitable employment.

The services provided under this option may include training at a college or university, vocational or technical schools, on-the-job training, internships, apprenticeship programs, work-study programs, work monitoring, job shadowing, and public/private job partnering.

*Remember that one very important thing to remember about Chapter 31 benefits is that even though you may qualify for benefits under this program. You still may not qualify for the last option, which is the employment through long-term services portion of Chapter 31. Your counselor must determine that your service-connected disability is basically the root of your un-employability problem and without long-term training, you are likely to stay unemployed.

A Closer Look at the Specialized Training and/or Education Services

Although many disabled veterans apply for the Chapter 31 program based on specific needs and for particular portions of the program. The vast majority of disabled veterans that apply are in search of long-term training / educational benefits.

Because disabled veterans that qualify for educational benefits under Chapter 31 can receive a great deal of free educational benefits. These include:

- Tuition and fees.
- Books.
- School supplies (and equipment needed to achieve your program).
- Tutorial assistance.
- Medical and dental coverage.

Chapter 31 Subsistence Allowances

Depending on your household income, the VA can also pay you a monthly subsistence allowance while you are training. This amount is paid in addition to any other VA amount that you may be receiving. Such as disability compensation that was explained in chapter 5. Additionally, this money is tax free as well.

Subsistence Allowance Rates

Depending on which program that you are enrolled into, the number of dependents you have and the pace at which you will be training at, will determine which subsistence allowance rates that you qualify for. The rates listed are effective as of October 1, 2010. Current rates can easily be found at: http://www.vba.va.gov/bln/vre/doc/sa_rates.pdf

The following is Table 10-1 which are the 2011 monthly rates for students enrolled into either college, university, independent living programs, extended evaluation programs, and work experience programs (that are non-pay or nominal pay work experience in a federal, state, local, or federally recognized Indian tribe agency).

Vocational Rehabilitation and Employment (Chapter 31)

The following Subsistence Allowance rates are paid for training

in an Institution of Higher Learning

Rates Efective - October 1, 2010

TABLE 10 - 1

Institutional Training			
Number of Dependents	Full Time	Three Quarter Time	One Half Time
No Dependents	$554.22	$416.43	$278.64
One Dependent	$687.47	$516.35	$345.23
Two Dependents	$810.13	$605.69	$405.81
Each Additional Dependent	$59.05	$45.41	$30.30

Disabled veterans that are enrolled into the following categories can also receive the subsistence allowance at the full-time rates:

- Vocational course in a rehabilitation facility or sheltered workshop.
- Institutional nonfarm cooperative.
- Training in the home.
- Non-pay or nominal pay on-job training in a federal, state, local, or federally recognized Indian tribe agency.

- Disabled veterans that are in combined college and on-the-job training courses (that are in school for over one half of their time).

Then there are reduced rates for disabled veterans that are enrolled into other various programs. The reduced rates are because these veterans typically earn wages while working in their particular programs. Take a close look at Table 10-2 which is the reduced subsistence rates for 2011:

Subsistence Allowance is paid for full-time training only in the following training programs

farm cooperative, apprenticeship or other on-the-job training

Rates Effective - October 1, 2010

TABLE 10 - 2

Number of Dependents	Full Time
No Dependents	$484.57
One Dependent	$585.99
Two Dependents	$675.36
Each Additional Dependent	$43.93

These rates apply to the following categories of disabled veterans:

- Disabled veterans enrolled into full-time nonfarm cooperative / on-the-job training.
- Apprenticeships, farm cooperatives, or other on-job training.
- Disabled veterans that are in combined college and on-the-job training courses (that are in school for less than one half of their time).

Applying for Chapter 31 Benefits

To apply for Chapter 31 benefits, you will need to download VA Form 28-1900, which is the Disabled Veterans Application for Vocational Rehabilitation form. You can download this form at: http://www.vba.va.gov/pubs/forms/VBA-28-1900-ARE.pdf

Once completed, you will need to send your application to the VA regional office that services your area. This was explained in chapter 2. Once the VA has reviewed your application, they will have you meet with a VRC.

*Remember that if you disagree with your VRC findings for benefits even if you meet the requirements for the Chapter 31 program. To appeal their decision, you will need to file an appeal with your VA regional office. This was covered in chapter 3.

Students with Disabilities

I strongly encourage disabled veterans that plan to attend college whether on Chapter 31 or any of the various GI Bills to check in with the students with disabilities department that is located on most college and university campuses. They can become a huge asset for disabled veterans that have special needs or that are limited by physical restraints. I feel that this bears mentioning because oftentimes disabled veterans will just work through the pain instead of seeking an alternative or asking for help. An important thing to remember about college is that you are there to learn. Which means that you should be judged on what you have learned, not by how fast you can write, type, or the speed that you can complete the assignments.

Dependents' Educational Assistance Program Known as DEA (Chapter 35)

The DEA program was instituted to assist the spouses/widows and children of service members or veterans that were either severely injured or lost their lives while serving our country. This program offers up to forty-five months of full-time educational benefits to qualifying participants.

Qualifying for DEA Benefits

This program provides educational assistance to the spouse/widow, son, daughter, stepchild, or even adopted child of a service member or veteran that meets one of the following sets of circumstances to qualify for DEA benefits:

- A veteran who either died or is permanently and totally disabled (see the P&T section of chapter 5) as a result of a service-connected disability. The disability must arise out of or be aggravated by their active duty in the armed forces.

- A veteran with a permanent and total service-connected disability that dies from any cause while the P&T service-connected disability was in existence.

- A service member that is currently being forcibly detained or interned in the line of duty by a foreign government or power.

- A service member who is missing in action or that is captured in the line of duty and is currently being held by a hostile force.

- A service member that the VA determines has a P&T service-connected disability, that at the time of the VA's determination is a member of the armed forces who is hospitalized or receiving outpatient medical care, services, or treatment and is likely to be discharged or released from the service for their service-connected disability. This was a new category that took effect as of December 23, 2006. For service member's families to be eligible for the DEA program. If you meet these qualifications and were previously denied for DEA benefits. I strongly urge you reapply for this benefit.

Eligibility Period for DEA Benefits

Depending on if you're the spouse/widow or child of a qualifying veteran or service member will help to determine your eligibility period for DEA benefits because depending on your individual cases circumstances can often determine if and how long you're eligible for DEA benefits.

Spouses of veterans that have a P&T service-connected disability are generally eligible for DEA benefits for ten years from the date that the VA notifies the veteran of their permanent and total status.

If the P&T veteran and spouse decide to divorce, then the spouse's DEA benefits end on the date of the divorce decree. In the event that the spouse is presently in training and the divorce occurred through no fault of the qualifying spouse. The VA can extend your benefits for a period of up to twelve weeks or to the end of the semester or course.

Spouses of service members that are either being held or missing, as either a POW, MIA, or that are forcibly held by a foreign government or power, then your eligibility period is for ten years as well and begins on the ninety-first day after the date that the service member was listed as either missing or captive.

*Remember that if the service member is either released from captivity or is determined to be alive and no longer missing, then your eligibility period ends on that date. If you are already currently enrolled, then your eligibility can be extended to the end of the semester or course.

Widows of veterans that have died from a service-connected disability have a ten-year period of eligibility as well. The period of eligibility will be chosen by the widow and must start between the date of the veteran's death and the date the VA determines that the death was due to the service-connected disability because it often takes some time to prove that the death was from a service-connected disability.

Widows of veterans that had a P&T service-connected disability, these widows have a ten-year period of eligibility as well. Your eligibility period begins on the date that the veteran passes.

Widows of service members that have died while on active duty are eligible for DEA benefits for twenty years from the date that the service member passes.

*Remember that prior to December 10, 2004 widows of service members that died on active duty only had ten years of eligibility to use their DEA benefits. These widows now have twenty years and may now still find themselves having eligibility under the new rules.

The Effects of Remarrying

Widows that qualify for DEA benefits will probably want to think long and hard before deciding to remarry prior to age fifty-seven, if they are using DEA benefits. Because widows under the age of fifty-seven that remarry will lose their eligibility for DEA benefits, unless their remarriage ends through divorce or death. Then the widow can reestablish their eligibility for DEA benefits.

Widows that remarried on or after January 1, 2004, and that are fifty-seven years or older can still be eligible for DEA benefits.

If you're a qualifying child, adopted child, or even stepchild that is eligible for DEA benefits, you're typically eligible for these benefits from the time that you turn eighteen until you turn twenty-six. There are a few exceptions to these rules though:

    a. You become ill.
    b. A death or illness within your immediate family.
    c. You're participating in an official missionary capacity.
    d. Unavoidable conditions of your employment that require you to stop your training.

e. Immediate family or financial obligations that require you to stop training. Such as taking employment to support your family.

f. You join the military. In which case, you will still qualify for DEA benefits after your discharge (assuming that your discharge was not dishonorable of course). In these cases, your eligibility period is extended for eight years from the date of your unconditional release from active duty. This extension cannot go beyond your thirty-first birthday though.

*Remember that as a qualifying child, the only way to extend your benefits beyond your thirty-first birthday. Is if you served on or after September 11, 2001, and you were called to active duty under Title 10 (federal authority) or section 502F of Title 32 for the National Guard, which is involuntarily ordered to full-time National Guard duty. In which case, the VA can extend your eligibility period by the number of months and days you spent on active duty plus four months.

Also, children that decide to marry will not lose their eligibility under the DEA program as well.

Preparing Your Children for College

I strongly encourage parents that have children who qualify for this program to speak with the child's high school guidance counselor. Oftentimes, not only will the guidance counselor be able to help the child realize the opportunities that are available to them, but they can often also help them to formulate and execute a strong educational plan.

Making Use of the Free Counseling

Before deciding on an educational program under DEA, it is usually best to utilize the free counseling services that the VA will provide you with. These counseling services can also include testing to help you select an educational, vocational, or professional objective and help develop a plan to achieve that goal. This counseling can also help you overcome any personal or academic problems that can interfere with the successful completion of your goals.

To schedule a free counseling appointment so that the VA can help assist you with picking out an educational plan, contact the VA's educational counseling at 1(800)827-1000.

For hearing impaired, call 1(800)829-4833.

Programs Offered under DEA

Family members that qualify for benefits under the DEA program can use their entitlement for many different types of educational programs. These include the following:

- Degree programs offered at colleges and universities. Including cooperative training programs and accredited independent study programs that are offered through distance education.
- Certificate programs at colleges, universities, technical, vocational, or business schools.
- Programs overseas that lead to college degrees.
- Preparatory courses for college or graduate school entrance exams.
- High school programs after the age of eighteen. If you are not a high school graduate.
- Correspondence courses. If you're a spouse or widow.
- Farm cooperative training courses.
- Apprenticeship or on-the-job training programs.
- Special restorative training or specialized vocational training. For those that are handicapped by either a physical or mental disability.
- You can also receive reimbursement for the cost of tests for licenses or certifications. Up to $2,000 per test. These benefits are paid even if you don't pass the test. You can also use these benefits to renew or update your licenses or certificates.
- You can also receive benefits for national tests required for admission into various colleges and universities. These include SATs, LSAT, GRE, GMAT, AP, and CLEP tests.

Getting Ready to Use DEA Benefits

Another important piece of the puzzle to remember before you start in training is that you can receive DEA benefits for refresher courses to help you get prepared for an approved education program. This can be very helpful for spouses and widows that were not planning on going back to school, that due to their spouse's medical circumstances are being pushed back into the workforce. For these refresher, remedial, or deficiency courses, your entitlement will not be charged for the first five months of training.

The Importance of Completing Courses

You will want to seriously consider the consequences before deciding to drop courses after the school's drop period has ended while using DEA benefits because by dropping courses, you can end up paying back any benefits that you have received, unless there are mitigating circumstances that are beyond your control, such as unexpected illnesses or a death in your family.

DEA Program Rates

Depending on which type of training and the pace that you pursue your educational goal at will determine your monthly rates that you are entitled to. Since you are entitled to forty-five months of full-time educational benefits under DEA, this will work in the same fashion as the other educational benefits. In that if you train at a half-time pace, you will be charged half a month's entitlement per month of training and will receive payments at the half-time rates, and full-time training uses the full-time rates.

Take a look at Tables 10-3 through 10-6, these are the rates for 2011. These rates are adjusted annually on October 1 of each year. To check the current rates for the DEA program, go to: http://www.gibill.va.gov/resources/benefits-resources/rates-tables.html

Survivors' and Dependents' Educational Assistance Program

(DEA / Chapter 35)

All rates are effective October 1, 2010

TABLE 10 - 3

Institutional Training	
Training Time	Monthly Rate
Full Time	$936.00
3/4 Time	$702.00
1/2 Time	$466.00
Less than 1/2 time; more than 1/4 time	$466.00 **
1/4 time or less	$234.00 **

** Tuition and Fees ONLY. Payment cannot exceed the listed amount.

Correspondence - Entitlement charged at the rate of one month for each $936.00 paid.

Farm Cooperative Training
All Rates are Effective October 1, 2010

TABLE 10 - 4

Farm Cooperative Training	
Training Period	Monthly Rate
Full Time	$753.00
3/4 Time	$565.00
1/2 Time	$466.00

OJT All Rates are Effective October 1, 2010

TABLE 10 - 5

Apprenticeship and On-the-Job Training	
Training Period	Monthly Rate
First six months of training	$682.00
Second six months of training	$511.00
Third six months of training	$337.00
Remaining pursuit of training	$170.00

Special Restorative Training
All Rates Effective October 1, 2010

TABLE 10 - 6

Special Restorative Training	
Training Period	Monthly Rate
Full Time	$936.00
Accelerated Charges - Cost of Tuition and Fees in Excess of	$290.00
Entitlement Reduced 1 day for each	$31.20 (1/30 of Full Time Rate)

Receiving a Free Tutor through DEA

Another competitive advantage that the DEA program can provide you with is a special allowance for free tutorial assistance for the subjects that you are weak in. To qualify, you must have a deficiency in that subject that makes the tutor necessary.

Additionally, the institution must certify the tutor's qualifications and the hours that you are being tutored. If eligible for this assistance, the qualifying student can receive a monthly payment of up to $100, up to a maximum of $1,200 without being charged from your entitlement.

Things to Remember before Applying for DEA Benefits

If you are the child of a deceased veteran, children typically are eligible to receive death benefits from ages eighteen to twenty-three, if you continue attending school. The thing to remember is that if you are also eligible for DEA benefits. You must elect which benefit to receive. If you elect DEA benefits, the death benefits will stop when you begin receiving the DEA benefits.

In some cases, you may also want to defer your DEA benefits. This can be useful for dependents that are in programs that require more than forty-five months of training.

If you're the spouse/widow, then your DEA benefits will have no effect on your benefits as either a dependent on the veteran's disability compensation or pension as explained in chapter 5, or their Dependency and Indemnity Compensation (DIC) as explained in chapter 5.

Applying for DEA Benefits

To apply for DEA benefits, just download and complete VA Form 22-5490. You can download this form at:
http://www.vba.va.gov/pubs/forms/VBA-22-5490-ARE.pdf

Once you have completed VA Form 22-5490, you will need to mail it to the VA regional processing office that corresponds to where you live. This information is on the last page of the application form. If you have questions about filling out the application or questions about

specific programs that are accepted under the DEA program, call
1(888)442-4551.
For hearing impaired, call 1(888)829-4833.

Other Scholarship Opportunities
While not all veterans may not qualify for additional educational
scholarships, it is always smart to evaluate either your military service or
your parents (in the event that you're a dependent). In some instances,
you may find that either your past service or a parents past service can
lead you to free money for college.

For example: Veterans or the qualifying dependents of veterans that have
received a Purple Heart are eligible to apply for scholarships that are
only available to Purple Heart recipients and their family members. This
makes for much smaller pools of potential applicants than traditional
scholarships. By carefully examining which scholarships that you may
be eligible for, based on previous military service. Oftentimes, veterans
and their families can help to reduce their educational expenses by
thousands of dollars per year.

Section 4

Life after the Military

The chapters within this section deal with many of the advantages that your military service can offer you throughout the rest of your life. Whether you're seeking employment or wanting to start your own business. From purchasing a home to reducing or eliminating the property taxes on it. By reading these chapters, you will not only know about the opportunities that are out there for you, but more importantly know how to cash in on them!

Chapter 11

Employment

In this chapter, we will be discussing all of the advantages that veterans and sometimes even their family members, as well, have when it comes to post-military employment. Although most veterans know that they receive a certain amount of preference when it comes to getting federal government jobs, by reading this chapter, you will learn quite a bit about several of the various career paths that are out there for veterans. We will be discussing:

- Veteran's federal job preference points.
- Crossover jobs.
- Government contractors.
- Small business loans for veterans.
- Advertising your veteran-owned small business.
- Executive Order 13360.

If you look back throughout our country's history, you will see that we have been giving preference to veterans that are seeking federal jobs ever since the Civil War era. This has been a long-standing practice and is a cornerstone of our country's heritage. This hiring practice is not intended to guarantee that only veterans will fill all of the federal job vacancies. What it is intended to do is recognize the sacrifices that veterans have made by giving up a part of their life to serve and protect our country, by giving special consideration to qualified veterans that are seeking federal employment.

Over the years, Congress has enacted several laws that prevent veterans that are seeking federal jobs from being penalized due to their time spent while serving our country in the military. These laws are meant to ensure that we as veterans will remain competitive when it comes to hiring for federal positions. Furthermore, it helps to recognize the economic losses that veterans have suffered while serving in the armed forces. After all, we know that many private-industry jobs pay considerably more than the military does, without constantly having to put yourself in harm's way.

This is also a way to ensure that disabled veterans and their spouses, widows, and mothers of surviving or severely disabled veterans are afforded the best opportunities when it comes to seeking federal jobs. After all, they have sacrificed the most and rightfully deserve every advantage that we can give them for the sacrifices that they have endured.

Determining If You Qualify for Federal Job Preference Points

Depending on which category you fit into, the majority of veterans qualify for either five or ten preference points. Since not all veterans qualify for preference points, you will need to meet the minimum qualifications to become eligible to receive them. Once qualified, you can add these preference points onto your passing civil service examination score or rating.

First off as with all veteran's benefits, you will need to determine your eligibility. To become eligible for veteran's preference points, you must have either an honorable or general discharge. Then you will need to fit into one of the following categories as well based on your personal situation to be eligible to claim them.

Five Veteran's Preference Points

To be eligible for five veteran's preference points, you must have served in the armed forces and meet one of the following circumstances:

- Served during the World War II period. Between December 7, 1941, and April 28, 1952.
- Served during the Korean War period. Between April 28, 1952, and July 1, 1955.
- Served for more than 180 consecutive days (other than for training), any part of which occurred after January 31, 1955, and before October 15, 1976. The Vietnam War period.
- Served during the Gulf War. Between August 2, 1990, and January 2, 1992.
- Served for more than 180 consecutive days (other than for training), any part of which occurred during the period beginning September 11, 2001, and ending on the date that is prescribed by law or presidential proclamation as the last day of Operation Iraqi Freedom.
- Served in a campaign or expedition for which a campaign medal was authorized. Any armed forces expeditionary medal or campaign badge that you have received that is documented on your DD Form 214 will qualify you for the five-point veteran's preference. There are many of these campaigns and expeditions.

*Remember that if you are a campaign medal holder or Gulf War veteran that originally enlisted after September 7, 1980, or that first started active duty on or after October 14, 1982. You must have served for twenty-four consecutive months or the full period called or ordered to active duty to qualify for the five-point veteran's preference. This twenty-four-month service requirement is waived for those that separated due to disabilities that were incurred or aggravated in the line of duty (which would qualify them for the ten veteran's preference points instead).

*Another thing to remember is that military retirees at the rank of lieutenant commander or higher are not eligible for veteran's preference points unless they are disabled veterans. (This rule does not apply to reservists who will not begin to draw retired pay until the age of sixty.)

Ten Veteran's Preference Points

To be eligible for the ten veteran's preference points, you must have served in the armed forces and meet one of the following circumstances:

- Be a disabled veteran with a service-connected disability that is properly documented by either the VA or DOD.
- A veteran that received a Purple Heart.
- The spouse of a veteran that is incapable of working due to their service-connected disability. This is typically veterans with 100 percent disability ratings from the VA.
- The unmarried widow of a service member that has died while on either active duty (without negligence) or from a service-connected injury or disability.
- The mother of a permanent and total service-connected disabled veteran. Or a service member that has died during a war under honorable conditions or in a campaign or expedition that a campaign medal has been authorized. She may receive preference assuming that she is either divorced, widowed, legally separated, or the father is totally disabled and incapable of supporting her.

* Remember that both the mother and the spouse/widow of a service-connected disabled or deceased veteran may each be entitled to preference based on the same veteran's service (if they each meet the requirements). However, neither may receive this preference if the veteran is qualified for federal employment.

The Importance of Preference Points

Having veteran's preference points will not guarantee that you will be hired into a federal position. What it will do is give you a competitive edge in the federal hiring process. This edge can often be the difference between if you get the job or not. Here's basically how it works.

When the federal government decides to hire an employee, there are numerous laws, executive orders, and federal regulations that govern federal employment and their hiring practices that are considerably different than those within private industry. Therefore, in most instances, they use a scale from 1-100 to rate each applicant.

Previously, most positions required that you took and passed a civil service exam to become eligible, but now most positions require only that you apply online and that you submit a resume through USAJOBS. In order to be considered for the position that you are applying for. That is, assuming that you are eligible to apply for the opening and meet all of the necessary qualifications.

Once the application period has ended, each applicant's information is reviewed and assigned a rating from 1-100. Assuming that your rating is over 70 (which is passing), then you will have either five or ten veteran's preference points added to your score.

This can be a huge advantage because if everyone else can score a possible 100, then we can potentially be scored at 105 or 110 depending on how many veteran's preference points you qualify for, especially seeing as the selecting officials from the agency that is hiring only select from the top 3 rated candidates. This means that your veteran's preference points will not guarantee that you get the job, but quite often they can get you that all-important interview so that you can sell yourself as the most qualified applicant.

*Remember that even if you qualify for both the five and ten veteran's preference points. The most preference points you can receive is ten.

Understanding KSAs

Another very important part of the hiring process is the knowledge, skills, and abilities, better known as the KSAs section. This is your opportunity to shine and tell them about what you can bring to the table if hired. This is probably the most important part of the hiring process. Seeing as millions of people apply for federal jobs each year and the majority of them do not even get an interview. To stand out from the millions of other applicants, you really need to shine in the KSA section because depending on how you answer your KSAs will determine if you separate yourself from the pack or not. Otherwise, you will more than likely just be wasting your time in continually applying.

*Remember that if you plan on applying for federal jobs, there are several great books on the topic of KSAs and how to be successful at applying for federal positions. I strongly encourage you to pick one up and read it prior to applying because the information contained within this section is just a brief overview of how the system works. If you plan on applying, you will want to know what they are looking for because the strength of your KSAs will have a strong impact on if you're successful or not.

On August 1, 2010 President Obama issued a memorandum instructing the federal agencies to overhaul the current hiring system. Although these changes will take time to be implemented, eventually they plan to do away with KSAs as well as allow hiring managers to choose from a group of qualified applicants instead of just the top three that they are currently instructed to choose from.

The Importance of Federal Jobs

Everyone knows that federal jobs have their advantages. Especially throughout this current economic crisis where everything has been so unstable and so many people are unemployed. Seeking a federal job can create stability and long-term job security. The real trick is getting into the federal system. Once you have been employed for a while though, there is plenty of room for advancement throughout your career.

Finding Your Way into Federal Jobs

Probably, the most confusing part of the federal hiring system is knowing who is eligible to apply for each job. After all, if you're applying for positions that you're not eligible to be considered for, then you're just wasting your time, right? There are basically two different categories that federal jobs fall into. These are competitive civil service jobs and excepted service jobs.

Competitive Civil Service Jobs

When filling competitive service jobs, the hiring agency must post their vacancies on USAJOBS and can choose from three different types of candidates. These are the following:

- A competitive list of eligible candidates—This list consists of all applicants who applied and met the qualification requirements for a specific vacancy announcement. These applicants are rated, and then your veteran's preference points are added, which can give you an advantage in the hiring process. This is also the most common entry route into federal service.

- Merit promotions—this basically means hiring from within. These applicants are eligible for noncompetitive movement within the competitive service because they either presently or previously served under career-type appointments in the competitive service.

In layman terms this allows current employees to change positions or agencies and often allows previous employees to return to federal service without having to compete against the general public. It basically allows current and previous federal employees to be promoted, reassigned, transferred, or reinstated. Veteran's preference points cannot be used in merit promotions.

- Special noncompetitive appointing authority—this allows agencies to hire certain veterans such as veteran's recruitment appointments better known as VRAs and 30 percent or more service-connected disabled veterans without competition. Veterans can be appointed to these positions up to GS-11 positions. Veteran's preference is used when applying for these types of positions.

Excepted Service Jobs

The other category of federal jobs is called excepted service jobs. These excepted service agencies set their own qualifications and requirements. They are not subject to the normal appointment, pay, and classification rules as competitive service jobs are. They are in most cases subject to veteran's preference though. Some agencies such as the FBI and CIA have only excepted positions due to the nature of their work. In other instances, certain specialized positions such as attorneys and chaplains may be excepted from civil service procedures as well due to their specialized fields.

Applying for Federal Jobs

To apply for federal positions, I would suggest first contacting the agency that you would like to apply with. This can be a great way to pick their brain and make sure that you do not have anything that may disqualify you from being considered for the position ahead of time. Then to submit your resume, just visit: http://www.usajobs.gov/

This is a really great Web site that is relatively easy to use. Once online, you can search thousands of jobs by category and location. It also has a resume builder, and you can apply right online fairly easily. If you are serious about seeking federal employment, you will want to become proficient at using this site. This Web site is run by the Office of Personnel Management, better known as the OPM, which does the majority of hiring and firing for federal positions; and unlike most veteran's benefits, the OPM manages the veteran's preference points program.

To apply online, you will need to open an account at USAJOBS and then build one if not several resumes. If you are eligible for five veteran's preference points, all you will need to do is prove your eligibility by submitting a copy of your DD Form 214 when you apply as proof that you meet the eligibility requirements. If you are eligible for ten preference points, you will also need to download and complete form SF 15. This is the Application for Ten-point Veteran Preference form. Once completed, you will want to make several copies of this form to submit along with proof of your disability so that you can receive your ten veteran's point preference each time you apply for a position. You can download this form at:
http://www.opm.gov/forms/pdf_fill/SF15.pdf

Crossover Jobs
Some jobs in the military have little to no applications within the private sector, while other military occupations can cross over into the civilian world with hardly any retraining whatsoever. Oftentimes, by using the training and experience that the military has equipped you with, many military occupations can lead into great careers with nothing more than a few courses or a certification.

For example, in many states, veterans that worked in the law enforcement community for the military for a few years can cross over into local law enforcement positions after only a brief training course that explains all of the local statutes, although this hiring practice is determined by each state's laws and regulations. This can be a great way to reenter the workforce in a minimal amount of time. This is also a great way to utilize your military experience and turn it into a profitable long-term career.

Additionally, in many areas, apartment complexes are authorized to offer either free or reduced rent to one or two law enforcement officers per property, in exchange for courtesy-officer duties that are in the officer's spare time. This act of bartering can often work out really well for both parties, because the apartment complex can receive free security and peace of mind for their residents, and the veteran can receive free rent for their family in return for a minimal amount of their off duty time.

Government Contractors

Then there are government contractor jobs that work alongside the federal government. These companies oftentimes recruit their employees straight from the military as service members are exiting the service. These companies typically prefer to employ veterans due to their specialized training, unique technical skills, and security clearances that many service members have to offer. These companies often pay top dollar with excellent incentives to employ certain veterans for their expertise in numerous fields.

Small Business Loans for Veterans

For veterans or their spouses that are looking to start a small business or expand an existing small business. There is a great new program being offered by the Small Business Administration (SBA), not the VA, called the Patriot Express Pilot Loan Initiative for veterans. This is a great new program that is intended to help support the entrepreneurial side of the military community by providing low interest loans to veterans and their spouses during this extended war on terror. These small business loans can provide up to $500,000 for veteran-owned small businesses, even during this current economic crisis.

The Patriot Express program was established on May 14, 2007, and is guaranteed to be in effect at least until December 31, 2010. At which time, the SBA will reevaluate the program and decide whether to keep or end it. Until that time, they have guaranteed to loan at least one billion dollars annually to veteran-owned small businesses, which can be a great deal if you have a really good idea for a business and just need a loan to help get it off the ground.

Eligibility for Patriot Express Loans

Since many current and former service members can each be eligible for this program, you will either need a discharge that was not dishonorable (for veterans) or be in good standing, which means having done nothing that would warrant a dishonorable discharge (for current service members). Additionally, the borrower must own at least 51 percent of the company to qualify. The following groups of people are qualified to borrow under Patriot Express:

- Veterans (other than dishonorably discharged).
- Service-disabled veterans.
- Current reservists and National Guard members.
- Active-duty service members that are participating in the Transition Assistance Program (TAP), which includes retirees within twenty-four months of separation and active-duty service members within twelve months of discharge.
- The current spouses of any of these members.
- The widowed spouse of a service member who either died while in service or of a service-connected disability.

How Patriot Express Loans Work

Patriot Express small business loans work the same way as the VA home loan program does. This means that if you receive a small business loan from the SBA under Patriot Express, the government is not lending you the money. They act as a cosigner on the loan, and if your company defaults, the government will back the majority of the loan. In simple terms, it's like having your parents co-sign for your first car because the bank would not have otherwise approved the loan.

Under Patriot Express, the SBA will guarantee 85 percent of loans up to $150,000. For loans over $150,000 up to the maximum of $500,000 the SBA will guarantee 75 percent of the loan.

Patriot Express Loan Interest Rates

Since interest rates often vary depending on the loan's size, risk involved, and the length of the loan. Under Patriot Express, the following interest rate restrictions apply: businesses can be charged up to 2.25 percent over the prime rate for loans under seven years and 2.75 percent over the prime rate for loans of seven years or longer. These rates can be 2 percent higher for loans of $25,000 or less and 1 percent higher for loans between $25,000 and $50,000.

Collateral for Small Business Loans

By using a small business loan through Patriot Express. Depending on the size of the loan will dictate if you will need collateral or not. The following rules will apply:

- Loans of less than $25,000. Lenders are not required to take collateral.
- Loans of more than $25,000 but less than $350,000. Lenders must follow the collateral policies and procedures they have in place for their non-SBA-guaranteed commercial loans.
- Loans of $350,000 to a maximum of $500,000. Lenders must take all available collateral.

*Remember that business loans under Patriot Express are not allowed to be split into multiple smaller loans to avoid SBA fees or collateral requirements. Additionally, these small business loans cannot be used to finance more than 90 percent of the actual cost of any real estate that is being acquired or of the financing needs of a new business. These rules do not apply to non-real-estate financing of an existing business for things such as working capital or equipment and such.

Types of Businesses and Programs You Can't Use a Patriot Express Loan For

Although there are numerous types of small businesses and programs that you can own under Patriot Express. There are certain types of businesses that will not qualify though. These include:

- Energy conservation or pollution control programs.
- International trade.
- Disabled Assistance Loan Program (DAL).
- Qualified employee trusts (ESOP).
- Community Investment Adjustment Program.
- Defense Loan and Technical Assistance (DELTA).
- Cap Lines Program (including Builders Loan Program).

Additionally, businesses engaged in teaching, instructing, counseling, or indoctrinating religious beliefs. As well as businesses engaged in gambling, businesses of a mature or explicit sexual nature, nonprofit businesses, life insurance companies, businesses engaged in lending, pyramid businesses, speculative businesses, government-owned entities, cooperatives, passive holders of real estate, illegal businesses, businesses that restrict patronage, and businesses engaged in political or lobbying activities are not allowed to receive loans under Patriot Express.

*Remember that under SBA's Patriot Express program, if you have previously defaulted on a federal loan or federally assisted financing that caused any agency within the federal government to sustain a loss. Then you will not be eligible to receive a loan. For those of you that have had a bankruptcy in your past though. You may still qualify for loans under Patriot Express. It's at the lender's discretion.

Things to Remember before Applying

Just because you have an idea for a business and also qualify for a loan under Patriot Express doesn't mean that you will automatically be qualified for a loan. You must understand that the majority of small businesses in the United States fail within the first five years. The SBA and the federal government have no intention of backing a loan for small businesses that do not have a good concept and a solid business plan. Before applying, you must realize that the lender will want to see that you have done your homework and want to know not only what you intend to use the funds for, but more importantly how you plan to repay the borrowed money back.

If you plan to open a small business, I strongly encourage you to use some of your educational benefits on various business and accounting courses. Having to deal with the owning and running of a small business prior to deciding because getting in over your head with a small business is not a good idea and closing your doors means that you will default on your loans, which also means that the federal government will more than likely lose money on the loan, and owing the government is not a position that you want to be in.

Applying for Patriot Express Loans

Since the Patriot Express program is still a relatively new program, the number of lending institutions that are authorized to offer these loans is growing and changing pretty frequently and the current online list of lenders does not have the contact information for each lender. So the best way to find an authorized lender is by going to: http://www.sba.gov/localresources/index.html

Once there, you will see a map of the United States and its territories. Click on your state, and the contact information for the SBA regional office that services your area will come up. Then just contact the SBA and ask for the closest Patriot Express approved lender.

Hiring Veterans First

If you have a small business and are looking for new employees, I encourage you to consider hiring veterans as well. If you think about it, veterans typically make great employees; they are used to long hours, and they come with a strong work ethic. From a business perspective, nothing will tell your clients that you support veterans like employing them.

Advertising Your Veteran-owned Small Business

With over twenty-three million veterans and nearly three times that number when you factor in families and surviving family members. That is quite a sizeable market all by itself. We proudly make up close to 25 percent of this country, and we have tremendous spending power within the economy. This can be a tremendous market all in itself if you decide to market your products and services to the military community effectively.

As a small business owner myself, in addition to being a mother, grandmother, and the wife of a seriously disabled veteran. In business, I frequently have veterans as customers, and I prefer doing business with them; and it shows through the special attention they receive from my company. I also tend to seek out other veteran-owned businesses as my first option, and I try to spend my money with them first in an effort to support our own.

Recently, several Internet Web sites have been coming online that have really helped veterans to locate veteran-owned businesses efficiently that are within each community. If you're a veteran business owner, I encourage you to register your business so that other veterans can seek out your business. One of the largest Web sites is veteranownedbusiness.com.

You can register your business for free; that way, other veterans can find you. Or for a nominal yearly fee, you can get loads of additional advertising and even offer coupons. Veteran business owners can register companies at: http://www.veteranownedbusiness.com/

Another great tool for advertising your business that has recently come online is the warrior gateway directory. This search engine allows veterans to locate the different services they need within their geographical area. It also allows customers to review your business, which can help to generate new veteran customers over time (assuming that your businesses service was good). To register, go to: http://www.warriorgateway.org/

*Remember that although there are numerous laws that govern business practices, there is no harm in offering discounts to service members and veterans. After all, we make up a huge segment of society and have the power to make your business thrive. After all, nothing says thank you for your service to our country more than a discount. It is not only a great way to show appreciation, but also a practical way to network to other veterans because veterans tend to have extremely long memories when it comes to businesses that acknowledge the sacrifices we have made.

Executive Order 13360

Did you know that if you're a disabled veteran with a service-connected disability, that if you own a business that wants to pursue contracts or sub-contracts with the federal government. You have a very realistic chance of getting in on these government contract bids because of Executive Order 13360. This order was signed by former president Bush, back on October 20, 2004. In an effort to help increase the number of service-disabled-veteran-owned companies that get federal contracts to supply goods and services to the federal government. This has helped to boost the number of business opportunities available to veterans that became disabled through their service to our country.

The president established a goal of no less than 3 percent of these federal contracts are to be reserved for disabled-veteran-owned businesses, this order also gives agency-contracting officers the authority to reserve certain procurements exclusively to service-disabled-veteran-owned businesses.

Although 3 percent of these contracts may not seem like much at first glance, but when you stop and think about it, that's a lot of contracts, which means numerous opportunities that can turn into quite a bit of money. You must remember that we're talking about contracts for the entire federal government. When you start to consider how much is outsourced by the government, this can really become a profitable option.

Getting these contracts is still not that easy, though, and can require quite a bit of learning and know-how. I suggest that if you plan to pursue government contracts with your business, you should definitely contact APTAC, which is the Association of Procurement Technical Assistance Centers. They teach small businesses how to sell to federal government customers. You can find your local representative by going to: http://www.aptac-us.org/new/Govt_Contracting/find.php

You will also want to register your business with vetbiz.gov. By registering your business with the Center for Veterans Enterprise, better known as the CVE, you are authorizing the CVE to verify that your business is owned by either a veteran or service-disabled veteran.

Once verified, your business will have the opportunity to compete for VA contracts under the Veterans First Contracting Program, as well as numerous other opportunities. To start the verification process, you will need to complete and submit VA Form 0877. You can download this form at: http://www4.va.gov/vaforms/va/pdf/VA0877.pdf

Chapter 12

VA Home Loans

In this chapter, we will be discussing all of the advantages that veterans are offered when it comes to owning a home. By reading this chapter, you will learn about:

- The VA Home Loan Program.
- Purchasing foreclosures on VA guaranteed homes.
- Avoiding foreclosure in times of crisis.
- Refinancing into a VA guaranteed home loan.
- Reduced property taxes for service-connected disabled veterans.
- The different types of grants that are available to modify your home to accommodate disabled veterans.

Since its inception back in 1944, the VA has helped over 18 million active-duty service members, veterans, and surviving spouses to purchase homes through the VA's home loan program, by guaranteeing over $911 billion in home loans since the program began. Currently there are 1.4 million home loans that are still in effect that were purchased through the VA's home loan guarantee program.

By using a VA home loan to purchase your new home, many of us that may not have qualified otherwise to purchase a home can become pretty attractive borrowers because we have the VA backing a portion of the loan to the lender. This makes it so that not only do many veterans qualify for loans, but more importantly, it can make the loans more affordable, seeing as the loan is guaranteed by the government. Additionally, over 90 percent of VA-backed home loans were approved without a down payment as well.

Who Qualifies for VA Home Loans

As with all programs that are run by the VA, there are minimum service requirements to become eligible for the VA home loan program. Since both current and former service members can both qualify for these loans, depending on which era you served in will often dictate how long you must have served for to become eligible. The good thing is that most veterans qualify for this program because the service requirements are fairly easy to meet.

Meeting the Requirements

First off, veterans that are no longer serving will need a discharge that the VA does not consider dishonorable. This is covered extensively in chapter 1. For veterans that have other than honorable (OTH) discharge characterizations. The VA may still allow you to have a VA home loan if they determine that your discharge was under other than dishonorable conditions.

For those that are still currently serving whether on active duty or in a reserve component, you will need to be in good standing with your service component, meaning that you have not done anything that would warrant a dishonorable discharge.

Length of Service Requirements for VA Home Loans

Since the rules have changed a bit over the years, depending on when you served will have a huge impact on the amount of service that is required to be eligible for the VA home loan program. The following is a list of the basic lengths of service and the possible exemptions to these rules that are required to become eligible for VA home loans:

Wartime Service

Ninety days of active-duty service is required unless you were discharged for a service-connected disability between the following dates:

- WWII—from September 16, 1940, to July 25, 1947
- Korean War—June 27, 1950, to January 31, 1955
- Vietnam War—August 5, 1964, to May 7, 1975

Peacetime Service

One hundred eighty-one days of continuous active-duty service is required unless you were discharged for a service-connected disability between the following dates:

- July 26, 1947, to June 26, 1950
- February 1, 1955, to August 4, 1964
- May 8, 1975, to September 7, 1980 (for enlisted)
- May 8, 1975, to October 16, 1981 (for officers)

Service after September 7, 1980 (for Enlisted) or October 16, 1981 (for Officers) if you are a veteran that has separated from the service and you initially began after these dates. You must meet one of the following requirements:

- Completed at least twenty-four months of continuous active duty.
- Completed the full period of at least 181 days that you were called or ordered to active duty, for either the National Guard or reserves.
- Completed at least 181 days of active duty and been given a hardship discharge or been given an early-out separation.
- If you have less than 181 days of service, you can still qualify for the VA home loan program. If you were discharged for a service-connected disability, involuntary reduction in force,

convenience of the government, or released for certain medical conditions.

Gulf War Service from August 2, 1990 to a Date That Has yet to Be Determined

If you are a veteran that served on active duty during the Gulf War era, to be eligible, you must meet one of the following requirements:

- Completed at least twenty-four months of continuous active duty.
- Completed the full period of at least ninety days that you were called or ordered to active duty for either the National Guard or reserves.
- Completed at least ninety days of active duty and been given a hardship discharge or been given an early-out separation.
- If you have less than ninety days of service, you can still qualify for the VA home loan program. If you were discharged for a service-connected disability, involuntary reduction in force, convenience of the government, or released for certain medical conditions.

Rules for Active-duty Members

For those of you that are still serving on active duty, you can use a VA home loan to buy a home while still serving. To be eligible, you must have served for at least ninety days on active duty (not on active duty for training) during the Gulf War. Once the war has ended and the president has established an end date to the war. You will need 181 days of active-duty service to qualify.

Rules for National Guard and Reservists

In many cases, reservists and guard members can qualify for VA home loans based on their active-duty service during call-up periods that qualify them through one of the previous categories. In the event that you do not qualify based on meeting any of the other qualifying periods of service, and you are a member of an active unit that only attended the required weekend drills and the two weeks of annual active duty for training. You will need to have completed six years in the National Guard or selected reserves to become eligible for a VA home loan. After your qualifying period has been completed, you will need to meet one of the following:

- Continue to serve in the selected reserves.
- Receive an honorable discharge.
- Be placed on the retired list.
- Be transferred to the standby reserve or an element of the ready reserve other than the selected reserve after service that was characterized as honorable service.

* Keep in mind that reserve and guard veterans that were discharged for a service-connected disability are still eligible even if they did not complete the six years of initial service.

VA Home Loans for Spouses and Widows

Certain spouses and widows can qualify for the VA's home loan program as well. To be eligible, you must meet one of the following circumstances:

- Be the spouse of a service member that is either missing in action or a prisoner of war.
- Be an un-remarried widow of a veteran that either died while in the service or from a service-connected disability.

*Remember that a rule change for widows seeking VA home loans came into effect on December 16, 2003. The rule states that surviving spouses that remarry after the age of fifty-seven and on or after December 16, 2003, are eligible for the VA's home loan program. However, a surviving spouse who remarried before December 16, 2003, and on or after the age of fifty-seven is not eligible for the VA home loan program. Additionally, the children of qualifying veterans are not eligible for VA home loans as well.

Possible Uses for VA Home Loans

Since each qualifying veteran has a different set of needs and there are numerous types of dwellings. You may use your VA home loan for these different types of homes as long they are within the United States (or its territories) and as long as you plan to live there (so it can't be used for investment properties). You may use your VA home loan guarantee to do the following:

- Purchase a house, condominium, town house, and/or manufactured home.

- Build, repair, or improve a home. (This includes energy-efficient improvements such as installing solar panels.) Under the 2009 federal stimulus package, there are numerous types of rebates for some of these home improvements. These can lead to some pretty good savings.
- Buy a mobile home and/or the land to put it on.
- Build a home.
- Purchase and then fix, alter or otherwise improve the home all at the same time.
- Refinance an existing loan to a lower interest rate or better terms of the loan.

Why VA Home Loans Are Better

For those that qualify (see the previous section), a VA home loan does not promise nor does it guarantee that you will meet the numerous other qualifications that lenders have put into place to qualify you for the purchase of a home. What it does give you is not only a great tool for negotiating your interest rates, but it can also act as a sizable down payment as well. Here is how it works.

As with all home loans, you will have to apply for the loan directly through the lending institution (which is not hard because almost all lenders accept VA loans). When the loan is approved, the VA will guarantee part of it, although the amount of the VA's guarantee will usually depend on the size of the loan. The basic entitlement for loans of $144,000 or less is $36,000. If the loan itself is for less than $36,000, the VA will guarantee the amount that you borrow. This $36,000 is seen as a down payment from the lender's perspective because even if you fail to make the first payment (hopefully this will not happen), the lender will receive $36,000 if you default and the home goes into foreclosure. So in their eyes, you're a pretty safe bet.

This is why over 90 percent of people that use VA home loans do not need huge down payments to close on their home loans, although this $36,000 does not come out of yours nor the VA's pocket. The lender will feel much more comfortable in loaning you the amount that you need to purchase the home. Which means the safer an investment you are to them, the lower your interest rates will often be.

For home loans over $144,000 up to $417,000, which is the maximum amount the VA will guarantee a loan for in the continental United States, except for a select few counties which have higher rates, the VA will guarantee up to 25 percent of the conforming loan limit, which is the amount that the Federal Housing Administration, better known as the FHA, advises the banks to limit all mortgage loans to homes that are located in each specific part of the country, all the way down to each individual county. For areas outside of the continental United States, the limit is $625,500. This limit applies for Alaska, Hawaii, the U.S. Virgin Islands, and Guam.

These rates are for the year 2010 and can be adjusted annually on the first day of each year. To find out the current conforming loan limits for the particular county you are looking to purchase a home in. I strongly suggest that you contact a real estate agent or mortgage lender because they have this information readily available. You can also view this information yourself on the FHA's Web site or at: http://www.fhainfo.com/frameloanlimits.htm

*Keep in mind that if you plan to purchase a new home, you will want to pay very close attention to the conforming loan limits for the county that you plan to purchase in. Because if you intend to purchase a home that is over the county's limit, you will need a down payment to make up the difference between what the VA will guarantee and the amount that the lender needs as a down payment, which is normally 25 percent. This can end up being thousands of dollars easily that must come out of your own pocket to make up the difference.

I remember the first time that my family decided to purchase a home using a VA home loan guarantee. We had contacted a local mortgage broker, and he insisted that VA home loans were not a good option. We listened to every reason and complaint that he listed and, in the end, came to realize that he was only looking out for his own best interest and not ours. Buying a home is a complex situation and one that most of us will only do a few times in our lives.

Knowing this, some lending institutions, real estate companies, and mortgage brokers will try to take advantage of this situation and ultimately can cause great financial distress to your family by putting you into a non-VA loan with bad terms and ridiculous constantly changing rates. Luckily, we figured this out in time and walked away before we made a huge mistake. Many people often do not realize this in time, though, which was one of the major causes of the housing market crisis over the last few years. So be cautious. A great question to ask your mortgage company is if a VA loan is right for you. Their answers can oftentimes be quite revealing as to if they have your best interests in mind or theirs.

Getting Your Certificate of Eligibility

Another great part about the VA home loan guarantee program is that it's very easy to use. All you will need to do after you find the property that you wish to buy is inform the mortgage company that you will qualify for a VA home loan. They will ask you for a copy of your DD Form 214 and then submit your information to the Automated Certificate of Eligibility system better known as ACE. The ACE system can confirm your eligibility in a matter of minutes in most cases and can allow the mortgage company to print out a certificate of eligibility. If you would like to do this manually, you can also download and complete your very own VA Form 26-1880. You can find this form at: http://www.vba.va.gov/pubs/forms/VBA-26-1880-ARE.pdf

Surviving spouses will need to use VA Form 26-1817. They can get this form by going to: http://www.vba.va.gov/pubs/forms/VBA-26-1817-ARE.pdf

Once completed, you will need to mail the form and proof of eligibility to:

The VA Loan Eligibility Center
P.O. Box 20729
Winston-Salem, NC. 27120

*Remember that after your eligibility has been established for a VA home loan guarantee, you will need to have a VA-licensed appraiser come and determine the reasonable value of the property. The mortgage company typically handles this aspect of the sale for you. I suggest that in addition to the appraisal, you have the property inspected by a licensed home inspector, although you will probably have to pay for this out of your own pocket. It can keep you from purchasing a home with numerous hidden problems, these inspectors are trained to find hidden issues

before you purchase the home, and for a few hundred dollars, they can really help keep you from buying a home that has major problems.

Moving in to Your New Home

This may sound crazy, but it needs to be addressed. There are rules in place due to the fact that previously, some veterans used their VA loans to purchase rental properties and houses to resell immediately without ever living in them. This program is intended to make veterans and service members' homeowners, not landlords and real estate agents. As the new owner of the property, you have sixty days to move in from the date of closing. This means that either the veteran or the spouse needs to be residing there. In certain instances (such as for major renovation purposes), the VA can extend this period up to twelve months.

Although there is no specific amount of time when it comes to how long you must live there. After all, most people rarely live in the same place for twenty or thirty years. The rules state that you must be the first people to live there. If you decide to live in the house for a week then move out. Chances are that the VA will decide that you were trying to scam them and you can get into big trouble for fraud. So don't try to play the system because it only causes problems for those of us that really need the program.

Purchasing Foreclosures on VA Guaranteed Homes

One man's loss is another man's gain. Unfortunately, this saying is extremely true these days, for those of you that are in the market for a new home and are flexible in where you are looking to buy. I sure have a deal for you.

Due to the recent mortgage crisis, many VA-guaranteed and VA-financed loans have been foreclosed on. These VA-acquired properties are listed for sale online at some serious discounts. Seeing as the VA isn't necessarily equipped to handle the massive amount of VA loans that have been foreclosed on, they have chosen to list these homes online. To see the list and information on VA foreclosures, go to: https://va.equator.com/index.cfm?

Once there you will see a map of the United States. You can search for homes based on city, state, zip code, or price range. When you find a property that you're interested in, contact the agent that is listed on the Web site for that particular property. This can be a great tool for veterans and service members that are looking for great deals on foreclosed properties.

Avoiding Foreclosure

Nobody buys a home with the intention of losing it to foreclosure. The problem is that with all of the uncertainty in the job and housing markets, sometimes losing your job can just happen these days. Then without enough income, and jobs being as scarce as they are, it's easy to see why so many people are losing their homes to foreclosure.

Nobody wants to lose their home through foreclosure. Especially if you have a VA home loan because knowing that the government is going to lose money due to your foreclosure does not sound like a very good position to be in.

If you ever find yourself in this position, be proactive. The VA realizes that the economy is bad and that a great number of homeowners have had an extremely hard time making their mortgage payments. The VA has put financial counselors in place to help you keep your home by speaking to the lender on your behalf. In an effort to pursue options that will help you keep your home. These skilled professionals are trained to help each veteran by seeking repayment plans, patience on the lender's part, and also help with loan modifications. All of which can help veterans to keep their homes.

These VA loan counselors have helped over 74,000 veterans, active-duty service members, and surviving spouses to keep their homes since 2000. By doing this, the VA has saved the government nearly $1.5 billion, so remember that the VA has a vested interest in seeing you succeed. These loan counselors are available to all veterans, whether your home loan was guaranteed by the VA or not. To obtain a VA loan counselor, call 1(877)827-3702.

In the event that you have lost your home to foreclosure and the government does end up losing money by paying your guarantee. You will not be able to receive another VA home loan guarantee until that money is paid back. This is not a place that you want to be in, especially if your loan was fraudulent or you accepted the loan in bad faith because then the government will use numerous ways to recover their money.

Refinancing into a VA Home Loan

As part of the Veterans' Benefits Improvement Act of 2008, the VA is allowing veterans with subprime and conventional home loans to refinance up to 100 percent of the value of the property into safer and more affordable VA-guaranteed loans. By doing this, the VA is hoping to help veterans that are stuck in loans with very unfavorable terms, by allowing them to use VA loans that are more reasonable. This can lower your interest rates and potentially avoid foreclosure all together.

Reduced Property Taxes for Disabled Veterans

Seeing as it is up to each individual state to determine if and how much they will charge for property taxes. Depending on which state you live in, you may or may not be eligible for a reduction in your property taxes if you are a service-disabled veteran. Since each state has different laws concerning taxing its residents' homes. I encourage you to spend a little bit of time researching the states' veterans' benefits before you purchase your new home. This can save you thousands of dollars each year alone, which can really help, especially if you live on a fixed income.

Some states offer very little or nothing in the way of reduced taxes for service-disabled veteran residents. While other states offer numerous tax advantages based on your service-connected disability rating percentage.

For example, Florida offers numerous savings through tax advantages for service-connected disabled veterans, those with VA disability ratings of 10 percent up to 100 percent (without the P&T status). Receive an additional $5,000 property tax exemption in addition to their homestead exemption on their property taxes.

Veterans that have the 100 percent permanent and total status (as explained in chapter 5) are tax exempt when it comes to property taxes and must merely pay for household chemical and solid waste, which is considerably less. By having the P&T status, veterans can reduce their property taxes down to only a few hundred dollars per year, which can take hundreds of dollars off their mortgage payments each month.

In addition to reduced property taxes, service-connected disabled veterans can also receive other advantages by choosing to live in Florida. These include the following:

- One free license plate for disabled veterans that are rated at 100 percent.
- $1.50 per disabled parking permit for disabled veterans who are rated at 50 percent or higher. You will additionally need a statement signed by your physician saying that you need the permit. There is also a limit of two disabled parking permits per veteran.
- Free hunting and fishing licenses for disabled veterans that are rated at 100 percent permanent and total.
- Free toll pass stickers are issued to disabled veterans that have a permanent impairment that impedes their ability to deposit the coins into the basket on toll roads. You will need a physician's approval for this as well.

These are all advantages that service-disabled veterans can qualify for, just in Florida. To learn about the various tax advantages that your state may offer, I suggest asking your VA counselor about state-run benefits for veterans you may qualify for in your particular state. There is also a nifty tool that explains each state's veteran's benefits on military.com. You can find this information at: http://www.military.com/benefits/veteran-benefits/state-veterans-benefits-directory

*Remember that each state has different state-run veteran's benefits. For each benefit that you qualify for, you will need to apply for that benefit (and submit the proper documentation) with the proper taxing authority, which means for example, if you are trying to reduce or eliminate your housing taxes as a disabled veteran, you will need to file the proper documentation with the County Property Appraisers Office because they determine your property taxes.

Government Grants to Adapt Your Home for Disabled Veterans

There are three basic types of grants that disabled veterans can qualify for, to modify their homes to make them more accessible and to increase the veteran's level of independent living. Depending on the severity and types of injuries the veteran has will dictate which grant or grants they will qualify for.

Specially Adapted Housing (SAH) Grant

This type of grant is used to build, modify, remodel, or at times help to offset the cost of purchasing a home that is already accessible and useable for severely disabled veterans with service-connected disabilities. Veterans that are eligible for SAH grants can receive up to $63,780 to help modify or build homes to make them better suited for their disabilities. These grants are often used to make homes wheelchair accessible. The SAH grants are available to both veterans who are and service members who will be entitled to disability compensation for permanent and total disabilities due to the following reasons:

- The loss or loss of use of both lower extremities. Such as if it were impossible for the veteran to walk or move around without the aid of braces, canes, crutches, or a wheelchair.
- Blindness in both eyes, having only light perception. Plus the loss or loss of use of one leg.
- The loss or loss of use of one leg along with either:
  a. Side or aftereffects of an organic disease or injury.
  b. The loss or loss of use of one arm, which affects your balance or propulsion so that it is impossible for the veteran to move around without the aid of braces, canes, crutches, or a wheelchair.

- The loss or loss of use of both arms. This means you have no use of the arms at or above the elbow.
- Severe burn-injury victims.

*Remember that if you qualify for an SAH grant, you can receive up to $63,780. This is the rate for 2011 and is adjusted annually on October 1 based on the cost-of-construction index. If you plan to purchase a home that already has the necessary upgrades to accommodate the veteran's disabilities. The SAH grant will pay for 50 percent of the property up to the $63,780 maximum.

Special Home Adaptation (SHA) Grant

The SHA grant is used to modify an existing home to help meet the veteran's needs. By adapting the home to fit the veteran's mobility needs.

Under the SHA grant, veterans and service members can receive up to $12,756 to modify the residence. These rates are for 2011 and are adjusted annually as well.

To qualify for an SHA grant, veterans will need to be receiving disability compensation for a 100 percent service-connected disability that has a permanent and total status as explained in chapter 5. Service members will need to be entitled to disability compensation with a P&T status due to one of the following types of injuries:

- Blindness in both eyes with 5/200 visual acuity or less.
- The anatomical loss or loss of use of both hands or extremities below the elbows.
- Veterans with severe burn injuries.

Applying for SAH and SHA Grants

To apply for both the SAH and SHA grants, you will need to download and complete VA Form 26-4555. Once completed, you will need to submit the forms to the VA regional office that services your area. Veterans can download this form at: http://www.vba.va.gov/pubs/forms/26-4555(1-09).pdf

Temporary Residence Adaptation (TRA)

Veterans that qualify for SAH or SHA grants can also use part of the grant money to modify a family member's home so that they may reside there temporarily. This can seriously help severely disabled veterans that often need to rely heavily on family members and can provide them with the ability to visit and stay with family more frequently. Veterans are limited to using $14,000 of their grant to adapt the family members' home. The TRA grant program is also scheduled to end on December 31, 2011. So if you plan to apply, you should hurry.

Home Improvements and Structural Alterations (HISA) Grant

The HISA grant is to help veterans with any home improvements necessary for the continuation of treatment or for disability access to the home and essential bathroom facilities. HISA grants are available to veterans that have received medical determinations that indicate that these structural alterations and improvements are necessary for the effective and economical treatment of their disability.

HISA grants are available to disabled veterans whether their disabilities are service-connected or not. Veterans with service-connected disabilities can receive up to $4,100 under HISA, while veterans with non-service-connected disabilities are limited to $1,200. Veterans are also allowed to use a HISA grant along with either a SAH or SHA grant as well.

Applying for a HISA Grant

To apply for a HISA grant, you will need to download and complete a VA Form 10-0103. Once completed, you will need to submit the forms to the VA medical center that you are seen at. Veterans can download this form at: http://www.prosthetics.va.gov/docs/vha-10-0103-fill.pdf

Section 5

Discounts on Shopping and Travel

The chapters within this section can really help you to save quite a bit of money, if you learn how to use these tools effectively. All service members whether active duty or reservists and many veterans as well have numerous opportunities when it comes to discounts on both shopping and travel discounts. As you're reading the chapters within this section, I challenge you to think about the different things that you already spend money on each month because oftentimes you will find that by simply inquiring about military and veteran's discounts, you can receive some pretty good discounts on the things that you already spend on each month anyway.

Chapter 13

Bargain Shopping and Veteran Discounts

This chapter is loaded with information about many of the shopping and discount opportunities that service members/veterans and their families are offered because of their military service. By reading this chapter, you will not only learn about many of the numerous ways that you can save money in these tough economic times, but how to find the hidden gems as well. We will cover:

- Reasons to shop in exchanges and ways to save.
- Using your commissary privileges.
- Using base privileges to save on entertainment.
- Evaluating and trimming your monthly expenses.
- Veteran's discounts from local businesses.

No matter which branch of service you come from. Everyone knows about the deals that come from shopping on base through the military's exchange system, the commissary network, and Morale Welfare and Recreation better known as MWR. After all, they pretty much run everything on the bases in the way of shopping, restaurants, lodging, and entertainment. Although the names may vary depending on which branch you may have served in. The core philosophy never changes. Which is good, products at competitive prices, with no taxes.

Oftentimes, depending on which branch you may have served in, many people may have only shopped in their particular branch's exchanges in the past, although they are each separate entities from one another. Service members, qualifying veterans, and their family members are all welcome to use all of them depending on which one is most convenient. The four different exchange networks are as follows:

- The Navy Exchange, more commonly known as the NEX.
- The Marine Corps Exchange, more commonly known as the MCX.
- The Army and Air Force Exchange Service (AAFES), more commonly known as the PX for army members and the BX for air force members.
- The Coast Guard Exchange, more commonly known as the CGX.

How the Exchange System Works

Depending on the size of the military base and the number of service members, qualified veterans, and family members (see the Shopping Eligibility section later in this chapter) that are located nearby within the community that shops at the exchange. Will help determine the size and amount of facilities they make available. Larger bases often have massive exchanges the size of superstores, while smaller military bases can literally have exchanges the size of convenience stores. It really all just depends on the size of their customer base and the needs within the community.

For over 115 years, the exchange system has been there to provide support to all of the men and women that have been serving our country. Allowing them to buy the same products and services they would find in America. No matter where they serve around the world. The exchange system continues to be successful (even in this declining economy) for several reasons. The most important of which is because they are a non-appropriated fund activity of the DOD.

Being a non-appropriated fund activity means that although the exchanges are government activities (seeing as they are on military installations), they are operated and funded through the sale of merchandise and services to service members, certain veterans, and their families. The only money that the government spends on the exchanges is to help get the merchandise overseas to the forward-deployed exchanges and providing utilities and military salaries. The majority of their operating budget, which pays for civilian employee's salaries, inventory, vehicles, facilities, and capital investments for equipment, comes directly from the sale of merchandise, services, and food to their customers. This makes it so that the exchanges fund 98 percent of their own operations.

Anyone that has ever been to a larger base knows that military bases are a self-contained city. With large department stores, food courts, movie theaters, and much more. These are all run by the exchange network with the sole intention of supporting the military community and helping to meet their needs.

While researching for this section, I was amazed to learn exactly how the exchange system works. As a frequent shopper at exchanges myself, I began to have a newfound appreciation for the exchange system as I learned about how they spend their profits.

I was quite impressed with the exchanges business model and how it is geared entirely toward the military community. The goal is simple: try to keep prices low while offering quality products. Employ the spouses and family of service members when available. Make modest profits, and return all of that money straight back to the military community. This philosophy is rarely practiced outside of the military.

For example, let's take the Army and Air Force Exchange Service (AAFES), which is the largest of all the exchange networks. In fiscal year 2008, which just so happened to be a one of the worst years ever for retailers. The AAFES network continued to remain competitive against the larger retailers by offering name-brand merchandise at an average of 20 percent less than other comparable stores. (This doesn't even include the tax savings.) AAFES alone had annual sales of $10 billion in 2008 and had earnings of over $376 million.

Why You Should Shop at the Exchange
Here is the important part that will hopefully make you think twice before you spend elsewhere. Other major retailers would take that $376 million and pay huge executive salaries, buy corporate jets, and give the rest away to shareholders as dividends.

AAFES doesn't squander their earnings that way. They take roughly 33 percent of their profits to build new, and expand or renovate existing facilities without any expense to the federal government. These include new shopping centers, movie theaters, gas stations, laundry facilities, and many other things that service members, veterans, and their families need wherever they may be living at. This makes for better facilities around the world for all of us.

The remaining 67 percent of the earnings goes toward increasing the quality of life services for those in the military community. In fiscal year 2008, AAFES alone paid out $264.5 million of their profits to help increase the quality of living for all service members by contributing this money to MWR (Moral Welfare and Recreation) services. This money helped to fund parks, golf courses, military hotels and resorts, bowling centers, and numerous other activities that increase the quality of life for all service members and their families.

Over the last ten years, AAFES alone has given back more than $2.4 billion, to help improve the quality of life for all service members and their families. Additionally, in 2008, the Navy contributed $45.4 million to MWR, and the Marine Corps contributed $48.8 million to MWR. That makes a total of $358.7 million in 2008 alone. That went directly back to our service members to help make their lives better and increase their standards of living while they serve.

*On a personal note, writing this book to me has always been about helping veterans and service members. The thing is that shopping on base just makes sense if you are allowed to. Not only does it save you money, it also is a great way to give back to the younger service members that rely heavily on MWR services and discounts. Each veteran can remember back to the days when they first started in the military. How little they made financially and how oftentimes the difference between going out and enjoying life versus not being able to afford going out on their off time. All came down to MWR's cheap entertainment and free services.

Hunting Down Discounts at Exchanges

Although some products may offer very little savings at the exchange, other products can offer significant savings if you're just willing to shop around a bit, high-ticket items such as jewelry, large appliances, and electronics as well as the private-label collections of merchandise. These products not only tend to have the largest savings, but when you factor in the tax savings alone, the amount you save really starts to add up.

Then you have the bonus buy and price cuts. This is a new pricing strategy that alerts customers to special buys that are only available for a limited time and merchandise that has had the price reduced for the bargain shoppers, as well as the generic product lines that are considerably cheaper.

Timing Your Purchases

Next you have the tent sales that some of the larger stores offer. These are often held to make room for new inventories. They are usually held a few months before the holidays, so the exchanges can clear out the store, to make room for the seasonal products. This can be a great way to get huge savings if you keep an eye out for them.

Since traditionally customers are purchasing BBQ grills and outdoor supplies in the spring. By waiting until the fall to make these types of purchases, you can often find these products for half off with no taxes, which can save you hundreds of dollars off your purchases. The exchanges also have flyers at the front doors regularly, and by using them to time your purchases, you can often save quite a bit of money.

Price-matching Guaranty

To help remain competitive against larger retail chains, the exchanges have also implemented an old strategy with a new twist. It's called price matching. At NEX's and MCX's, you can challenge their prices against those of a local competitor's advertised items. If the exchange has the same product for a higher price, they will refund you the difference. This can ensure you the lowest price, and you will still get the product tax free as well.

If you find a product at the exchange that is more expensive than a competitor's, just tell the cashier that you saw an identical item for a lower price in a local competitor's store. If the price difference is less than $5.00, they will take you at your word and give you the difference. If the difference is over $5.00, a supervisor will need to verify that it's the same brand and model (so it's best to bring in the competitor's advertisement). Once they match the price, you can still end up saving the taxes. The AAFES exchanges offer the same deal, but they will give you the difference up to $10.00 without needing to verify.

Things You Typically Will Not Save On at the Exchange

Certain things such as alcohol and tobacco products typically are not much cheaper at the exchanges anymore, although both of these used to be considerably less to purchase in the exchanges rather than off base. Now they are both limited to only 5-10 percent cheaper than the average off-base prices. As with anything averaged, though, you can often find them cheaper elsewhere outside the gates. This stems from an ongoing DOD initiative to help reduce alcohol and tobacco use by service members.

The gas stations on military bases are often more expensive than off base as well, due to the Hayden-Cartwright Act. Although military exchanges are exempt from charging taxes, they are not exempt from fuel taxes. Otherwise, the base gas stations would have a very unfair advantage and be able to sell gasoline for far less than anywhere else.

The good and bad thing is that on-base gas stations only adjust their prices a few times each month. This can be great if there is a huge upward spike in gasoline prices. Because most gas stations off base will raise their prices immediately, while on base, it can take several days to rise. The bad part is that when prices are relatively stable or dropping. Off-base prices may drop considerably lower for several days before the on-base gas station can catch-up.

Using Your Commissary Privileges

Another great way to save money is by shopping at one of the 254 commissaries (which is the military's term for grocery stores) that are located around the world. Unlike the separate exchange networks, commissaries have been consolidated into one massive system that operates stores to four different branches of the military. Which are run by the Defense Commissary Agency known as DECA.

Commissaries are also not tasked with making a profit to support the MWR fund. They are strictly there to provide the cheapest possible grocery store items to military members, qualified veterans, and their families, by selling grocery store products at only 5 percent over cost (to help build new commissaries and modernize existing ones). Another advantage of shopping there is that your purchases are tax free as well. All of this causes substantial savings to frequent shoppers over time and can take over 30 percent off your annual grocery bill.

In fiscal year 2009 alone, commissaries saved the average family of four nearly $3,300 off their grocery bill, while single members saved an average of $1,100 over the course of the year, which was an annual savings of 31.7 percent to the average customer off their grocery bill.

As times have gotten tougher for everyone over the last few years, more people have started to look to commissaries for savings. In 2009, DECA posted sales of over $5.98 billion. Which was an increase of 3 percent over the year before. As other grocery stores' prices continue to soar, these savings can put extra money back into your household by shopping there regularly.

Using Your Base Privileges to Save on Entertainment

Beyond shopping, there are many other ways to save money on base, especially within the entertainment department. On-base movie theaters are a great source of affordable entertainment. They actually show new movies (unlike the old days) for far less than you will find outside the gates. This can be a great way to enjoy a family night-out. Without having to worry about if your children can still go to college and see a movie in the same lifetime.

Moral Welfare and Recreation

Then there are Moral Welfare and Recreation known as (MWR) services. Depending on which base you're at will often dictate the types of services they offer. Bases near the ocean often rent boats, fishing equipment, and many other types of beach gear at extremely low prices. While inland bases often rent outdoor equipment, camping gear, and other types of things to help make life enjoyable for the service members that are stationed there and those that are visiting. Many bases' MWR services also offer everything you could possibly need for large gatherings and children's birthday parties as well. Some offer gazebos, dunk tanks, grills, turkey fryers, picnic areas, and various other things to help make your party complete. Without breaking the bank.

MWR Reduced Ticket Prices

Another great service that MWR offers is reduced ticket prices. Current service members are not the only ones eligible for these deals. Retired service members and 100 percent service-disabled veterans can usually get in on these reduced tickets as well (unless the attraction is specifically only offering the reduced tickets to service members). By visiting an MWR Information Ticketing and Travel (ITT) or Information Ticketing and Reservations (ITR) office, you can find out about various discounts on local events and areas of interest.

Or you can plan a great vacation at a fraction of the price using reduced ticket prices. Oftentimes theme parks and tourist attractions run great deals for service members, retirees, 100 percent disabled veterans, and their family members. As a way to say thank you for your service, these incredible deals are offered quite frequently, so using MWR to help plan your next trip can really save you a bundle.

*Remember that when planning your next vacation, you will really want to keep MWR in mind before you decide where to vacation at. Although by reading chapter 14, you will understand many of the travel benefits for hotels and transportation that are offered to service members, certain veterans, and their families. By going to MWR before you decide where to vacation at and keeping an open mind to the available discounts. They can really help you to plan a dream vacation on a realistic budget.

Different deals on great vacations start and end all the time at MWR. So contemplate and examine them carefully. By putting off that trip to Hawaii until next year so that you can cash in on a really cheap trip to Orlando this year can be a great way to enjoy your vacation instead of having to worry about how much you're spending on it.

For example, the reason that I used Orlando is not only because it is a great vacation destination. More importantly, they have a military resort with beautiful inexpensive rooms, and they also offer great deals on a regular basis to the theme parks so that your whole family can enjoy the parks without having to pay the full admission prices.

In 2010 alone, Disney World Orlando offered a deal that ran from January 3 through August 31, 2010 for active and retired military members. They offered a four-day military promotional ticket for $99.00. This was good for up to six people. That way, you get four days at the parks for close to the price of a one-day admission.

Sea World Orlando also has a program that is called Here's to the Heroes. Throughout 2010, for current military members, they are offering a free one-day admission to the park and up to three additional dependents can receive a free one-day pass as well with proper identification. These passes normally retail for $78.95 per adult at the gate. That's a deal no matter how you look at it.

Additionally, Universal Studios often runs similar deals, so check frequently.

These were all just examples on some of the great deals that MWR can help you find, although these deals sometimes have pretty small windows of opportunity. The fine people at MWR can help you to locate the deals and time your vacation to save money. Nothing is more satisfying than knowing that you are saving a fortune while still having a great time.

Shopping Eligibility for Veterans

The rules are fairly stringent when it comes to who is eligible to use base facilities for shopping and entertainment discounts among veterans. By referring back to chapter 6, you will see who is eligible to retain their military identification cards after their service has ended so they can continue to shop at base facilities.

The vast majority of people that qualify to retain their ID cards can use base facilities. There is one category of veterans that are not eligible to shop on base though. These are disabled veterans with less than 100 percent service-connected disabilities that are rated through the VA. This makes up the majority of disabled veterans that were given their disability ratings after separation through the VA.

Service members that are rated at 30 percent disabled or higher for their injuries are medically separated and considered medically retired. These members can shop on base because they are considered military retirees and have proper military identification cards.

There have been several congressional bills over the years that have failed that would change this rule. To allow disabled veterans with service-connected disability ratings of 30 percent or higher through the VA to shop on base, and those with 50 percent or higher service-connected disability ratings to use Space-A travel (which is covered in chapter 14). The problem is that certain veterans groups have lobbied extensively to help keep it this way because they do not want to have to share and oftentimes compete for many of these valuable benefits. This makes it so that less of the honorably discharged veterans that were injured while defending our country can use them.

Trimming Your Monthly Expenses
Whether you're a hard-core bargain shopper who is always looking to save a dollar or you're the type of person that rarely ever looks for the discounts. There are ways to trim your monthly budget if you are just willing to do a little research.

The easiest way to reduce your monthly bills is by first writing down all of your monthly expenses. Then closely examine each thing that you're spending on each month. Although some things such as your electric and water bills are not really negotiable, other items on the list may offer a veteran's discount if you just ask for it. Oftentimes a twenty-minute call to your cell phone carrier can save you 10 percent to 15 percent on your monthly cell bill. Just by inquiring if they offer a discount for veterans.

Many large companies with several competitors offer these savings to service members, retirees, and veterans; but they do not advertise these discounts to the general public. So you must ask specifically for them. For those of you that rarely bargain-shop, this can still be a great way to save because you need only to find the discount once, but the savings will continue on each month.

Another great trick is to inquire about veteran's discounts while you are already shopping. Many people annually shop for things such as lower car insurance rates (when they are up for renewal). Anyone that has ever inquired about better rates on car insurance knows that the insurance companies ask plenty of questions about your driving record, the car being insured, and numerous other things to help determine your rates. Many of these questions are already geared toward finding the discounts that you qualify for. By simply informing them about your veteran status, you may find yourself qualifying for a discount based on your past service. Veterans that are currently in school using their educational benefits will find that car insurance companies offer discounts based on their student status as well.

Veteran's Discounts at Local Businesses

Many large companies and small businesses offer discounts to veterans and service members as well. Oftentimes the difficult part can be finding which companies offer these discounts to veterans because many large companies tend to not advertise these discounts to the general public, which can sometimes make it pretty difficult for veterans to find them.

The other issue is that oftentimes businesses will only offer these discounts to veterans at certain times. While many large retail and restaurant chains will only offer discounts during certain patriotic holidays, such as the Fourth of July weekend or Veterans Day. Other businesses such as Bass Pro Shops, which offers a 10 percent discount to service members and retirees with valid military identification cards, they only offer these discounts starting on the fifteenth of each month, and the 10 percent discount lasts for one week. Additionally, retailers often reserve the right to exclude certain merchandise from discount, in this case, such as boats and other high-end items.

Finding the Discounts

Since businesses are free to start and stop offering discounts to veterans as they see fit. There really is no all-inclusive list of companies (and the discounts they offer) that exists at this time. There are certain things you can do, though, that can greatly increase your ability to find these discounts. Try the following:

- Do a word search on your computer. Then add the words *military discount* or *veterans discount* after the business or product that you're searching for. Although this takes a little bit of time to research on your computer. You will be surprised by how often that this extremely simple technique can pay off.

- Keep your retired military ID card (if you're retired) or your VA or VFW card handy. The majority of veterans, whether retired or not, have an ID card that proves their status as a veteran. By keeping your ID card clearly visible in your wallet or pocketbook. Oftentimes employees that are veterans themselves will see that you're a veteran as well and inform you of any veteran's discounts that are available. Oftentimes this leads to discounts when you were not even expecting them.

- Checking for military and veteran's discounts online. There are several online Web sites that have massive lists of businesses that offer discounts to current service members, retirees, and veterans that may have only served for a single enlistment as well. While some of these Web sites such as military.com offer free information to members on over 1,500 discounts that are offered to service members and veterans. Other Web sites such as "Veterans Advantage" charge membership fees and provide veterans discount cards to their members to become eligible to save. Another great way to learn about different companies that offer discounts to veterans is by visiting the "Discounts for Veterans" forum on hadit.com. This allows people to post different veteran's discounts that are out there. To visit each of these Web sites, go to:

  1. http://www.military.com/discounts/
  2. http://www.veteransadvantage.com/
  3. http://www.hadit.com/forums/

Chapter 14

Travel Benefits

This chapter explains all of the different travel benefits that service members, many veterans, and their families are allowed to use, even after their military service has ended. By reading this chapter you will learn how to utilize these valuable benefits effectively, and it can help you to save plenty of money while on your next vacation, while still having a great time. This chapter will cover:

- Flying Space A.
- Other discounts while on vacation.
- Staying in Military lodging when traveling.
- Roughing it at military campgrounds.
- Enjoying yourself at an (AFRC) Resort.
- Cashing in on cheap timeshare condos.

It seems that when talking to veterans about Space-A travel, everyone has one of three opinions about it. They either love it, hate it, or have never tried it because they had heard negative stories. Those that love Space-A will tell you that although it can be a bit frustrating at times, Space-A is the only way to travel if you want to see the world. While others do not like Space-A largely due to the fact that they have had a bad experience or two, and have given up on trying to use it. Then there are those that have never tried it because they have heard several horror stories. These people often think they do not have the patience that is often required to fly Space-A.

Oftentimes each of these things can be true. Space-A travel is not for everybody, but for those of you that have flexible schedules, plenty of patience, and a sense of adventure. Space-A can allow you to visit many parts of the world that most other people only dream of seeing, without having to spend your life savings to get there.

Understanding How Space-A Works

Oftentimes in life, having a basic understanding of how things work can allow you to decide if something is right for you or not. This statement definitely applies when determining if you want to fly Space-A, or commercially.

Our military has bases all over the world and is tasked with performing various types of operations in many places. Therefore, a massive air transit system (that is operated by the Air Mobility Command better known as the AMC) is required to provide support to the numerous places that our military service members are serving at around the world. Numerous planes are constantly traveling around the world day and night to delivery supplies, equipment, and service members and their families to wherever they may be needed. Oftentimes, though, not all of the available room on these planes are being utilized, which paves the way for Space Available, more commonly known as Space-A flights.

By realizing that many times these flights have ample room left over to transport people and their luggage, the military came up with a system that allows people to hop on for free instead of having to purchase expensive airline tickets. Over the years, this has become a giant network and the preferred way to travel for many people that are flexible and looking for great travel deals.

*Remember that although passengers travel for free using Space-A, they are still responsible for taxes, immigration/customs inspection fees, and meals that are served while aboard military aircraft. If you are departing from the United States on a military commercial contract aircraft from a commercial airport, you must pay $7.30 as an airport departure tax. This goes toward airport improvements. All Space-A passengers that are departing on commercial contract missions that are inbound to the United States will need to pay an $11.30 head tax and a $12.50 federal inspection fee for immigration/customs. Although these fees may vary from time to time, they are still much cheaper than flying even the cheapest of commercial airlines.

Additionally, on normal Space-A flights from air force bases, passengers are given the option of purchasing a box lunch. These are available for under $5.00 and typically have quite a bit of food in them, which is way better than the salted peanuts that commercial airlines offer. In the event that you do not wish to purchase a box lunch, passengers are allowed to bring their own food on Space-A flights, but be aware that you must finish your food and drink before you land because you cannot take it through customs. Also, alcoholic beverages are not allowed on these flights.

What Stops Many People from Traveling Space-A

Traveling Space-A can be a tricky game sometimes. After all, traveling this way is a benefit to those that qualify and is not a guaranteed right. You must first understand that military supplies and equipment as well as required passengers (which are military members that are on orders and other official duty passengers) are the priority, and rightfully so. Everyone else is then competing for the available space that is left. Sometimes, there may be enough room for everyone that wishes to travel that day. While other times, there may only be a few spaces available and hundreds of people seeking them.

Additionally, military life is very fast paced, and everything runs on a schedule, which can often be difficult for service members that are looking to travel this way on vacation. Your superiors do not really care about why or how that you became stuck somewhere else when your leave has ended; you're still considered AWOL or unauthorized absence. Also, service member's leave time is very valuable, so many choose not to spend their limited vacation days transiting.

Determining Who Can Fly Space-A

Many different types of people are authorized to travel using Space-A. These include current service members, both active duty and reservists / National Guard, twenty-year retirees, and the dependents of each of these groups as well.

There are numerous other groups of people that are authorized to travel this way as well. Seeing as this is a book for veterans and service members, though, I am limiting the information to only these groups of people.

Who Is Not Allowed to Fly Space-A

After extensive research on this single question, I was appalled to find that disabled veterans with 100 percent service-connected disabilities and widows/widowers of both active-duty and retired military personnel are not eligible to fly Space-A. While there have been numerous attempts made to correct this long-standing policy, by adding these groups of people to the list of eligible Space-A passengers. Each attempt has failed in Congress though.

DOD 4515.13-R is the directive that determines who is eligible for Space-A flights, and until amended, this practice of denying travel benefits to those who were either injured while protecting our country or that have lost their qualifying spouse (therefore may no longer travel using Space-A) will continue.

Determining Which Space-A Priority Category You Fit Into

There are several factors that help to determine which of the six priority travel categories that each person fits into. Depending on which status you are traveling under will dictate what the priority is that you catch the next available flight. Many times there is enough room for everyone that is attempting to make the flight to fit on the plane. So everyone from each category will make it when their name is called.

In the event that there is not enough room for everyone, when roll call begins, as they start calling the names, each person will be selected in the order that they signed up in each category. This means that all of the names in category 1 will be called in the order they have signed up. Then they will move onto category 2 and so on until there is no more space left available on that flight. Each person that answers the call, when their name is selected, will be manifested for the flight.

To determine which priority travel category that each person fits into, you will want to use the following basic guidelines:

Category number 1. Emergency leave unfunded travel—This is a fast way home for service members and dependents as well, in the event that there is a life-threatening illness, severe injury, or death in the immediate family. Immediate family is defined as parents/step-parents, sisters, brothers, sons, and daughters of both the service member and their spouse. This can also be extended to grandparents as well, if the grandparent raised the service member or spouse for at least five years of their childhood. To qualify for emergency leave status, you must have the Red Cross verify the emergency condition and the emergency must be indicated in your leave orders.

*Remember that emergency leave allows service members and their dependents to travel around the world quickly so they can get home in times of crisis to be with family.

Category number 2. Environmental morale leave (EML)—This type of leave is for service members that are stationed overseas in harsh environments such as Iraq or Afghanistan. The DOD realized that service members assigned to these types of unique places require frequent rest and relaxation known as R&R. So the DOD sometimes designates certain overseas areas to qualify for one EML per year. That way, service members that are serving in harsh environments can get home quickly to maximize the amount of time they have with family. Additionally, service members and their dependents can travel together anywhere while on approved EML orders using category number 2.

Category number 3. Ordinary leave, Medal of Honor holders, house-hunting permissive (TDY)—This category is for active-duty service members (including reserve component members on active duty). That are on ordinary leave, that is not considered an emergency or EML. Service members and their accompanying dependents can travel anywhere using category number 3 while on leave. Also, Medal of Honor recipients and their accompanying dependents are authorized to travel under category number 3 as well, but they must present a copy of their Medal of Honor certificate to qualify.

Additionally, when traveling to your next duty station to look for and secure new housing, while on house-hunting permissive TDY orders. Service members may only bring one dependent while traveling Space-A. Category number 3 travelers can fly anywhere as well.

Category number 4. Unaccompanied dependents on EML—Oftentimes service members are sent to some pretty distant locations. When their EML comes around, many times the family is looking to join them somewhere other than at home. By using category number 4, dependents are allowed to use Space-A to travel without having the sponsor present. This can allow the family to meet up with the service member without having to come home. Dependents are allowed to travel from one overseas location to another. As well as to and from overseas locations back to the continental United States commonly referred to as CONUS. The one thing that dependents cannot do is use Space-A category number 4 to travel from one location in CONUS to another location in CONUS without the sponsor being present.

Category number 5. Permissive (TDY) for non-house-hunting, dependent students and others—This category entails a few different groups of travelers. These are as follows:

    a.   Military service personnel that are traveling without dependents while on temporary duty orders other than for house-hunting. These travelers can travel to all locations.

b. Dependent children that are college students that are attending an overseas branch of an American university. That is in the same overseas area in which they reside with the sponsor. These dependent children may travel unaccompanied to and from the school one round trip per year, under category number 5.

c. Dependents who are command sponsored and are stationed overseas with their sponsor who is in the armed forces. These dependents are permitted to travel unaccompanied to and from the nearest overseas military academy testing site. In order to take scheduled entrance examinations for entry into any of the U.S. service academies.

Category number 6. Retired military members, reservists, and National Guard—This category entails a few different groups of travelers as well. These are the following:

a. Retired uniformed services members. These retirees and their dependents that are accompanying them are entitled to travel to all locations with the sponsor present.

b. Authorized Reservists and National Guard members and retired reserve and National Guard members that are entitled to retired pay at the age of sixty (gray-area retirees) can travel Space-A in the CONUS. Additionally, they may travel directly between the CONUS and Alaska, Hawaii, the U.S. Virgin Islands, Puerto Rico, Guam, and American Samoa (Guam and American Samoa travelers may transit Hawaii or Alaska), or travel within Alaska, Hawaii, Puerto Rico, or the U.S. Virgin Islands.

Deciding Where to Fly

Now that we have determined who is eligible to fly Space-A in each category, it's time to take a look at how you go about picking a destination. Here is where being flexible in your travel plans can really pay off. When signing up for Space-A flights, it really helps to think outside the box to maximize your travel opportunities because traveling

Space-A is not an exact science and oftentimes it may require multiple flights to get to the destination you're seeking.

The key here is to remember that they are doing you the favor by allowing you to travel for free. The military is not on your schedule; you're on theirs, so learning how to make your travel needs fit into the military's travel plan, and being creative in picking your travel destinations can really help you get there more efficiently.

When signing up for Space-A travel, passengers are allowed to choose up to five destinations. If you're only looking to go to a certain specific destination, then the real trick will be to find a path that leads there. Don't worry though; there is a great Web site that addresses this issue. By doing a little research at pepperd.com, you can usually find a solution to your travel problem. This Web site is a massive Space-A message board. Where other fellow Space-A travelers find and leave travel tips on how to get from one place to another efficiently. By following the bread crumbs of others that have traveled before you, most times you can find the most efficient path to your destination because these flights are usually on a regular schedule. You can visit this Web site at:
http://www.pepperd.com/cgi-bin/spacea/discus.cgi

For people that are more flexible in their travel plans. Who are just looking for an adventure without having to be in a specific place at a specific time, when signing up for Space-A, you have the option to choose either specific locations to travel to or you can pick entire countries. By picking entire countries instead of only selecting a particular location, oftentimes Space-A travelers can get pretty close to where they want to go. Once there, they often find it much easier to find additional hops to their ultimate destinations.

Another option when selecting destinations is choosing "All" as one of your choices. This allows you to be put on the waiting list for all of the flights that are departing from that particular military air terminal. That way, if you can't make the cutoff for one particular flight, you can oftentimes hop on a different flight to a different destination. This is a great alternative for people that are extremely flexible, that want to see different parts of the world.

*Remember that although there are flights going on constantly around the world, many places are not accessible from certain air terminals. In layman's terms, this means that it's much easier to get to and from countries that are located in the Pacific Ocean (such as Asia) from the West Coast, and it's much easier to get to and from European countries (which are in the Atlantic Ocean) from the East Coast of the United States.

Additionally, timing is everything when it comes to Space-A travel. Just like commercial travel, Space-A has peak travel periods as well. While trying to hop a flight as a priority category 6 passenger is next to impossible during the holidays and when the children are out of school for the summer. There are other periods when traveling Space-A can be much less challenging. Statistically, the best times to travel Space-A are February through March and October through early November.

Signing Up for Space-A Travel

There are three different ways that you can sign up for Space-A travel. Once registered, your name will remain on the list for sixty days from the day that you signed up, the duration of your leave orders (for service members), or until you fly out. Whichever of these comes first. Active-duty service members will also want to remember that they cannot sign up for Space-A travel prior to the date their official leave orders begin. To sign up, you can do the following:

1. Sign-up in person—although this is by far the most inefficient way to sign-up for Space-A travel, it can really be helpful the first few times until you get the hang of it. First, you will need to determine the air terminal that you will be departing from. There is a list of all Space-A air terminals that are located around the world and their contact information in appendix B. Then just stop by the terminal and speak with a passenger service representative. They can guide you through the process and inform you of where flights are departing to, as well as which documentation that you will need to fly, and any other things you will need, such as immunization records, and border-crossing documentation such as passports and visas. This form of sign-up is especially helpful the first few times because nothing will frustrate you more than being turned away at the last second because your paperwork is not in order.

2. Self sign-up—most air terminals have started to allow people to sign up for Space-A flights without having to wait in line. The majority of air terminals each have a self-sign-up counter that allows people who are qualified to fly Space-A an option that doesn't require waiting in line. These self-sign-up counters are easy to use, and they offer easy-to-follow instructions for registering.

3. Remote sign-up—This is the way of the future for Space-A travelers. This allows travelers to put their name on the Space-A waiting list without having to stop by the terminal. By allowing you to fax copies of your proper service documentation and desired destinations without having to go into the air terminal itself. This is a huge time-saver. The fax numbers for each military air terminal are furnished in appendix B as well.

*Remember that when signing up for Space-A flights, you will want to submit the proper documentation of all people that will be traveling, because adding travelers after you have signed up can cause your name to get bumped back down to the bottom of the list. Also, if you want to check exactly how far down on the list you are (so you will know if you have a reasonable chance of making the flight), you can stop by the terminal and check the Space-A register or call the air terminal and ask. Additionally, you can sign up for travel from multiple locations, which is great because if you plan on traveling to a certain destination, you can sign up for your return trip prior to leaving, then as you're out sightseeing, your name will be slowly moving up the list.

Preparing for Your Trip

One of the major advantages that Space-A travel offers to passengers is that you can actually bring quite a bit of luggage with you without the fear of being charged extra for trying to take your clothes on vacation with you. Each passenger is allowed to bring two bags weighing up to seventy pounds each with them. That's 140 pounds of luggage per person maximum, and families that are traveling together may pool their baggage together for up to five family members. In other words, five passengers equals ten bags with up to seven hundred pounds. Each piece of baggage must also be less than sixty-two linear inches (which is the sum of the length plus width plus height) as well.

Passengers may also have one carry-on item to take with them, such as a small backpack, briefcase, baby stroller, or baby-supply bag. This bag must be able to fit either underneath your seat or in the overhead compartment, and on most flights, carry-on luggage may be no larger than forty-five linear inches.

*Remember, these rules are in place for the majority of flights. Some smaller planes that offer Space-A flights will only allow you to bring up to thirty pounds of luggage. So by packing lightly, travelers can greatly increase their odds of making it on smaller planes while others must pass on them. After all, thirty pounds is still quite a bit of luggage to travel with. Packing lighter can also make traveling on long trips easier as well. Every additional pound of luggage you bring is an additional pound that you have to carry all over the place with you, and that can tire you out.

The other important factor that you need to consider when preparing to travel Space-A is what to wear. Common sense really plays a large role here because you must remember that these flights are government run. If your shirt says something that is considered offensive, chances are you will get turned away. Also, open-toed footwear is not allowed on cargo aircraft for safety reasons. The best way to dress is in comfortable clothes and dress in layers. Since you never can tell what the temperature will be like on different types of aircrafts. Also, if you get warm, a sweater balled up can make a comfortable pillow.

It's Showtime

Ever since 9/11, the restrictions have been tightening concerning travel information for military flights, and rightfully so. Therefore, departure and arrival time information on these aircrafts is only given out typically three days in advance. So it really makes sense to call the terminal ahead of time to check for updated travel times; that way, if your flight changes missions, you will not be wasting your time. Most air terminals also have a flight information recording. By referring to appendix B, you can get the number for the air terminals recording and find out information on future flights.

On the day that your flight is scheduled to depart, you will want to arrive at the air terminal a minimum of two to three hours before the scheduled departure time. That way, you can declare yourself present and verify that your sign-up date and time has been properly entered into the system. Shortly before "showtime," the passenger representative will post a list of all the people that are present for the flight. This can give you a pretty good idea as to if you will make the cutoff or not.

Once showtime starts, a passenger representative will start calling the names of all the people that are marked as Present in the computer. This goes in order by priority category and date/time they signed up, once your name is called (assuming that you answer), your name will be manifested for that flight, and you will be on your way shortly. That is unless you get bumped by a space-required passenger or cargo that can come on at the last minute because they have priority. In which case, you can reregister using your original date and time.

*Remember that schedules can and often do change at the last minute for military flights, so be prepared. Smart travelers will plan for this because arriving late can oftentimes make you lose your seat. In the event that you are unable to make a flight that you desire, you can either try and take another flight (which is why it is advisable to sign up for more than one location), you can try and stay on base at the lodging facilities (which is covered later in this chapter), come back and try again at a later date, or fly commercially. In any event, travelers will need to have sufficient funds on them for their journey because even in the event that you can stay on base, it's still going to cost you and commercial airline tickets are often most expensive when purchased at the last minute.

Spending Time at the Air Terminal
Space-A terminals often have the same comforts that commercial airports have. Many terminals have snack bars, exchanges, baggage lockers, USO lounges, televisions, and even children's nurseries. The larger the air terminal, the more facilities they typically offer. Also, if you get stuck in one location for several days, it's best to try and secure a room on base, assuming there is availability, then research other alternative routes so that you can get closer to your destination. Using flexibility, creativity, and timing are much cheaper than staying put for several days until the next flight or purchasing commercial airline tickets.

Other Discounts while on Vacation

If flying Space-A is not your cup of tea, don't worry. There are plenty of other ways to save when planning your next trip. Several commercial airlines have come to realize that many service members prefer not to travel Space-A. Therefore, they have started offering greatly reduced rates to service members if you just ask for them. These reduced fares are not typically offered through the airline's online reservation systems, so you will need to call the airlines directly to inquire.

Other great discount opportunities are out there as well, such as discounts on cruises, rental cars, hotels, and reduced airfares that are not only offered to service members, but to all veterans and dependents as well. Although some of these discounts may be minimal such as 5-10 percent off or free upgrades. Other times with a little bit of research on your computer, veterans can find huge discounts on vacation deals up to 65 percent off. There are numerous Web sites that are dedicated just to travel discounts for military service members, veterans, and retirees; so whichever category you fit into, there are discounts available if you just take a little time and look. These deals begin and end all the time, so it's best to either check with several of the online sites or contact MWR directly.

Staying in Military Lodging

This alone can be a great way to save a ton of money when you're traveling. The problem is that most veterans tend to forget about these on-base lodging opportunities after they have left the service. Others of us that are old-timers also remember back in the days when it was truly Space-A because you never really knew if you could get a room until late in the day, and that's if there was space available that was left over for that night. Then you always ran the risk of being bumped out the following morning due to other families that were coming in as space-required travelers on orders.

My how times have changed, now that all the lodges are computerized, and most have central reservation systems, so you can make your reservations well in advance. Once your reservations are confirmed, you can't get bumped out by those with official travel orders, it kind of sounds like a regular hotel, right? With one major exception—the price, military lodges are much more affordable than comparable hotels that are located outside of military bases. Rooms tend to be 45 percent cheaper in military lodges than hotels that are located close by off base.

Eligibility to Stay at Military Lodges

Not everyone is allowed to stay at military lodges after their military service has ended though. To qualify, you will need to have a valid military ID and be in one of the following categories:

- Active-duty military members.
- Reservist or National Guard members.
- 100 percent disabled veterans with service-connection.
- Retired military members (including gray-area retirees).
- Medal of Honor recipients.
- Dependents of the above.
- Surviving spouses and their family members.
- Former spouses when accompanied by dependent children.

Keep in mind that eligibility for this benefit means that people who meet the eligibility criteria are authorized to reserve rooms and check in. Guests may stay there with them, but as with all things on military bases, the sponsor is responsible for their actions. Also, the eligible person must be the one to check in. If you're still not sure if you're eligible to stay in military lodges, check your military ID card. Newer ID cards will say which on-base benefits you're entitled to use in the lower right-hand corner. If the ID card says MWR, you're authorized to use this benefit.

*Remember that these are the basic eligibility requirements, while these groups of people are eligible to stay at on-base lodging facilities. It is still first and foremost for those that are space required, which means that Space-A rules apply, so it's best to try and use them during off-peak-seasons or when they are not at full capacity. Additionally, certain smaller bases with minimal lodging facilities that are in desirable destinations oftentimes put numerous restrictions on who can stay at these facilities and for how long, that way, they have the necessary facilities available for those that truly need them, instead of those that want them for vacation.

Pick a Lodge, Any Lodge

For those of us that are eligible to stay at these facilities (see the Lodging Eligibility section). This can really be a fun way to travel and save at the same time. Military lodges come in all shapes and sizes. Some are large with hundreds of rooms, while others are small with only a few dozen rooms. Some are brand-new and state-of-the-art, while others are WWII barracks that have been converted into hotel rooms that may be really outdated, but are still an inexpensive way to put you up for the night. The good thing is that the facilities offered are pretty much reflected in the price. The best part is that if you're eligible to stay at on-base lodging, you can use the lodges of each military branch. In other words, you can stay at an Air Force lodge even if you served in the Army. So that's a pretty big network of places to stay while you're traveling.

Making Your Reservations

When making reservations to stay at military lodges, it's always better to make reservations sooner than later. As a general rule of thumb, active-duty members and their dependents can make reservations up to sixty days in advance. Everyone else can make them thirty days in advance. By doing it this way, lodges can plan well in advance and take the necessary steps to make accommodations available to those that will be needing them. That way, vacation travelers can still have the opportunity to plan trips a good month in advance.

The Army, Navy, and Air Force each have plenty of bases with lodging facilities, so they have centralized reservation systems. That way, no matter which base you are wanting to stay at, all you will need to do is call a single number to make a reservation for any of the lodges that are in that branch. These are the following:

To make a reservation at any of the Army lodges, call (866) 363-5771.
To make a reservation at any of the Navy lodges, call (800) 628-9466.
To make a reservation at any of the Air Force lodges, call (888) 235-6343.

There is a great Web site available that can help you locate military lodges that are available wherever you may be traveling to as well. Just go to: http://www.dodlodging.net/

Since the U.S. Marine Corps and Coast Guard do not operate nearly as many lodges as the Army, Air Force, and Navy does, they haven't felt the need to switch to a centralized reservation system yet. So you will have to contact the base lodges directly to make reservations. The good thing is that they each have nice lodging in some really beautiful places to view the different types of lodging facilities that the Marine Corps and Coast Guard have available, which can be anything from cabins to chalets and even beach houses and cottages in certain places. Just go to: http://www.usmc-mccs.org/lodging/reclodging.cfm?sid=rf&smid=3 or
http://www.uscg.mil/mwr/lodging/Lodging.asp

*Remember that while many military lodging facilities have started to allow patrons to bring their pets into the lodging facilities. Not all lodges are accepting pets, so it's best to ask when making your reservations ahead of time.

Roughing It at Military Campgrounds
This is a great new program that MWR offers called Paths Across America. This allows those with MWR privileges (see the Eligibility for Staying at Military Lodges section) to stay at numerous RV parks and campgrounds that are located all across America at reduced rates, while many of these parks offer RV hookups and campsites at reduced prices for those that are vacationing. Others offer cabins and motel units at reasonable prices with MWR activities nearby as well. To locate the different parks that are participating in this program, go to: http://old.armymwr.com/portal/travel/paths/default.asp

Enjoying Yourself at an AFRC Resort
The armed forces recreation centers better known as AFRC can be a great alternative to regular resorts. Although there may only be five of them, they are scattered around the world in some of the best vacation destinations on the planet. These full-service resorts offer top-notch service and breathtaking views to service members and veterans alike. They offer unparalleled service yet are affordable enough for everyone that is on a military budget.

These AFRC resorts are a great way to stay in a high-end resort on a low-end budget. After all, these resorts are joint-service facilities that are managed by the U.S. Army Family and Moral, Welfare, and Recreation Command, which means that since MWR helps to manage and operate these resorts, you will not be paying an arm and a leg to stay in them. Even though they are in some pretty desirable destinations.

A Look at the Resorts

Although there may only be five AFRC resorts, they are located in very strategic places that allow for some great rest and relaxation. The one common factor they each share is that they are all really nice vacation resorts, in great locations at a fair price. Let's take a look at each:

Shades of Green

This resort is located on Walt Disney World property in sunny Orlando, Florida. This resort is great for families (especially with young children) that are looking to enjoy the theme parks without having to spend their life savings to do it. The property itself has everything that you could possibly need to make your stay enjoyable. From four great restaurant choices to two heated pools and hot tubs. There are also several great golf courses located close by and an on-site ticket sales office (that way, you're not waiting in line at each park's gates). They even offer shuttle transportation to all of the parks.

As a longtime resident of Orlando, I can personally tell you that Shades of Green is the best place in town for the price. Over the years I have had the opportunity to visit just about every hotel and resort in Central Florida. Hands down, there is nothing comparable for the price. Other resorts that are located on Disney property while they may be beautiful, they each cost considerably more, often two to three times more. To make reservations at each resort, see the Making Reservations at AFRC Resort section later in this chapter.

Cape Henry Inn and Beach Club

This is the newest AFRC resort and is located on Chesapeake Bay near Virginia Beach. This beautiful resort is relaxing to put it mildly and the perfect way to reconnect with loved ones in a relaxing quiet beach atmosphere. This AFRC resort is much smaller than each of the others, and that's what helps to keep it so intimate.

The Cape Henry Inn may only have fifty beautiful hotel rooms, but they also offer log cabins, bungalows, and cottages as well. Which make for a great relaxing and secluded vacation with those that you truly want to be with. Consider it your own little mellow and relaxing hideaway, from the busy world.

For those that are looking for activities on their visit. First off, the sunrises are incredible. Also, there are two lighthouses close by and a boardwalk to stroll as well. The resort also has two pools and a beautiful pristine beach with sand dunes. There is also good fishing, whale, and bottlenose dolphin watching as well. With many great restaurants located nearby.

The Hale Koa

This is by far the largest of the AFRC resorts, with 817 guest rooms between the two towers that are located on beautiful Waikiki Beach in Hawaii. The view is incredible, and the atmosphere and staff are very relaxed. Which makes many first-time visitors of the Hale Koa tend to be very pleasantly surprised with their stays because when making their reservations, newcomers often do not realize exactly how enjoyable a vacation they have planned.

The resort itself has just about everything you could possibly need to make your vacation enjoyable, from surf and snorkel equipment to tennis and sand volleyball. Then when you're finished with those activities, you can unwind in one of the pools or visit the spa for a massage. As for dining and entertainment, there are many great options both in the resort and close by, including both a really fun authentic luau and a magic-and-comedy dinner show that are both located on the property. All this while staying on one of the most beautiful beaches in the world, which is why so many people who qualify to stay there end up returning to have their weddings and renewing their vows at the resort.

Dragon Hill

The Dragon Hill resort is located in Seoul, South Korea. This beautiful resort provides a great avenue for some well-deserved R&R for both families that are stationed overseas in Southwest Asia and for those that just love to travel the world. The world-class shopping is the real draw here for many travelers, while others choose to take up the sites and learn about the Asian culture.

The resort itself has five different types of American-style restaurants and two American fast-food restaurants as well. Then feel free to unwind at Bentley's English Pub or relax at Whisper lounge. Additionally, they have a health club, twenty-five-meter indoor lap pool, racquetball court, bubbling spa, and various other types of fitness equipment.

Edelweiss Lodge and Resort

The Edelweiss Lodge and Resort is located in the Bavarian Alps in Germany. This picturesque resort offers not only some of the most beautiful scenery imaginable, but also some of the best skiing, mountain climbing, and hiking in the world. For those that are more into sightseeing, there are endless possibilities to choose from. So it's best to prioritize by what is truly important for you to see during your stay. Just make sure you make time for the Neuschwanstein Castle that's really a must-see.

The resort itself has several different types of rooms and cabins that have a variety of amenities depending on your needs and desires. They also have an indoor pool, outdoor hot tub, game room, and fitness center. As for dining at the Edelweiss, they offer four different choices to choose from, including a mountain-style alehouse bistro, casual dining, upscale or fine dining, and a snack bar that has smoothies and Starbucks coffee.

Eligibility for AFRC Resorts

Not everyone is eligible to stay at AFRC resorts. To make a reservation and stay there, you must fit into one of the following categories:

- Active-duty military service members.
- Reservist or National Guard members.
- Retired military service members. (This includes gray-area retirees.)
- Disabled veterans with 100 percent service connection.
- Medal of Honor recipients.
- Involuntarily separated service members under TAMP.

- Personnel that were separated under VSI or SSB are authorized to stay there for two years after your separation.
- Dependents of the above-mentioned veterans.

Reserving Rooms at AFRC Resorts

There are a few things that you will want to remember before making a reservation at any of these resorts. To start with, those that are eligible to stay at these resorts can only stay there for thirty days out of the year. You can, on the other hand, book up to three rooms for your stay (that way, the whole family can come). Also, each of these facilities does not allow pets and are smoke-free facilities.

*Remember that each of these resorts' rates is determined not only by the type of room and the amenities that you have requested, such as a larger room or a better view. In AFRC resorts, the room rates are also based on military rank as well. Realizing that lower-ranking service members do not make nearly as much money as higher-ranking service members do, the rates are adjusted accordingly. This makes it so everyone in the military family can afford to stay at each resort.

Reservations at each of these resorts are on a first-come-first-served basis. Which means you will really need to plan your trips well in advance. Reservations are accepted up to a year in advance, and it can often take up to several months to find availability. After all, these resorts are in some pretty great locations.

AFRC resorts also offer discounts on a regular basis, so it's best to check online before trying to make your reservations. Oftentimes ten minutes of research on the resort's Web site can literally save you 25-50 percent off your room rates. Just by looking carefully at the Vacation Specials section on the Web site before you book your stay. To reserve rooms at each of these resorts, you can either make a reservation over the phone or online. The contact information for each resort is:

Shades of Green
(888)593-2242 or http://www.shadesofgreen.org/

Cape Henry Inn and Beach Club
(757)422-8818 or http://www.capehenryinn.com/

The Hale Koa
(800)367-6027 or http://www.halekoa.com/

Dragon Hill Lodge
(011-82-2)790-0016 or http://www.dragonhilllodge.com/main.html

Edelweiss Lodge and Resort
From the USA call: (011-49)8821-9440
From Europe call: 8821-9440
Or online at: http://www.edelweisslodgeandresort.com/home.html

The New Sanno Hotel

Although this is not technically an armed forces recreation center, it definitely does bare mentioning.

The New Sanno Hotel is a U.S. Naval Joint Services Activity that is located in downtown Tokyo, Japan. This luxury hotel has 149 exquisite rooms that cost far less than anything you will find in the Tokyo area.

They offer a heated pool, hot tub, fitness center, four different shops onsite, and a beauty salon that offers massages as well. As for dining, there are five different restaurants with everything from fine dining to traditional Japanese fare. There is also a really nice American cocktail lounge.

Nightly rates are determined the same way as AFRC resorts are. Which means the type of room and your rank are both considered when determining your nightly rates. To be eligible to stay at the New Sanno Hotel, you must fit into one of the following categories: active duty, active-duty dependents, active Reservist or National Guard member (on orders or EML orders to Japan), retired service members, retired Reservists, and disabled veterans with 100 percent service-connected disabilities. To make reservations, you can contact them at:

The New Sanno Hotel
(03)3440-7871 extension #7121
http://www.thenewsanno.com/

The Armed Forces Vacation Club

In the event that you don't wish to stay at any of the other options, or you are just looking to get away from everything that is military while on your vacation. Let's try this one on for size. It's called the Armed Forces Vacation Club or AFVC for short. AFVC is part of Wyndham Worldwide, which is one of the world's largest hospitality companies. They have teamed up with MWR to offer service members and eligible veterans a really great vacation alternative for those of us that are just looking to get away.

How AFVC Works

People around the world purchase time-share condos all the time. The problem is that oftentimes after a few years have passed, many time-share owners may decide to skip their week of vacation or just decide not to go anymore, instead of letting the unit just sit there empty for the week, they came up with a great alternative that has been implemented. Which is, allowing active-duty service members, active and inactive reserve and guard members, retired military members, 100 percent service-disabled veterans, and their adult dependents to use these time-share condos. They offer these condos at a greatly reduced flat rate of $369 per week, but they frequently offer $20 discounts for online booking as well, so it's usually $349 if you book your room online.

As soon as AFVC becomes aware that each condo is not going to be used, they post it on their Web site. Which can be anywhere from 2-360 days in advance. Then anyone that is eligible to reserve that unit is free to make a reservation and firmly secure their vacation condo. Once the reservation has been made, the unit is taken out of the available inventory pool of condos, and the room is yours to enjoy. Although this is considered Space-A vacationing, all condo reservations are on a first-come-first-served basis.

Where You Can Stay Using the AFVC

Since these vacation condos become available and are reserved at a pretty quick pace, it's often difficult to say exactly what will be available when you check. The good part is that there are plenty of vacation rentals to go around for everyone, and the Web site is quite helpful. AFVC regularly has accommodations at more than 3,500 resorts, vacation apartments, homes, and condominiums in over eighty countries, which can provide you with some fantastic vacationing opportunities that few people are ever offered, spanning across over eighty countries.

They regularly have vacation rentals located throughout the United States, Mexico, and the Caribbean. Or you can get a bit more adventurous and try the ancient ruins of Greece or one of the many options available overseas.

Vacation Rentals versus Hotels

By using the AFVC Web site, you can really scope out some great deals. Most of the time-shares and resorts have several pictures of their properties and a full explanation of the amenities that they offer. When staying in most hotels, all you get is a basic room. While most condominium-style vacation resorts typically offer considerably larger rooms often with kitchens, dining rooms, washer and driers as well as numerous other on-site amenities, which can give you far more bang for your buck.

Reserving Your Vacation Condo

To be eligible for these spectacular deals, you must first call AFRC and sign up. You can reach them at 1(800)724-9988. Once the people at AFRC verify your eligibility, they will issue you an account number and password. That way you can browse available resorts and make reservations using the Web site. If you're not sure if this option is something that you would be interested in, try visiting the Web site first, and take a look at some of the deals. You can visit the Web site at: http://www.afvclub.com/

*Remember that if you're eligible to stay at AFVC resorts, you can book multiple vacation condos at the same resort for the same time period. This is really a great option for family gatherings. Additionally, although these condos are for a set price, some all-inclusive resorts can and do charge additional fees. This is due to the fact that all meals, drinks, tours, and entertainment are wrapped into the price. These additional all-inclusive fees can easily turn your $349-a-week vacation condo into a $2,000-a-week condo, so be careful. These fees are set and implemented by the individual resorts, and AFVC has no control over them. AFVC clearly marks these all-inclusive vacation resorts on their Web site, and if you have questions, the vacation guides that work at AFVC will gladly tell you about any all-inclusive conditions and rates before you confirm your reservations.

Section 6

The Golden Years and Beyond

The chapters within this final section of the book contain quite a bit of information on many of the different benefits that are available to service members, veterans, and their families toward the later stages of each veteran's life. While we never truly know which day will be each person's last, there are numerous benefits available to veterans and their families when that time comes. Although most of us try not to spend too much time focusing on the inevitable. By educating ourselves now about the necessary steps to take in the future, we can each lessen both the burden and financial impact on our families during the latter stages of life. I like to think of it as being responsible by getting prepared.

Chapter 15

Planning for your Retirement

In this chapter, we will be discussing everything pertaining to your retirement plan. While each person has a different idea as to what they want their retirement years to look like. By spending just a little bit of time now, thinking about your future. This can oftentimes help each of us to chart a course that will make you secure and free to enjoy your retirement years. Instead of having to constantly worry about survival, when the time arrives. The information in this chapter pertains to:

- Coming up with a retirement plan.
- The advantages of growing older as a veteran.
- Finding a suitable retirement home as a veteran.
- The armed forces retirement homes.

When it comes to retirement, each person has a different idea of where they want to be when the time comes. Some people really want to be able to travel the world, and others just merely want to keep living the same way they always have with family and friends. While yet other people really just want a nice retirement home or community living center to live in so they can be around other retirees for companionship. Without having to worry about the daily inconveniences of such things as cooking, driving, being alone, and even smaller issues like going to get their prescriptions filled. The thing to remember is that as each person gets older, time will take its toll. The older each person gets, chances are the more assistance they will require.

The Advantages of Being a Veteran

No matter what your retirement plan looks like, being a veteran is a good thing when it comes to getting older. While many people that never served may have had an opportunity to amass more wealth over the years, they oftentimes end up spending every penny of it early in their retirement years. Largely due to the ever-rising costs of health care and overpriced assisted-living facilities.

Veterans, on the other hand, are offered numerous types of assistive services at little or no cost to the veteran. The services available and costs associated with them are typically based on several factors such as the severity and type of disability or illness, amount of military service completed, if they are faced with financial hardships, and the amount of space and resources that are available at the time.

*Remember that even if you plan to live independently at home throughout your retirement years, it still makes good sense to have a solid backup plan because by not being aware of which extended care benefits you're entitled to, as a veteran, it can easily evaporate your life savings, especially seeing as the VA has numerous options available for older veterans, when it comes to the different types of extended care programs for elderly veterans at controlled costs. These programs are explained thoroughly in chapter 7 in the Extended Care section.

Retirement Homes for Veterans

When it comes to locating a suitable retirement home, assisted-living facility, or VA community living center as a veteran, there are several very important factors that you will want to take into consideration before making a decision. While cost and cleanliness are obviously two of the most important factors to consider, there are several other variables that one must contemplate before making that all-important decision, such as if your spouse is eligible to reside there as well, the type of medical facilities they offer, are meals included, are activities offered, can you come and go freely, can you have visitors regularly, are the staff and residents generally happy to be there, and are these facilities for both officers and enlisted veterans as well. This may sound crazy, but many retirement facilities are for veterans that were either officers *or* enlisted members, not both. These are all-important issues that should factor into your decision-making process before moving in.

The good thing is that there are literally thousands of retirement facilities for veterans located throughout the U.S., while many are operated or contracted by the VA (see chapter 7); others are run by various veterans' service organizations such as the VFW. Part of the trick is determining which area of the country that you wish to live in and then searching for which facilities that are designated for veterans, luckily, by utilizing the Internet, this process of comparing retirement facilities has become relatively easy to do and doesn't take very long anymore.

Armed Forces Retirement Homes
Did you ever wonder what the military does with all the money from the fines and forfeitures when service members get into trouble? Between all of the money from the fines, forfeitures, and the fifty-cent payroll deduction that each active-duty-enlisted service member pays out of their paychecks, all of this money goes directly into the AFRH trust fund. Which helps to maintain both of the armed forces retirement homes, more commonly known as the AFRHs, there are two such facilities; one is located in Gulfport, Mississippi, while the other is located in the heart of Washington D.C.

The Gulfport Campus
Although Hurricane Katrina had her way with this veterans' retirement home back in August of 2005. Congress has decided to rebuild this massive retirement home for veterans on its original site. Scheduled to reopen in October 2010, this AFRH will have rooms for 584 residents,

providing veterans with independent living, assisted living, and long-term-care facilities.

This beautiful 660,000 square-foot main facility will end up costing $240 million to demolish the older facility and build the new one. When you consider the fact that for over 150 years, thousands of our elder veterans were given the opportunity to spend the latter part of their lives enjoying the outdoor recreation areas right near the ocean on the beautiful Gulf Coast. It really was worth rebuilding.

The Washington Campus

This AFRH is located in the middle of our nation's capital, on 272 gorgeous acres. This massive AFRH has been assisting older and disabled veterans for over 155 years, by offering them a nice safe refuge in one of the retirement home's 1,021 private rooms. This campus offers its veteran residents literally every amenity you could possibly imagine and is considered the premier retirement home for veterans.

The residents of the Washington campus are free to enjoy their retirement years with plenty of activities both on and off campus. On-campus residents can play golf on the nine-hole golf course complete with a driving range, go fishing on two stocked ponds, try a game of bowling at the six-lane bowling alley or become part of the bowling league, or take in a movie or enjoy a game of bingo in the 667-seat fully equipped theater. Other activities that are offered to residents include a complete fitness center, walking trails, garden plots (for gardening), computer center, reading/audio/video libraries, auto shop, card and game recreation rooms, ceramic/painting work areas, great dining selections, and a lounge with cold beer and snacks for vets to sit and watch sports in. These were all just some of the amenities; trust me, there are plenty more. Outside the gates, veterans can take in all of the sights of the D.C. area or head over to nearby Andrews Air Force Base and catch a Space-A flight for a vacation.

Taking Care of Your Health Care Needs at the Washington Campus

Residents of AFRH facilities have plenty of options for their health care needs. The Washington campus has an on-site two-hundred bed, long-term care facility that provides primary, intermediate, and skilled health care. As well as physical/occupational/recreational therapists, speech-language pathologists, on-site pharmacy, clinical and dental services as well.

For veterans that have more severe medical issues, AFRH offers free transportation to the surrounding hospitals. This includes the Washington D.C. VA Medical Center and the Walter Reed Army Medical Center.

Eligibility to Stay at an AFRH

Although all active-duty-enlisted service members have helped to pay for these facilities, not everyone qualifies to stay there. To qualify to live at either of the AFRH campuses, you must meet one of the basic eligibility rules, which are as follows:

- Be a veteran with twenty or more years of active-duty service and are at least sixty years of age.
- Veterans unable to earn a livelihood due to a service-connected disability.
- Veterans unable to earn a livelihood due to an injury, disability, or disease and that served in a war theater or that received hostile fire pay.
- Female veterans that served prior to 1948.

*Keep in mind that veterans are eligible to stay at either of the AFRH facilities if their active-duty service was at least 50 percent enlisted, warrant officer, or limited duty officer, and they meet one of the above-mentioned criteria. Additionally, married couples are welcome, but only if they are both eligible in their own right.

Passing the Screening to Live at AFRH

Veterans that qualify and that are interested in spending their retirement years at either of these veterans' retirement homes should definitely plan ahead. The baby boomer generation is not getting any younger, and although the waiting list is not long at this time, it will continue to grow in the coming years.

One of the major hurdles in applying to live at either of the AFRH campuses is the health-screening process. Once the health screening has been completed and you have been accepted. Your name will be placed on the waiting list. Then once your name reaches the top of the list, you're free to move in. The one thing to remember is that your health screening is only good for five months. Therefore, applicants may need to have an additional health screening to prove they are capable of self-care to become eligible to move in.

Because new resident applicants must be capable of self-care and psychologically stable when they arrive, they must also be free of alcohol, drug, and psychiatric problems as well. Additionally, to apply, applicants must never have been convicted of a felony.

*Remember that it's better to move in early before any serious health conditions arise. Once you have moved in to either of the AFRH homes, if your health deteriorates and you need increased health care. They offer both assisted-living and long-term care at each of the campuses. That way, you're not having to spend the later stages of your life bouncing from one facility to another.

Keeping You Medical Insurance at an AFRH

As each of us gets older, having good health insurance tends to become much more important, especially if you plan to spend your retirement years at either of the AFRH campuses. Residents are required to keep good health care coverage. The exact type of coverage, though, often depends on your status; so you may want to refer back to chapter 8, TRICARE to make sure you're eligible. Here are the basic guidelines AFRH uses:

- Medicare parts A and B coverage is mandatory before entry into either AFRH (assuming you qualify).

Military retirees over the age of sixty-five:
- If you have no Medicare benefits, then you are required to obtain and keep TRICARE Prime.

Military retirees under the age of sixty-five:
- If you have Medicare benefits, then you need only to obtain and keep TRICARE Prime as secondary coverage. (At no charge).

- If you do not have Medicare benefits, you must obtain and keep TRICARE Prime coverage. (In this case, you will have to pay for coverage and co-pays as well for private doctor's visits.)

Nonmilitary retirees:

- If you're a veteran with a 100 percent service-connected disability. Then you must use a VA or military medical facility.
- If you're under the age of sixty-five and without any Medicaid, Medicare, or VA benefits. Then you must purchase and maintain a major medical insurance policy.
- If you have Medicare benefits, then you will need to additionally secure one of the following as well:
  1. Secure Medicare supplemental insurance.
  2. Enroll into and maintain a Medicare HMO.
  3. Enroll into and maintain Medicaid.

Calculating How Much It Will Cost to Live at an AFRH

Another advantage that AFRH homes offer is that the amount that you're required to pay each month is based on a percentage of what you make versus the level of care that you require. These rates are computed annually and are adjusted for inflation. By doing this, residents really never have to worry about losing everything they have at the first sign of illness. Here is how it works.

- If you're an independent-living resident, you're required to pay 35 percent of your total current income, but not to exceed $1,238 each month.

- If you're an assisted-living resident, you're required to pay 40 percent of your total current income, but not to exceed $1,856 each month.

- If you're a long-term-care resident, you're required to pay 65 percent of your total current income, but not to exceed $3,094 each month.

*Monthly fees are based on your total current income. Which are based on both your taxable and nontaxable incomes.

Your taxable income is considered all of your income that is reportable as adjusted gross income on your individual U.S. income tax return and is adjusted by adding your tax exempt income that is received during the same year.

Your nontaxable income includes your benefits that you receive from the VA, social security, pensions, disability-retired pay, annuities, and IRA distributions that are not included in your adjusted gross income.

Touring the AFRH Campuses

Before deciding to apply at either of these veteran retirement homes, it's always smart to make sure that it's exactly what you're looking for. Because making the right decision the first time means never having to move again.

Veterans that meet the eligibility criteria and that are considering a move into either of these retirement homes are encouraged to visit and tour both of these locations. Each of the AFRH homes offer a complimentary two-night stay so that the veteran and their family may take a look around the property. The Washington campus additionally offers a limited number of meals to those that are visiting. This is a great way to make an informed decision, and it really shows that the AFRH homes are proud of the product they offer.

To schedule a visit to the Gulfport campus, call (800)332-3527.
To schedule a visit to the Washington campus, call (800)422-9988.

Applying to Become an AFRH Resident

The best way to start the application process to become a resident at either of the campuses is to call the campus directly at the above-mentioned phone number. Or you can request information; download the new resident's application and the medical examination forms online at: https://www.afrh.gov/afrh/newres/visit.htm

Chapter 16

Military Funerals

The prospect of passing away someday is not exactly something that most people (myself included) really like to put much thought into. We each know that someday it's going to happen, so why should we spend even a few minutes of our lives thinking about it now? The answer is simple: because anyone that truly loves their family would not want to leave them panicked. Left to scramble around afterward, not knowing what to do. Trying aimlessly to figure out exactly what their loved one would have wanted. In the end, leaving the family with nothing more than a huge funeral bill and no time to grieve the passing of the one they had loved so much. It doesn't have to be this way. Families should not have to worry about what to do with their loved one's remains, how to memorialize them to honor their memory and how they intend to pay for it. Luckily, there are numerous services that the VA and government can provide you with. This chapter will help you by providing a blueprint of services that veterans' families can receive, when the time comes. Also, keep in mind that the information contained within this chapter will be limited and pertain only to veterans, service members, and their families. We will then close with how both the VGLI and S-DVI life insurance programs work.

Coming Up with a Burial Plan

This may sound completely obvious, but the fact is that the majority of veterans and their spouses that have never been struck with a serious illness or injury more than likely have never seriously discussed their final wishes. Couples that have talked about what they would like oftentimes haven't even considered exactly which benefits the government and VA will provide them with. While other families may have already come up with a solid plan and come to realize that they do not qualify for the burial benefits they desired shortly after their spouses have passed. Then they are left scrambling at the last minute, trying to figure out an acceptable alternative.

*Remember that as you continue reading throughout this chapter, you will come to realize that many different veterans and their families are often eligible for many different types of benefits. So it's best to read this chapter carefully then come up with a plan that applies to your individual situation and needs.

Deciding Which Route to Take

Each of us has a different idea of what we want to happen after we have passed away. While many of us would like a military funeral and then to be buried at Arlington or a national cemetery, others want nothing more than a small private ceremony and then to be buried in a local private cemetery. That way, family can come by and visit more frequently. While other veterans may wish to be cremated and have their ashes placed into an urn. Then kept with family or placed into a columbarium or mausoleum. The thing to remember here is that there is no right or wrong decision when it comes to your final wishes. It's entirely up to each family's wants and desires.

Who Takes Care of Each Part of the Funeral and Burial Process

For better or worse, the military community is a giant family. This is never more apparent than when it comes to the passing of one of our own. While the DOD is responsible for providing veterans with military honors, the VA can help with several other details such as burial and plot allowances (if buried or inurned in a private cemetery, mausoleum, or a state-run veterans' cemetery). Headstones and markers, burial flags, Presidential Memorial Certificates, and even assistance with burials themselves in one of the VA's 131 national cemeteries that are located throughout the United States and Puerto Rico can all be arranged and received through the VA.

For those that are contemplating a burial at Arlington? The U.S. Army has the distinct honor of operating and managing burials that are within the Arlington National Cemetery, which subsequently has the strictest rules on who is eligible for burial there and will be explained later in this chapter.

*Remember that no matter where you choose to be buried at, each of these benefits are intended to help offset the costs associated with giving proper burials to those who have made numerous sacrifices to our country through their military service.

Eligibility for Basic Military Burial Benefits

There are many options available when it comes to choosing a final resting place for veterans. Therefore, it's typically best to first determine who is eligible for basic military burial and memorial benefits prior to making that all-important decision. These benefits can be used for burials in VA national and state-run veterans' cemeteries, National Park Service cemeteries, and privately owned cemeteries as well. The following groups of veterans are eligible for burial and memorial benefits:

- Any member of the U.S. Armed Forces that has died while on active duty. This also includes reserve component members.

- Any veteran that was discharged under conditions that the VA does not consider to be dishonorable. With service beginning prior to September 7, 1980 (for enlisted), or October 16, 1981 (for officers).

- Any veteran that was discharged under conditions that the VA does not consider to be dishonorable. With at least twenty-four continuous months of active-duty service or the full period for which the person was called to active duty, which is common with reserve component members, with service that began after September 7, 1980 (for enlisted), or October 16, 1981 (for officers).

- Any citizen of the United States who, during any war in which the United States has or may be engaged, served in the armed forces of any government that is allied with the United States during that war, whose last active service ended honorably by death or otherwise, and who was a citizen of the United States at the time of entry into such service and at the time of death.

- Reservists and National Guard members that died while hospitalized or undergoing treatment at the expense of the United States for any injury or disease. That was contracted or incurred under honorable conditions while performing either active or inactive duty for training or that was undergoing such hospitalization or treatment.

- Reserve component members that were disabled or died from either an injury or disease that was incurred or aggravated in the line of duty during a period of either active or inactive duty for training.

- Retired reservists and National Guard members who, at the time of death, were entitled to retirement pay or that would have been entitled to retirement pay, but that were under the age of sixty (gray-area retirees).

- Spouses and surviving spouses of eligible veterans are also eligible for burial benefits in most cases. Even if the veteran is not buried or memorialized in the cemetery, which in most cases means that even if the spouse pre-deceases the veteran, they still qualify. Additionally, surviving spouses of eligible veterans that have decided to remarry. If the subsequent marriage is to a non veteran and whose death occurred on or after January 1, 2000. Then the widowed spouse is eligible for burial in a VA national cemetery based on the widowed spouse's marriage to the eligible veteran.

- Minor children of eligible veterans are also eligible for burial benefits as well in many cases. For burial-benefit purposes, *minor children* are defined as "unmarried children that are under the age of twenty-one." This is extended to age twenty-three if the child remains in school full-time at an approved educational institution.

- Unmarried adult children can also qualify if the child became permanently physically or mentally disabled and incapable of self-care prior to the age of twenty-one. This can be extended to age twenty-three if the child was a full-time student. Either way, the parent must be able to provide proper supporting documentation to verify the child was disabled.

Who Is Not Eligible for Military Burial Benefits

Although most current and former military service members will qualify for burial benefits, there are a few groups of people that are *not* eligible for this benefit. These include the following:

- Reserve component members whose only service was for active or inactive duty for training. Unless they meet one of the above-mentioned eligibility categories.

- A former service member whose only separation from the armed forces was under dishonorable conditions. Or whose character of service resulted in a barring from veteran's benefits. If you're not sure if this applies to your situation, then it's best to contact your VA regional office (see appendix A).

- Former spouses of eligible veterans whose marriage ended in either a divorce or annulment.

- Persons that are found guilty of state or federal capital crimes. Or that would have been convicted of a capital crime if not having been unavailable for trial due to death or having taken flight to avoid prosecution.

- Any person that is convicted of a subversive activity after September 1, 1959. In these very few instances, eligibility can be restored with a presidential pardon.

*Remember that these are only the general military burial guidelines. Sometimes cases such as veterans with multiple discharges from active duty with varying discharge characterizations can require further review by the VA regional office before final approval. In these types of cases, it's best to check your eligibility by calling the VA at 1(800)827-1000.

A Closer Look at Burial Options

There are five basic options when it comes to burials for eligible veterans and service members. Depending on which option that you choose, though, in many cases certain family members (being the spouse and children) can qualify for free burial in certain types of cemeteries as well. It really all just comes down to the wants and needs of each individual family. While nobody really wants to spend a small fortune to bury a loved one in a cemetery, it can easily happen, especially, if you choose not to exercise the valuable benefits that are available to you. This is why it absolutely makes sense to weigh your options now. Then collect the proper paperwork, which is typically only copies of the veteran's discharge paperwork in advance. That way, when the time comes, everyone will be in agreement and know exactly what to do. Here are your different burial options:

- Burial in a VA national cemetery.
- Burial in a National Park Service cemetery.
- Burial in a state-run veterans' cemetery.
- Burial in a privately owned cemetery.
- Burial in the Arlington National Cemetery.

VA National Cemeteries

The VA operates and maintains 131 national cemeteries throughout the United States and Puerto Rico. Although not all VA national cemeteries have space available to accommodate new veterans and their families. The VA is opening new national cemeteries on a pretty regular basis to help keep up with the never ending demand.

There are several advantages to being buried in VA national cemeteries. The most obvious reasons are the price and level of assistance. Eligible veterans, spouses, and their minor children as well are all eligible for burial in VA national cemeteries free of charge. The services that are offered are the opening and closing of the grave, a government-furnished headstone or marker, and perpetual care as well. This may not seem important to everyone, but the thing to keep in mind is that many private cemeteries will only provide regular upkeep until they have reached capacity. Then once they are at capacity, the private cemetery's standards will often quickly decline and family members are left struggling to locate the grave site, as where VA national cemeteries provide regular upkeep indefinitely.

The veterans themselves, not the family members, are also eligible for a burial flag, Presidential Memorial Certificate, and in many cases, veterans that choose to be buried at VA national cemeteries are often also eligible for burial allowances. Each of these benefits is explained later in this chapter.

The other major reason that many veterans and their families use VA national cemeteries is because of the high level of service. Those tasked with helping veterans and their families make it through this ordeal are typically very compassionate and quite committed to making sure that everything is done correctly when it counts the most. They truly believe in what they are doing and feel as if every veteran deserves their finest service.

The one major disadvantage is that oftentimes, depending on where you live, there may not be a VA national cemetery close by. This can make it quite difficult for families. Especially for those that are located in one of the eleven states that do not have a VA national cemetery.

Making Arrangements at VA National Cemeteries

To locate your nearest VA national cemetery or to begin the process of scheduling a burial in one, the easiest way to find the closest national cemetery to you and the cemeteries current contact information. Just go to: http://www.cem.va.gov/cems/listcem.asp

National Park Service Cemeteries

Although there are technically fourteen national park cemeteries that are operated by the National Park Services, which falls under the jurisdiction of the U.S. Department of the Interior. Only two of these parks are still actively burying veterans and their dependents at this time though. These are as follows:

1. The Andersonville National Historic Site, which is located in Andersonville, Georgia. This site was home to one of the largest Confederate stockades of the Civil War.

2. The Andrew Johnson National Historic Site, which is located in Greenville, Tennessee. This site is not only the final resting spot for numerous veterans, but also the burial site of former president Andrew Johnson.

Burials at National Park Service Cemeteries

Those that meet the eligibility requirements for military burials, which was explained earlier in this chapter, are also eligible for burial in either of these National Park Service cemeteries as well, the good thing is that those who wish to be buried at either of these historical sites are eligible for the same burial benefits as those who are buried in VA national cemeteries. That is with one major exception, which is that spouses and children do not receive a free government-furnished headstone or marker.

Veterans, on the other hand, that meet the eligibility criteria described earlier in this chapter, are eligible for government-furnished headstones and markers, but the family is responsible for ordering them. The other negative is that there are only two of these sites that are still active, which can really make burials difficult, unless you live in the southeast.

To request a burial using your military burial benefits in either of the National Park Service cemeteries, you must contact the Department of the Interior directly. You can do this by calling (202)208-4747 or in writing at:

Department of the Interior
National Park Service
1849 C Street, N.W.
Washington, D.C. 20240

State-run Veterans' Cemeteries

Realizing the growing need for additional cemeteries for veterans and their family members, the VA has been helping to fund numerous state-run veterans' cemeteries. Here is how it works. Each individual state can apply for and is eligible to receive a VA grant to help fund cemeteries that are strictly used for burying eligible veterans and their dependents.

Although these state-run veterans' cemeteries have similar eligibility requirements to VA national cemeteries, they are owned strictly by the individual state and often have residency restrictions as well to ensure that only resident veterans and their dependents are buried there.

The good thing is that these state-run veterans' cemeteries have standards they must maintain and can also help with making burial arrangements. After all, they specialize in military burials, which is quite helpful when it comes to providing family members with the correct information.

*Remember that state-run veterans' cemeteries are operated by the individual states and not the VA. This means that the services they offer can vary greatly from one cemetery to another. Additionally, some of the services they offer can often require a fee, especially when it comes to dependents of qualifying veterans, so it's best to inquire ahead of time. The good thing is that veterans and dependents also qualify for free government-furnished headstones or markers in state-run veterans' cemeteries. To find a complete list of state-run veterans' cemeteries, go to: http://www.cem.va.gov/scg/lsvc.asp

Privately Owned Cemeteries

Although many veterans and their families often find this the most convenient route to take, they typically also find it as being the most expensive way. While convenience should always factor into your decision-making process before choosing, you must understand that the assistance that will be available to families will be greatly reduced. This means that the family will need to pay for the entire burial upfront and then submit the proper paperwork if they qualify for partial reimbursement of the funeral and burial expenses. Which are explained in the Helping to Offset the High Cost of Funerals and Burials section of this chapter.

Things to Consider at Private Cemeteries

The thing to remember here is that deciding to be buried in a private cemetery is your decision. Which means that details such as government-furnished headstones or markers, Presidential Memorial Certificates, burial flags, and a military honor's details will each need to be requested by the family or funeral director. As where the other burial options typically offer much more assistance throughout the process during these difficult hours.

Additionally, dependents are not eligible to receive burial benefits or free government-furnished headstones and markers in privately owned cemeteries. Veterans themselves, though, are eligible for these free headstones and markers. The problem is that many private cemeteries often require the family to purchase a special base for the marker or they charge extra for placing and caring for the headstone itself. Then if the headstone or marker becomes damaged over time or while the cemetery is performing regular maintenance (such as mowing the grounds). The family will be forced to argue with the cemetery caretakers, attempting to have them fix the damage they have caused.

The good thing is that no matter where the veteran is laid to rest. The VA will provide upon request a government headstone or marker free of charge anywhere in the world. Even to privately owned cemeteries. To make arrangements for funerals and burials in privately owned cemeteries, you must contact the funeral home directly.

Burials at Arlington National Cemetery

The eligibility criteria for burial at Arlington National Cemetery is considerably stricter than any of the other burial options. The veteran's last period of active duty must have been considered fully honorable. Additionally, the veteran must meet at least one of the following standards. Keep in mind that these are only the rules that pertain to service members and veterans for ground burial purposes. To be eligible, you must meet one of the following conditions:

- Any member of the armed forces that dies while on active duty, except for those that have died while on active duty for training only.
- Veterans that are retired from active duty.

- Former reserve component members that are retired from either the National Guard or reserves and that are in receipt of retired pay (which is at least age sixty) at the time of death. Additionally, the veteran must have served a period of active duty that is considered as other than for training purposes.
- Former prisoners of war who served honorably. That died on or after November 30, 1993.
- Honorably discharged veterans that were separated prior to October 1, 1949, for medical reasons that received a medical discharge rated as 30 percent disabling or higher from the military upon discharge.
- Veterans that have received any of the following awards: the Medal of Honor, the Purple Heart, the Silver Star, the Distinguished Service Medal, the Distinguished Service Cross, the Navy Cross, or the Air Force Cross.
- The spouse, un-remarried widow, minor children, and permanently dependent children of a veteran that is eligible for burial at Arlington National Cemetery.

*Keep in mind that if the spouse or child pre-deceases the veteran, they can be buried at Arlington National Cemetery. That is, if the eligible veteran agrees in writing to be buried at Arlington as well.

- The widow or widower of any service member that is determined to be missing in action already interred in Arlington as part of a group burial or is already interred at a U.S. military cemetery that is overseas, which is maintained by the American Battle Monuments Commission.

Eligibility for Inurnment in the Arlington Columbarium

The rules regarding eligibility requirements for entering cremated remains for inurnment into the columbarium at Arlington National Cemetery are a bit more relaxed. Although anyone that is eligible for ground burials may instead elect to be memorialized in the columbarium. Certain other fully honorable veterans and their qualifying dependents are eligible as well. These include the following:

- Service members who die while on active duty.

- Any veteran who previously served on active duty (other than for training).
- Any citizen of the United States that served in the military of any government that was allied with the United States during that particular war, and whose service ended honorably by death or otherwise, and that was a citizen of the United States at the time of their death.

Members of the U.S. reserve components that die under any of the following conditions:

a. While on active duty for training or that are performing full-time service while under Title 32. This includes during authorized travel to and from that duty.
b. While on authorized inactive duty for training. This includes training performed by the Army and Air National Guards.
c. While being treated or hospitalized at the expense of the United States for injuries or diseases that were caused or contracted by their duty or service.

*The spouses, minor children, and certain adult children of the above-mentioned eligible veterans.

Exception to Interment/Inurnment Policy

*Remember that these are the general guidelines concerning eligibility for burial/inurnment at Arlington National Cemetery. Sometimes there may be an instance where a veteran should absolutely be given the opportunity for burial at Arlington, but due to the strict guidelines, they may fail to meet one of the criteria listed above. In these certain instances, the family should request an application for an exception to the interment/inurnment policy. This is a way for families to ask for special consideration to be given based on the merit of the extraordinary circumstances that the veteran may have displayed during their military service.

The thing to remember here is that this is for extraordinary circumstances. Families should not attempt this unless they are reasonably certain and can provide the necessary proof that the veteran's military or civilian service contributions and acts directly and substantially benefited the U.S. military. The Secretary of the Army will be the one making the decision, which means you better have your proof ready. This process typically takes seven to ten business days from the day they receive the request. To start this process after the veteran has passed, the families may fax their request letters to the superintendent of the Arlington National Cemetery at fax number (703)607-8583.

Why Many Veterans Choose Arlington

If you have never had the privilege of seeing a burial service at Arlington National Cemetery, I strongly encourage that you watch one prior to making a decision. There really is nothing like it anywhere else in the world. Members of the elite 3rd U.S. Infantry, often referred to as the Old Guard, provide families of eligible veterans with the most respectful and professional burials imaginable. It truly is an amazing sight and leaves little doubt as to why over three hundred thousand people have chosen to be buried there.

Requesting Burial or Inurnment at Arlington National Cemetery

Whether your final wish is to be buried at Arlington or to have your ashes inurned in the columbarium at Arlington, the process is similar in each case. The best way to request burial or inurnment is to inform the funeral director at your local funeral home. They can help with the necessary arrangements (such as transporting the remains) and can also fax off the necessary paperwork to show eligibility. If you need to contact the cemetery staff at Arlington with any questions concerning burials, just call (703)607-8585. To fax over eligibility paperwork, fax it to (703)607-8583.

Families that would like to have the ashes inurned at Arlington. They must make arrangements ahead of time and are welcome to carry the remains there themselves, as long as they are in a tightly sealed urn.

Special Circumstances for Those That Have Died while on Active Duty

If a service member dies while on active duty, active duty for training, or inactive duty for training. The military branch itself will usually pick up pretty much all of the additional costs incurred with allowing for a proper burial, this includes transporting the remains, cremation and urn costs, or for normal embalming and casket costs for those that wish to be buried. These are all costs that the VA generally will not cover.

Helping to Offset the High Cost of Funerals and Burials

Oftentimes the family can be reimbursed by the VA for a portion of the funeral and burial expenses they have incurred. This can be a huge difference maker when you consider the fact that normally funerals are quite expensive. Here is how it works.

You may be eligible for a burial allowance from the VA if you meet *all* of the conditions listed below:

1. The veteran was discharged under conditions that the VA considers other than dishonorable.
2. You have paid for the veteran's funeral or burial.
3. You have not been reimbursed by any other source such as another government agency.

Additionally, the veteran must have been meeting at least one of the following requirements at the time of death:

- The veteran was receiving VA disability compensation or a VA pension at the time of death.
- The veteran was entitled to receive VA compensation or a VA pension, but decided not to reduce their military retirement or disability pay.
- The veteran died from their service-related disability.
- The veteran died while traveling to or from an authorized VA medical appointment. That was for the purposes of examination, care, or treatment. That was properly authorized and at the VA's expense.
- A veteran that had either an original or reopened claim that was pending at the veteran's time of death, and the VA has determined that the veteran would have been entitled to either compensation or pension from a date that is prior to the veteran's date of death.
- A veteran who has died while in a VA medical facility or that was receiving care at a non-VA facility that is contracted with the VA to provide care and services to veterans.
- A veteran who died on or after October 9, 1996, while being an admitted patient at a VA-approved state nursing home.

Calculating Your Burial Allowance

The amount that a family member may receive for partial reimbursement is determined by if the veteran's death was service related or not and when the veteran died. Let's take a closer look:

A. For service-related deaths—The VA will pay up to $1,500 toward the burial expenses for service-related deaths that occurred prior to September 10, 2001. For service-related deaths that occurred on or after September 11, 2001, the VA will pay up to $2,000 toward the burial expenses. Additionally, if the veteran is being buried in a VA national cemetery, the VA can help with some or all of the costs associated with transporting the remains. The family will have to pay for this upfront and then ask for reimbursement.

B. For non-service-related deaths—The VA will pay up to $300 toward the funeral and burial expenses and $300 as a plot-internment allowance for veterans whose deaths occurred on or after December 1, 2001. For veterans whose deaths occurred prior to December 1, 2001, the plot-internment allowance is only $150. Additionally, if the veteran's death occurred while they were in a VA hospital or while under the care of a VA-contracted nursing home, then some or all of the costs associated with transporting the remains may be reimbursed by the VA.

Applying for Burial Allowances

The family member that paid for the funeral or burial will need to download and complete VA Form 21-530, which is the Application for Burial Benefits form. Once you have completed the application form, you must send the application, copies of all of the funeral/burial receipts, a copy of the death certificate, and copies of the veteran's discharge paperwork to the VA regional office. Keep in mind, though, that if the veteran's death was not service related, then you only have two years from the date of burial or cremation to file your claim. This two-year period does not apply if the veteran's death was service related. To download VA Form 21-530, just go to:
http://www.vba.va.gov/pubs/forms/VBA-21-530-ARE.pdf

Receiving Burial Flags

Veterans that were discharged under conditions that the VA does not consider dishonorable are entitled to a free burial flag from the VA. The flag is used during the funeral services to either drape the casket or accompany the urn of the deceased veteran. During the military funeral honors, which will be covered later in this chapter, the military honor guards will carefully fold the flag and then present it to the deceased veteran's next of kin or a close friend if no family is present. This is given as a keepsake to help honor the memory of the veteran's military service.

Obtaining a Burial Flag

A good funeral director will typically go ahead and order this for the family to help ease the burden. In the event that you're required to provide the burial flag, though, all you will need to do is download and complete VA Form 21-2008. Once completed, you can take the form, a copy of the death certificate, and a copy of the veteran's discharge paperwork to any U.S. post office or VA regional office, and they will provide you with a burial flag. To download VA Form 21-2008, just go to: http://www.vba.va.gov/pubs/forms/VBA-21-2008-ARE.pdf

*Remember that after the next of kin has been presented with the folded American flag, these flags are not suitable for displaying outside on a flagpole due to the elements. The best thing to do is purchase a flag case, which is similar to a shadow box. These are designed to display the folded flag properly. Flag cases typically cost anywhere from $30 up into the hundreds, depending on the type and quality of the case you desire.

Receiving a Presidential Memorial Certificate

Oftentimes, as with burial flags, the funeral director will help with the ordering of Presidential Memorial Certificates. These engraved paper certificates are signed by the current president of the United States and are intended to help honor the memory of each honorably discharged veteran.

Applying for Presidential Memorial Certificates

In the event that the family or close friends of the deceased veteran would like to order more than one of these certificates, or if the funeral director fails to order the certificate while making the necessary funeral arrangements. The family or friends can easily order them free of charge by submitting a completed VA Form 40-0247. Which is the Application for Presidential Memorial Certificate. To download VA Form 40-0247, just go to: http://www4.va.gov/vaforms/va/pdf/VA40-0247.pdf

Once completed, the easiest way to submit the application, honorable discharge paperwork, and death certificate is by faxing copies of these papers to fax number 1(800)455-7143. Or you can mail copies (do not send originals because they will not be returned) to:

> Presidential Memorial Certificates (41A1C)
> National Cemetery Administration
> 5109 Russell Road
> Quantico, VA. 22134-3903

Receiving a Free Headstone or Marker

When a veteran is buried in either a VA national cemetery, National Park Service cemetery, state-run veterans' cemetery, or at the Arlington National Cemetery, the cemetery staff will order the headstone or marker for the family. This happens after the family has informed the cemetery staff of any appropriate inscriptions or faith emblems that they wish to be placed on the headstone or marker before placing the order (this is explained in detail later in this section). This is quite important because once the order has been placed, it cannot be changed.

Veterans that have chosen to be buried in privately owned cemeteries are eligible for free government-furnished headstones and markers as well. The family's estate is responsible for any and all costs associated with the setting and placement fees.

A Closer Look at Memorial Options

When it comes to headstones and markers, the VA has three basic designs that they offer to veterans and their qualifying dependents. These are the following:

- The traditional headstone—which is 42 inches tall, 13 inches wide, and 4 inches thick, it is available in both granite and marble, and weighs approximately 230 pounds.

- The bronze niche marker—which is 8½ inches long, 5½ inches wide, and has a 7/16-inch rise. The bronze niche marker weighs approximately 3 pounds. Additionally, the mounting bolts and washers are included with the bronze niche marker.

- The flat grave markers—which come in granite, marble, and bronze. The granite and marble flat markers are 24 inches long, 12 inches wide, and are 4 inches thick. These weigh approximately 130 pounds. The bronze flat grave markers are 24 inches long, 12 inches wide, and have a ¾-inch rise. They weigh approximately 18 pounds.

*Remember that when deciding on either a granite, marble, or bronze flat grave markers, the VA will provide you with the necessary anchor bolts, washers, and nuts that are needed to fasten the flat grave marker to the base. The family will be responsible for the base, though, because the government does not furnish them if buried in a private cemetery. Additionally, many state-run veterans' cemeteries also charge the families estate a fee for setting the headstone or marker so inquire ahead of time.

Which Information Goes on the Headstone or Marker

The veteran's legal name, year of birth, year of death, and branch of service are all considered mandatory items that must be placed onto the headstone or marker. After that, if there is still space available, the family may choose to have other items inscribed at the government's expense as well. These include religious emblems, highest rank attained in service, month and date of birth/death, awards the veteran achieved in service, credentials or accomplishments such as doctor or judge, nicknames, and tasteful terms of endearment such as *my loving husband*. These are all examples of acceptable items and can be inscribed at government expense.

Ordering a Free Headstone or Marker

Unless the veteran is being laid to rest in a privately owned cemetery, this should automatically be taken care of on the family's behalf. In cases where the veteran is being buried in a private cemetery, though, the funeral director may or may not offer this service. Other instances such as if the headstone or marker is stolen, vandalized, or otherwise severely deteriorated by the elements. To order a new or replacement

headstone, all you will need to do is download and complete VA Form 40-1330, which is the Application for Standard Government Headstone or Marker. To download this form, just go to:
http://www4.va.gov/vaforms/va/pdf/VA40-1330.pdf

Once completed, you can fax the application, death certificate, and proof of military service to fax number 1(800)455-7143. Or you can mail the information to:

Memorial Programs Service (41A1)
Department of Veterans Affairs
5190 Russell Road
Quantico, VA. 22134-3903

Military Funeral Honors

Under the Honoring Those Who Served program, the DOD is tasked with providing military honors to service members and veterans that have passed away upon request by the family. This is a beautiful way to pay tribute to the men and women that have given up either a part of their lives or sometimes unfortunately their life itself while defending our nation. When each veteran remembers back to that day, when they raised their hand and took the oath to defend and protect our country. They had made a pact that day to be honorable and to do the right thing. This is why the military branch the veteran served in will send representatives (being a military honors guard detail) to acknowledge these sacrifices. This is the military's way of honoring those who have displayed honor.

Eligibility for Military Funeral Honors

For the most part, anyone that has served and that was discharged under conditions that the military does not consider dishonorable will qualify for a military funeral honors detail. As with everything that is run by the government, though, there must be rules. Here is a list of those that are eligible for military funeral honors:

- Current military members that were either on active duty or that were in the selected reserves.
- Former military service members that completed at least one term of enlistment or period of initial obligated service within

the selected reserve, then departed under conditions that were considered other than dishonorable.

- Former military service members that were discharged from the selected reserve due to a disability that was either incurred or aggravated in the line of duty.
- Former military service members that served on active duty and departed under conditions other than dishonorable.

Military Funeral Honors Guard Detail

The law states that every service member and eligible veteran that has died be able to receive a military honors ceremony, to include the folding and presenting of a U.S. burial flag to the next of kin or a close friend and the playing of taps at the ceremony. Furthermore, the law requires that the military funeral honors detail must consist of at least two or more properly uniformed military personnel with at least one of the members being from the veteran's parent service of the armed forces.

Although the law states that at least two members of the military must attend and present the military funeral honors. In most cases, if the resources are available, the military will send anywhere from a three to seven member team to properly carry out the ceremony. These military funeral honors teams are made up of current service members that often have other positions within the military, which is why it is always best to request honors guard details as soon as possible through the funeral director. That way, these service members who are volunteering their time can make the arrangements necessary to attend and perform the ceremony.

*Remember that although the military is required to provide the family with a folding and presenting of a burial flag and the playing of taps as part of the standard military funeral honors detail upon request. Depending on the amount of resources available, the amount of funerals scheduled for that particular day where the veteran's ceremony will take place, the wishes of the family, and the veteran's status are all factored into if additional manpower; hence, additional services will be available for the funeral. These additional services can often include a military rifle volley team or the military funeral honors members performing as pallbearers. Much of this depends on the level of the veteran's service.

Standard military funeral honors teams typically consist of two to three members as explained earlier and are reserved for veterans that do not fit one of the following categories:

a. Seven or nine-member details—these are reserved for retired service members, those that have died while on active duty, or that were still active in the reserves or National Guard, but were not killed in action. In addition to the standard military funeral honors, they receive three volleys of rifle fire.

b. Full military honors detail—this is reserved for E-9s, O-7 and above, Medal of Honor recipients, and service members that were killed in action. Full military honors consists of a sixteen to twenty one member team and provides six soldiers as pallbearers and three volleys of rifle fire in addition to the standard military honors.

Requesting Military Funeral Honors

No matter which different burial option that you have decided on, the DOD will assign you a military funeral honors detail if you request it, although most funeral directors will handle this task for you. On some occasions, the family may need to contact the particular representative that handles making arrangements for funeral honors for the veteran's particular branch of service in the state that they plan to have the ceremony. The easiest way to find the representative's contact information for the deceased veteran's state and military branch is by calling 1(877)645-4667, or you can find the contact information at: http://www.militaryfuneralhonors.osd.mil/hnrs/owa/director.show_select

Veterans' Group Life Insurance (VGLI)

Upon separation from the military, veterans have the option of converting their Service Members' Group Life Insurance policy, more commonly known as SGLI, into a comparable Veterans' Group Life Insurance policy, more commonly known as VGLI.

This coverage can be a valuable asset especially to those that are separated from the military due to severe medical conditions because while no privately owned life insurance company would even consider writing a policy for a disabled veteran with a pre-existing serious medical condition by converting your SGLI coverage to VGLI coverage within 120 days of separation from the military, veterans can switch without having to submit to a health screening exam. This can be a huge advantage for those with major medical issues because they cannot be denied life insurance coverage!

How VGLI Works

Service members, upon separation from the military, may elect to convert up to the full amount of their SGLI coverage to VGLI coverage. Depending on the amount of coverage each service member chooses while actively serving (which can range from $10,000 up to $400,000) of coverage, you have the option to transfer that coverage over to VGLI. Upon separation, veterans have up to 485 days to elect this coverage; but if you plan to transfer the coverage, you should do it within the 120-day period to bypass the health screening.

Although the rates are often substantially higher for VGLI coverage, seeing as rates are determined by age and the amount of the policy. Disabled veterans with severe medical conditions are often quite limited when it comes to acquiring life insurance policies.

Applying for VGLI

To apply for VGLI coverage, you will need to download and complete Form SGLV 8714, which is the Application for Veterans' Group Life Insurance. To download this form, just go to: http://www.insurance.va.gov/sgliSite/forms/8714(10-08).pdf

Once completed, just mail the forms and your initial premiums to:

OSGLI
P.O. Box 41618
Philadelphia, PA 19176-9913

Service-Disabled Veterans Insurance (S-DVI)

Veterans with service-connected disabilities are also eligible for S-DVI insurance policies in the amount of $10,000 in many instances. To be eligible, the veteran must meet all of the following criteria:

- The veteran was released from active duty on or after April 25, 1951, under other than dishonorable conditions.

- The veteran is in good health except for the service-connected medical conditions.
- The veteran is rated for the service-connected disability (even if only a 0 percent rating).
- The veteran applies within two years from the date the VA grants your new service-connected disability.

The one thing to keep in mind, though, is that an increased rating of an existing service-connected disability or the granting of a 100 percent disability rating or individual un-employability of a previously rated medical condition does not automatically entitle a veteran to this insurance by resetting the eligibility period for them. The veteran should apply for this insurance when they first file their claims for disability compensation or pension.

Applying for S-DVI

Typically, when veterans apply for their VA benefits with a veteran's benefits counselor or VSO, the representative applies for this insurance policy for them. In the event that you would like to apply for an S-DVI policy on your own, just download and complete VA Form 29-4364, which is the Application for Service-disabled Veterans Life Insurance. You can find this form at:

http://www.vba.va.gov/pubs/forms/VBA-29-4364-ARE.pdf

Once completed, you will need to mail VA Form 29-4364 to:

The Department of Veterans Affairs
Regional Office and Insurance Center (RH)
P.O. Box 7208
Philadelphia, PA 19101

In certain instances, veterans that qualify for S-DVI policies are eligible for a waiver of premiums. To qualify for a waiver, the veteran must meet one of the following conditions:

1. The veteran must have a physical or mental disability, which prevents them from performing substantially gainful employment.

2. A total disability must begin before the veterans sixty-fifth birthday and must continue for at least six consecutive months.
3. The total disability may not begin prior to the effective date of the policy unless the total disability is for a service-connected condition.

To apply for a waiver of S-DVI premiums, just download and complete VA Form 29-357, which is the Claim for Disability Insurance Benefits. Once completed, you will need to mail the form to the address listed above. To download VA Form 29-357, just go to:
http://www.vba.va.gov/pubs/forms/29-357.pdf

To file a claim after the veteran has passed away, the beneficiary will need to download and complete VA Form 29-4125, which is the Claim for One Sum Payment. Once completed, you will need to mail the form to the address listed above. To download VA Form 29-4125, just go to:
http://www.vba.va.gov/pubs/forms/VBA-29-4125-ARE.pdf

Appendix A

VA Regional Offices

The following is a list of the locations and mailing addresses for each state's VA regional offices. To contact your regional office by phone, you will need to call the VA at (800) 827-1000.

Alabama
Montgomery Regional Office
345 Perry Hill Road
Montgomery, AL 36109
Fax# (334)213-3461

Alaska
Anchorage Regional Office
2925 De Barr Road
Anchorage, AK 99508

Arizona
Phoenix Regional Office
3333 North Central Avenue
Phoenix, AZ 85012

Arkansas
North Little Rock Regional Office
2200 Fort Roots Drive Building 65
North Little Rock, AR 72114

California
Los Angeles Regional Office
Federal Building, 11000 Wilshire Boulevard
Los Angeles, CA 90024

San Diego Regional Office
8810 Rio San Diego Drive
San Diego, CA 92108

Oakland Regional Office
1301 Clay Street Room 1300 North
Oakland, CA 94612
Fax# (510)637-6111

Colorado
Denver Regional Office
155 Van Gordon Street
Lakewood, CO 80228

Connecticut
Hartford Regional Office
555 Willard Avenue Building 2E
Newington, CT 06111

Delaware
Wilmington Regional Office
1601 Kirkwood Highway
Wilmington, DE 19805

District of Columbia
Washington D.C. Regional Office
1722 I Street N.W.
Washington D.C. 20421

Florida
St. Petersburg Regional Office
9500 Bay Pines Boulevard
St. Petersburg, FL 33708

Mailing Address
P.O. Box 1437
St. Petersburg, FL 33731

Georgia
Atlanta Regional Office
1700 Clairmont Road
Decatur, GA 30033

Hawaii
Honolulu Regional Office
459 Patterson Road, E-Wing
Honolulu, HI 96819
Fax# (808)433-0478

Mailing Address
VBA Honolulu Regional Office
P.O. Box 29020
Honolulu, HI 96820

Idaho
Boise Regional Office
444 West Fort Street
Boise, ID 83702

Illinois
Chicago Regional Office
2122 West Taylor Street
Chicago, IL 60612

Indiana
Indianapolis Regional Office
575 North Pennsylvania Street
Indianapolis, IN 46204

Iowa
Des Moines VA Regional Office
210 Walnut Street
Des Moines, IA 50309
Fax# (515)323-7407

Kansas
Wichita Regional Office
5500 East Kellogg
Wichita, KS 67211

Kentucky
Louisville Regional Office
321 West Main Street, Suite 390
Louisville, KY 40202

Louisiana
New Orleans Regional Office
1250 Poydras Street, Suite 200
New Orleans, LA 70113

Maine
Togus VA Medical/Regional Office Center
1 VA Center
Augusta, ME 04330
Fax# (207)623-5776

Maryland
Baltimore Regional Office
31 Hopkins Plaza
Baltimore, MD 21201

Massachusetts
Boston VA Regional Office
JFK Federal Building
Boston, MA 02203

Michigan
Detroit Regional Office
Patrick V. McNamara Federal Building
477 Michigan Avenue
Detroit, MI 48226

Minnesota
St. Paul Regional Office
1 Federal Drive, Fort Snelling
St. Paul, MN 55111
Fax# (612)970-5415

Mississippi
Jackson Regional Office
1600 East Woodrow Wilson Avenue
Jackson, MS 39216
Fax# (601)364-7007

Missouri
St. Louis Regional Office
400 South 18th Street
St. Louis, MO 63103

Montana
Fort Harrison Medical and Regional Office
William Street off Highway
Fort Harrison, MT 59636

Mailing Address
3633 Veterans Drive
P.O. Box 188
Fort Harrison, MT 59636

Nebraska
Lincoln Regional Office
5631 South 48th Street
Lincoln, NE 68516

Nevada
Reno Regional Office
5460 Reno Corporate Drive
Reno, NV 89511

New Hampshire
Manchester Regional Office
Norris Cotton Federal Building
275 Chestnut Street
Manchester, NH 03101

New Jersey
Newark Regional Office
20 Washington Place
Newark, NJ 07102

New Mexico
Albuquerque Regional Office
500 Gold Avenue S.W.
Albuquerque, NM 87102

New York
New York Regional Office
245 West Houston Street
New York, NY 10014

Buffalo Regional Office
130 South Elmwood Avenue
Buffalo, NY 14202

North Carolina
Winston-Salem Regional Office
Federal Building
251 North Main Street
Winston-Salem, NC 27155

North Dakota
Fargo Regional Office
2101 Elm Street
Fargo, ND 58102
Fax# (701)451-4690

Ohio
Cleveland Regional Office
A.J. Celebrezze Federal Building
1240 East 9th Street
Cleveland, OH 44199
Fax# (216)522-8262

Oklahoma
Muskogee Regional Office
125 South Main Street
Muskogee, OK 74401

Oregon
Portland Regional Office
1220 S.W. 3rd Avenue
Portland, OR 97204

Pennsylvania
Pittsburgh Regional Office
1000 Liberty Avenue
Pittsburgh, PA 15222

Philadelphia Regional Office
5000 Wissahickon Avenue
Philadelphia, PA 19101

Rhode Island
Providence Regional Office
380 Westminster Street
Providence, RI 02903

South Carolina
Columbia Regional Office
6437 Garners Ferry Road
Columbia, SC 29209

South Dakota
Sioux Falls Regional Office
2501 West 22nd Street
Sioux Falls, SD 57117
Fax# (605)333-5316

Tennessee
Nashville Regional Office
110 9th Avenue South
Nashville, TN 37203

Texas
Houston Regional Office
6900 Almeda Road
Houston, TX 77030

Waco Regional Office
1 Veterans Plaza, 701 Clay Avenue
Waco, TX 76799

Utah
Salt Lake City Regional Office
550 Foothill Drive
Salt Lake City, UT 84158

Vermont
White River Junction Regional Office
215 North Main Street
White River Junction, VT 05009

Virginia
Roanoke Regional Office
210 Franklin Road S.W.
Roanoke, VA 24011

Washington
Seattle Regional Office
915 2nd Avenue
Seattle, WA 98174

West Virginia
Huntington Regional Office
640 Fourth Avenue
Huntington, WV 25701
Fax# (304)399-9355

Wisconsin
Milwaukee Regional Office
5400 West National Avenue
Milwaukee, WI 53214
Fax# (414)902-9415

Wyoming
Cheyenne VA Medical/Regional Office Center
2360 East Pershing Boulevard
Cheyenne, WY 82001

Guam
Guam Benefits Office
Reflection Center, Suite 202
222 Chalan Santo Papa Street
Hagatna, GU 96910

Philippines
Manila Regional Office
1131 Roxas Boulevard, Ermita
0930 Manila, PI 96440
Phone# (632)301-2000

Puerto Rico
San Juan Regional Office
150 Carlos Chardon Avenue
Hato Rey, PR 00918
Fax# (787)772-7458

Appendix B

Location	Phone number	Fax	Flight Info Recording
Altus AFB OK	DSN: 866-6428		DSN: 866-5333
	(580)481-6428		(580)481-5333
Anderson AFB, Guam	(671)366-5165	(671)366-3984	(671)366-2095
Andrews AFB MD	(301)981-1854	(301)981-4241	DSN: 858-5851
(NAS) Atlanta GA	(678)655-6359		
Aviano AB, Italy	39-434-66-7680	39-434-66-7782	
Baltimore-Washington IAP	(410)918-6900	(410)918-6932	(410)918-6900
(NAS) Brunswick MA	(207)921-2682		(207)921-2689
Ben Gurion IAP, Israel	((972) 3-935-4333	(972) 3-935-8697	
Cairo East AB,Egypt	20-2-797-3212	20-2-797-1290	
Charleston AFB SC	(843)963-3083	(843)963-3060	(843)963-3082
(NAS) Corpus Christi, TX	(361)961-2505		(361)961-3385
Davis-Monthan AFB, AZ	(520)228-2322	(520)228-7229	(520)228-2322
Diego Garcia	(246)370-2745	246-370-2787	
Dobbins ARB, GA	(678)655-4903	(678)655-6155	
Dover AFB, DE	(302)677-4088	(302)677-2953	(302)677-2854
Eilson AFB, AK	(907)377-1854	(907)377-2287	(907)377-1623
Elmendorf AFB, AK	(907)552-8588	(907)552-3996	(907)552-8588
Fairchild AFB, WA	(509)247-5435	(509)247-3399	(509)247-3406
F.E. Warren, WY	1(800)832-1959		
Forbes Field ANG, KS	(785)861-4210	(785)861-4555	(785)861-4210
(JRB) Fort Worth, TX	(817)782-5677		(817)782-6289
Grand Forks AFB, ND	(701)747-7105	(701)747-3448	(701)747-7105
NAS Guantanam0 Bay, Cuba	011-53-99-6408	011-53-99-6170	
Hickam AFB, HI	(808)449-1515	(808)448-1503	(808)449-1515
Hill AFB, UT	(801)777-3089	(801)775-2677	(801)777-1854
Holloman AFB, NM	(505)572-3150		
Homestead ARB, FL	(305)224-7518		
Incirlik AB, Turkey	90-322-216-6424	90-322-216-3420	
MCAS Iwakuni, Japan	81-6117-53-5509	DSN:315-253-3301	DSN:315-253-1854
(NAS) Jacksonville, FL	(904)542-3956	(904)542-3257	(904)542-3956
Jackson IAP, MS	(601)936-8761	(601)936-8698	(601)936-8761
Kadena AB, Japan	011-81-6117-34-2159	DSN:315-634-4221	
Keesler AFB, MS	(228)377-2120	(228)377-2488	(228)377-4538
Keflavik, Iceland	(354)228-6139	354-228-4649	
Lackland AFB, TX	(210)925-8715	(210)925-2732	(210)925-8714
Kirtland AFB, NM	(505)846-7000		(505)846-6184
Kunsan AB, Korea	82-63-470-4666	DSN:315-782-7550	
Lajes AB, Azores	351-295-57-3227	351-295-57-5110	
Langley AFB, VA	(757)764-3531	(757)764-3722	(757)764-5807
Little Rock AFB, AR	(501)987-3342	(501)987-6726	(501)987-3684
(NAS) Lemoore, CA	(559)998-1680		

Location	Phone Number	Fax	Flight Info Recording
MacDill AFB, FL	(813)828-2440	(813)828-7844	(813)828-2310
McChord AFB, WA	(253)982-7259	(253)982-6815	(253)982-7268
McConnell AFB, KS	(316)759-4810	(316)759-1032	(316)759-5404
McGuire AFB, NJ	(609)754-5023	(609)754-4621	(800)569-8284
March ARB, CA	(951)655-2397		(951)655-2913
Maxwell AFB, AL	(334)953-7372	(334)953-6114	(334)953-6760
RAF Mildenhall, UK	44-1638-54-2248	44-1638-54-2250	
(NAS) Miramar, CA	(858)577-4283		
Misawa AB, Japan	011-81-3117-66-2370	011-81-3117-66-4455	011-81-3117-66-2852
Naples, Italy	39-081-568-5247	39-081-568-5259	
Nellis AFB, NV	(702)652-2562	(702)652-2561	
Norfolk Naval Station, VA	(757)444-4148	(757)445-7510	(757)444-4118
(NAS) North Island, CA	(619)545-9567	(619)545-9532	(619)545-8273
Offutt AFB, NE	(402)294-8510		(402)294-7111
Osan AB, Korea	011-82-31-661-1854	011-82-31-661-4897	011-82-31-661-1854
Pease ANGB, NH	(603)430-3323	(603)430-3335	
(NAS) Pensacola, FL	(850)452-3311		(850)452-3311
Patrick AFB, FL	(321)494-5631	(321)494-7991	
Peterson AFB, CO	(719)556-4521	(719)556-4979	(719)556-4707
(NAS) Point Mugu, CA	(805)989-7731	(805)989-8540	
Pope AFB, NC	(910)394-6527	(910)394-6526	(910)394-6525
Ramstein AB, Germany	DSN:479-4440	011-49-6371-47-2364	
Randolph AFB, TX	(210)652-3725	(210)652-5718	(210)652-1854
Robins AFB, GA	(478)926-3166	(478)926-5835	(478)926-4446
(NAS) Rota, Spain	34-956-822411	34-956-821734	
Scott AFB, IL	(618)256-2140	(618)256-1946	(618)256-1854
Sigonella, Italy	39-95-86-5576	39-95-86-6729	
Souda Bay, Crete	302-821-02-1275	302-821-02-1525	302-821-02-1387
Spangdahlem AB, Germany	49-6565-61-8866	49-6565-61-8665	49-6565-61-8860
Stewart ANG, NY	(914)563-2226	(914)563-2228	
Tinker AFB, OK	DSN: 339-4339	DSN:339-3826	DSN:339-4360
Travis AFB, CA	(707)424-5770	(707)424-2048	(707)424-1854
Westover ARB, MA	(413)557-3453	(413)557-3147	(413)557-2589
Willow Grove JRB, PA	(215)443-6217		(215)443-6216
Wright-Patterson AFB, OH	(937)257-7741	(937)656-1580	(937)257-6235
Yokota AB, Japan	81-3117-55-5661	81-3117-55-9768	81-3117-55-7111

Index

A

Active Duty Montgomery GI Bill
(ADMGIB), 210
Agent Orange, 97-98
appeals
checking up on, 73
filing a motion to reconsider, 75
filing in U.S. Court of Appeals. *See*
notice of appeal
reasons for having, 61
reopening, 76
requesting speedup for, 72
Arlington National Cemetery, 334,
337, 341, 344
armed forces recreation centers
(AFRC), 313
Armed Forces Vacation Club
(AFVC), 318, 320
Army and Air Force Exchange
Service (AAFES), 285, 288
Automated Certificate of Eligibility
(ACE), 276

B

basic allowance for housing (BAH),
224
benefits, 35, 40
eligibility in getting, 19
government agencies handling, 40

guardsman, 47
questions when applying for, 38
rules for receiving, 12
various state, 85
blind veterans, 157-58
board hearing, 69, 71
Board of Veterans Appeals (BVA),
74-77
burial
allowances, 345
benefits, 334-37
flags, 346
plan, 332
Buy-up Program, 221-22

C

Cape Henry Inn and Beach Club,
314, 317
catastrophic cap, 189-90
cemeteries
national, 333-42, 348-50
private, 340
Central Medical Board (CMB), 90-
91
CHAMPVA In-house Treatment
Initiative (CITI), 198-200
Civilian Health and Medical
Program of the Department of
Veterans Affairs (CHAMPVA),
195-98

claims
  filing, 40
    being successful in, 42
    evaluating records when, 57
    keeping track of paperwork
      when, 55
    saving records on PC, 56
    Washington as place in, 70
  finding holes in, 58
  fixing errors in, 62
combat-related special compensation
    (CRSC), 116
combined disability ratings table, 103
Community Living Center, 161-62
compensation and pension exam
    (C and P), 57
Continued Health Care Benefit
    Program (CHCBP), 194
counsel, 66
counseling, 83-84, 86-87, 147, 149,
    156-58, 246-47, 264-65

D

Department of Defense (DOD), 16,
    40
dependency and indemnity
    compensation (DIC), 116,
    120-23
disability compensation, 46-48, 87
  calculating, 92, 108
  determining rate of, 107
  former POW, 97
  Gulf War veterans, 99, 101
  radiation-exposed veterans, 99-100
  reasons to receive, 92
  reserve and National Guard
    members, 102
  service connection for

  making, 94
  presumptive, 96
  proving existence of, 94
  Vietnam and Korean War veterans,
    29-30, 271-72
  See also Agent Orange
  ways in getting, 94
disability rating, 47, 61, 87, 92, 103.
    See also combined disability
    ratings table
discharge
  bad conduct (BCD), 22
  dishonorable (DD), 22
  entry level separation (ELS), 21
  general, 21
  honorable, 20
  improper, 33
  inequitable, 33
  other than honorable (OTH), 21
  punitive, 22
  upgrading, 26, 32, 34
Discharge Review Board (DRB), 33-35
discounts, 296, 310
domiciliary care, 163
Dragon Hill, 315-17
duty-to-assist law, 49

E

Edelweiss Lodge and Resort, 316-17
educational plan, 204
enrollment, 43
exchange system, 285, 287

F

federal records, 50-51
form
  annual clothing allowance, 159

Appeal to the Board of Veterans' Appeals, 65

Application for a HISA Grant, 283

Application for Burial Benefits, 346

Application for CHAMPVA Benefits, 196

Application for Dependency and Indemnity Compensation, Death Pension and Accrued Benefits by Surviving Spouse or Child, 120

Application for Presidential Memorial Certificate, 348-49

Application for SAH and SHA Grants, 282

Application for Service-disabled Veterans Life Insurance, 354-55

Application for Standard Government Headstone or Marker, 350

Application for Veterans' Group Life Insurance, 353

Appointment of Individual as Claimant's Representative, 67

Appointment of Veterans Service Organization as Claimant's Representative, 67

certificate of eligibility, 276

CHAMPVA Claim, 198

Claim for Disability Insurance Benefits, 354, 356

Claim for One Sum Payment, 355

disability compensation, 46

GI Bill benefits, 233

Request for and Authorization to Release Medical Records or Health Information, 60

G

geographical income threshold, 171, 173-74

H

Hale Koa, 315-17, 319

health and dental insurance, 176

health care, 144, 147, 166
    accepting financial responsibility for, 166
    benefits coverage for, 155
    eligibility exceptions for, 149
    eligibility requirements for, 147
    enrolling for, 154
    extended programs for, 163
    facilities for, 146

Home Improvements and Structural Alterations (HISA), 282

home loans, 268-70, 273, 278

I

improved death pension, 119

K

kickers, 220

M

maternity care, 156

medals, applying for, 34

medical appointments, keeping, 151

medical documentation, 54

military funeral honors, 350-52

military lodging, 298-99, 310-11

Montgomery GI Bill Selected

Reserve (MGBSR), 215

N

national income threshold, 171-72
National Veterans Legal Services
  Program, 66-67
New Sanno Hotel, 318
ninety-day rule, 70
nonfederal records, 50-51
notice of appeal, 76-77
Notice of Disagreements (NOD), 63
nursing home programs, 161-62
nursing homes, 115, 117, 147-48,
  162-64, 171-72

P

patient-driven scheduling, 49, 150
pension, 87, 116-18
  death, 120
  determining how much, 118
  Medal of Honor, 124-25
  qualifications for, 117
permanent and total disability
  (P and T), 112
Permanent Disability Retirement List
  (PDRL), 20-21, 53-54, 92-93
Physical Evaluation Board (PEB), 53,
  89-90
Post-9/11 GI Bill, 222-23, 225, 230
postmilitary life
  deciding on, 81
  picking the right place during, 84
  renting or owning home for, 85
  utilizing transitional assistance for,
    82
post-traumatic stress disorder
  (PTSD), 82-83, 156

Presidential Memorial Certificate,
  347-48
priority groups, 144, 149-51, 153-
  54, 161, 166-68, 170-71, 173

Q

Quick Start, 46-47

R

rejection letter, 61
representation. *See* Veterans Service
  Organizations (VSO)
Reserve Educational Assistance
  Program (REAP), 217
routine refill program, 170-71

S

secondary tier illnesses, 55
Service-disabled Veterans Insurance
  (S-DVI), 353
service records
  fixing errors in, 28, 32
  proving errors in, 28
  proving injustice in, 28
  reasons to upgrade, 27
Shades of Green, 314, 317
sixty-day rule, 65, 67
Space-A, 298
Special Home Adaptation (SHA),
  281
Specially Adapted Housing (SAH),
  280
special monthly compensation
  (SMC), 112-13
special survivor indemnity allowance
  (SSIA), 124-25

Spina Bifida, 99-100
state homes, 162
Statement of the Case (SOC), 64
Supplemental Statement of the Case
      (SSOC), 68
Supporting Evidence, 53
Survivor Benefits Program (SBP),
      124

T

Temporary Disability Retirement
      List (TDRL), 20-21, 53-54,
      91, 93
Temporary Residence Adaptation
      (TRA), 282-83
Transition Assistance Office (TAO),
      45
travel category, 302
traveling. *See* Space-A
TRICARE, 176
   Extra, 186-87
   for Life, 190
   and Medicare, 190-91
   Prime, 181-82, 329, 331
   Standard, 186
   See also catastrophic cap
Tricare Retiree Dental Program
      (TRDP), 200

V

veteran, 19
Veteran's Affairs (VA)
   annual budget, 16
   determination, 37
   guidelines, 48
   local office, 44
   medical center, 43

online applications (VONAPP), 46
Veterans' Group Life Insurance
      (VGLI), 352
Veterans Service Organizations
      (VSO), 66

Y

Yellow Ribbon Program, 233

Limit of Liability/Disclaimer of Warranty

While the publisher and author have used their best efforts in preparing this book and specifically disclaim any implied warranties of fitness or merchantability for a particular purpose. No warranty shall be created or extended through sales or promotional materials. The advice, as well as the strategies contained herein may not be suitable for every situation or individual. You should consult with a professional where appropriate.

Since information and links to other companies and websites are provided, mentioned companies, or persons, nor does any links indicate any association with or endorsement by the publisher or author. The readers need to be fully aware that internet websites listed in this book may have disappeared or may have changed after this book has been written as well as when it is read.

This publication is designed to provide information as well as personal knowledge to the subject matter covered. It is offered or sold with the understanding that neither the Author nor the publisher is engaged in rendering legal, accounting, or any other professional services. If legal advice or any other expert help is needed, the services of a competent professional should be sought. Neither the publisher nor the Author shall be held liable for any loss of profit, or any other commercial damages including but not limited to special, incidental, or any other damages.

Made in the USA
Lexington, KY
03 December 2011